John Hungerford Pollen

Acts of English martyrs

Hitherto unpublished

John Hungerford Pollen

Acts of English martyrs
Hitherto unpublished

ISBN/EAN: 9783741183126

Manufactured in Europe, USA, Canada, Australia, Japa

Cover: Foto ©Andreas Hilbeck / pixelio.de

Manufactured and distributed by brebook publishing software (www.brebook.com)

John Hungerford Pollen

Acts of English martyrs

ACTS
OF ENGLISH MARTYRS

HITHERTO UNPUBLISHED.

BY

JOHN HUNGERFORD POLLEN

Of the Society of Jesus.

With a Preface by

JOHN MORRIS

Of the same Society.

LONDON:
BURNS AND OATES
LIMITED.

1891.

PREFACE.

"ACTS" is the name that has been applied from the earliest times of Christianity to the records of all that concerned the last days upon earth, the judicial examinations, the sufferings and death, the sayings and doings, of the Martyrs. Everything that belonged to those who gave their lives for God and were the champions of the Church, was most highly prized; and certainly the example of their constancy and fidelity was not less held in esteem than the material relics of their bodies, their property, or the instruments of their martyrdom. The Church took pains to secure faithful narratives of what befell her most glorious children, and the first duty of the Notaries was to see to the compiling of such records. These were read in the assemblies of the Faithful, and we have still traces of them in the historical Lessons of the Breviary. The various persecutions, however, rendered the preservation of these official Acts very difficult, for they were eagerly sought after, and, whenever the tyrant could obtain possession of them, destroyed, together with the Sacred Books.

Not official records only were called "Acts," but the use of the word was extended to include similar narratives of martyrdoms and of the events preceding them, though drawn up without authority by private individuals. This, has in fact come to be the admitted meaning of the term. The splendid collection due to the unwearied industry of the Bollandists goes by the name of the *Acta Sanctorum*. In this sense the word is used in the title of this volume. There is nothing official in these records. They are, documents collected together for biographical, purposes, and they are here printed in their integrity that the reader may not only know something more than has hitherto been known, of the Martyrs themselves, but also of our sources of information respecting them.

Hitherto the English reader has practically, been limited to Bishop Challoner's *Memoirs of Missionary Priests* for his knowledge of the holy, men, not priests only, but laymen, too, in full, proportion, who, under Elizabeth and her, successors, gave their lives for their religion. That book, which was compiled with the most conscientious care by the good Vicar Apostolic of London in the last century, has kept alive the memory of the Martyrs. Until comparatively recent times it was a popular book amongst English Catholics, but of late years literary taste has so changed that it has fallen into neglect. The time has come when a new book is required to take its place. The Lives of the English Martyrs must be rewritten, and the present volume is a contribution towards that work, and will make its execution comparatively easy. The documents in this volume are hitherto unpublished. In one or two instances a document quoted by Challoner finds place among them, in order that the reader might have the full story before his eyes, and now and again a paper has been printed here, though it has previously appeared in Brother Foley's *Records;* but these cases are so rare, that they do not prevent the series of papers from rightly bearing the title of " Unpublished Acts."

Two different collections of these documents were possible, and each in its own way was desirable. For the Cause of the Canonization of the Martyrs it would have been most useful that a volume should have appeared in all respects resembling the two grand volumes, called *Records of the English Catholics,* for which we are indebted to the zeal and diligence of the Fathers of the London Oratory. Nothing could have been better for the purpose of the Postulators of the Cause of the English Martyrs than that the documents now published should have appeared, each in its own original language, edited with the care and skill that the Oratorian Fathers have brought to bear on their volumes. But such a book would not have been popular, and another form seemed necessary if it was to help to spread a knowledge of the sufferings of our Martyrs amongst Catholics in general. The documents that follow have all been translated from their respective original languages into English, and sufficient comment accompanies them to make them intelligible to all readers.

It must be remembered that this book does not profess to make mention of all our Martyrs. Its title is *Acts of English Martyrs,* that is to say, of some of them; and its object is in no way to supersede Challoner, but to supplement him. The book does not even profess to contain all that is not to be found in Challoner. It confines itself to hitherto unpublished matter; and information respecting the Martyrs drawn from manuscript sources in other publications, as for instance, the accounts of Martyrs given by Father

John Gerard in his Autobiography,[1] or again, the most interesting chapters contributed by the late Mr. Richard Simpson to the *Rambler*, find no place in this volume. If, however, it should be proved, by the sale of this collection of documents, that English Catholics care sufficiently for their glorious Martyrs to render such publications feasible, it is intended to produce another volume, or perhaps two, similar to this, containing documents which have already been printed, but notwithstanding are now, for the most part, practically inaccessible. Bishop Challoner's authorities are, many of them, well deserving of publication in full. He was obliged to be very cautious, writing as he did before the repeal of the penal laws, but there is no need for reticence now.

An example may illustrate this, and besides, be itself of some interest. Challoner, speaking of the Venerable John Kemble, says, "The following account of him was sent me from a worthy prelate in that part of the kingdom;" and he winds up the extract with: "Thus far my Right Reverend correspondent." The original letter addressed to

---

[1] *The Life of Father John Gerard, S.J.* By John Morris, S.J. Third Edition, re-written and enlarged. London: Burns and Oates, 1881. Many Martyrs are mentioned by Father Gerard, and in some cases his account is very full, for instance of the Venerable Anne Line and the Venerable John Rigby.

Challoner is preserved with the rest of Challoner's materials at St. Mary's Seminary, Oscott, and thus we come to know that the worthy prelate was Matthew Pritchard, the Vicar Apostolic of the Western District, who dates his letter from Perthyre, February 27, 174$\frac{9}{1}$, and addresses it to Bishop Challoner in this disguised form: "To Mr. Fisher, next door to Mr. Sherwood, surgeon, in Devonshire Street, near Red Lyon Square, London." Perthyre, whence Bishop Pritchard dates his letter, was a community of Franciscan Fathers, to which Order Bishop Pritchard himself belonged; and it makes a difference in the meaning of the Bishop's phrase, which Challoner prints as "three or four of the family of P——," to know that "the family of Perthyre" means the community of Franciscan Fathers living at that place.

The materials, then, exist for one or two more interesting volumes on the Martyrs, which, though they have in some way appeared in print already, would be almost as new and fresh to the reader as these which have never been printed; but it is a matter of doubt whether the publication of such volumes would not entail a loss. Those who would be inclined to subscribe for them, would probably be encouraged by knowing that the publication of such volumes would greatly facilitate the labours of the Postulator and the Roman lawyers, when the Cause comes to be heard in its later stages by the Sacred Congregation of Rites.

The collections in which the documents now published are found in manuscript, are all indicated in the lists prefixed to each chapter of the following book. It may be well, however, here to say that the chief sources of information of which Challoner knew nothing, are the following:

First the Public Record Office. The documents of all kinds that form the collection of State Papers are now easily accessible: and, as may well be imagined, they throw a great light on the history of the persecution. Some few reputations have suffered from the disclosures there made. Now and then a priest, whose character stood all the higher with his Catholic contemporaries in consequence of imprisonment borne for the faith, is now found to have given way under the pressure brought to bear upon him, and for a time to have tried to purchase gentler handling or money help by treacherous revelations, made to Elizabeth's Ministers, of the names and whereabouts and doings of other Catholics, and especially of priests. The temptation was so great that our surprise is not so much to find that such cases existed, as to know that they were not numerous.

An instance occurs in this volume, where Dr. Younger or Young writes an account of Martyrs for Father Persons, the accuracy of which is corroborated by letters written by him, when a prisoner, to Lord Keeper Puckering. One or two of the Lives of the Martyrs require re-writing in consequence of the further information afforded by the State Papers. This is the case with the Venerable Henry Walpole, S.J., as may be seen from the documents quoted by Dr. Jessopp, in his *One Generation of a Norfolk House*. The same may be said of the Venerable John Hambley, whose confessions were printed in the *Rambler* for November, 1858, by Mr. Richard Simpson. Mr. Simpson presses, as it seems to us, too hardly on the one, and Dr. Jessopp on the other, of these holy Martyrs. Both did what was inexcusably wrong, but their martyrdom is all the more glorious for the knowledge that we thus have obtained of the weakness, in spite of which they recovered themselves and persevered to the end in a fidelity and constancy that is enhanced by what had gone before.

The Privy Council Books at Whitehall can be seen, but they are far more difficult of access than the State Papers in the Record Office. We must be thankful for what we have obtained, but the Editor of this volume met with what would seem to be needless obstruction, when in his search for purely literary purposes, he was not allowed to make any complete transcript. The passage of the letter of the Lords of the Privy Council to the Lieutenant of the Tower ordering that, if Blessed Thomas "Sherwood shall not willingly confess such things as shall be demanded of him, he is then to commit him to the dungeon amongst the rats," is not published here for the first time. Other extracts from the Privy Council Warrant Book, given in chapters iv. and v. are new and interesting.

The Westminster Archives and those of Stonyhurst College are spoken of in very sufficient detail in the course of the book, to which they contribute by far the larger share. Of these great collections, with the exception of a very few papers, Bishop Challoner knew nothing. Our volume pretty nearly exhausts the documents contained in them, supplementary to Challoner's work. In several cases the story of a Martyr is not all gathered up into one place. This was inevitable, unless the documents were to be cut up and distributed more than seemed advisable. In some instances this has been done in such a way that the document can be easily reconstructed; but it was not feasible when many Martyrs were mentioned in the same paper, as for instance, the "Relation of the Penkevels," in chapter xiii.

Bishop Challoner's manuscript materials are, as has already been said, at St. Mary's Seminary, Oscott. They were collected for him chiefly by Alban Butler, and thus they have a peculiar interest as associated with two great men. In addition to this original information and all that was to be found at Douay, to which he had free access, Challoner had recourse besides to various scattered printed books, some of considerable bulk, such as Bridgewater's *Concertatio* and Yepez' *Historia Particular*, and others more fugitive, which have become rare and are as hard to get a sight of as the manuscripts themselves. These, as we have said, we propose to collect and publish, if Catholic readers share our sense of their interest.

And now for a few remarks called for by the contents of the following pages. Amongst the laymen who suffered, James Layburne is here included, whose name was omitted by Bishop Challoner as he denied Elizabeth's right to the throne. It will be understood that the insertion of his history amongst those of his fellow-sufferers, is not intended as in any way prejudging the question which the Holy See will one day be called upon to decide, that is to say, his right to the title of Martyr. It is no more in the power of private individuals to decide this, than it is in their power to say to which of those who died in prison the like honour is to be accorded. It cannot properly be said that the admission of others, whose case is similar to Layburne's, into the decree of equivalent beatification, is a virtual decision of his case by Rome; though no doubt it has made a great difference. The truth is that in that decree of beatification the various cases were not judged on their merits, but only on the single fact of whether or not they are included amongst those whose pictures were put up in the College Church at Rome under Gregory XIII. When Plumtree, Felton, Storey, and Woodhouse, who all now have the title of Blessed, come to be proposed for Canonization, their claim and right to the title of Martyr will be investigated and decided precisely in the same way as James Layburne's. Meanwhile it is our duty to regard the matter as undecided by the only tribunal that can speak in the name of the Church and with her full authority.

One or two Martyrs, hitherto unrecognized, find their place in these narratives. There is the interesting case of John Thomas, who suffered at Winchester in August, 1593.[2] He had been condemned to death with the Venerable James

[2] *Infra*, pp. 232, 234.

Bird, but through fear he had promised to go to church and was reprieved accordingly. He repented at once, and following the example of the "lapsed" in the primitive Church, he offered himself for martyrdom, his dread for which was changed into desire.

Another instance is that of a Martyr named Symonds, the omission of whose name from the Catalogues is perhaps to be attributed to a false report that he was a spy. Yet "at Tyburn he blessed himself, and kissing the halter said it was the happiest collar that ever went about his neck."[3]

It is less clear that the Queen Mary priest called William or Williams is a Martyr unknown to Challoner. The only difficulty of identifying him with one of those who come in Challoner, and now enjoy the title of Venerable, is the date. Our Martyr died in 1592. Challoner says: "About the same time (some say the same day) [as Ven. John Weldon,[4] October 5, 1588], Richard Williams, a venerable priest, who had been ordained in England before the change of religion, was also, for religious matters, hanged at Holloway, near London."[5]

[3] P. 289.   [4] Pp. 229, 289, 309.
[5] He may very possibly be the same, again, as Maurice Williams, who was committed to the Clink, June 17, 1586, and is called by Justice Young, "an old priest" (*Troubles*, ii. pp. 179, 232).

This seems to be a mistake of date, due to Williams having taken Symonds' place in some Catalogue of Martyrs, which Challoner has followed; Father Persons, in his *Responsio ad Edictum Elizabethæ Reginæ*,[6] gives both under their right dates.

The case of the Venerable Richard Williams, as we may safely call him, as described[7] by James Young and by Father Garnet, is well deserving of attention. He was ordained priest under Queen Mary, had become a minister in Elizabeth's time, and had married. Now the marriage of one in sacred orders, or of a Regular under solemn vows, though in itself invalid, is called in Canon Law, *bigamia similitudinaria*. Alexander III. declared it to entail irregularity, from which the Ordinary can dispense, and Clement V. punished those thus offending with excommunication *latæ sententiæ* reserved to the Ordinary. A dispensation was therefore needed for such a one to resume his priestly functions, and as Williams was found acting as a priest, it was presumed that he must have been reconciled. On this he was condemned to death and executed. We, in our turn, may draw an argument from this as to the feeling of the Catholics of those days about the validity of Anglican Orders,

[6] Edit. 1593, p. 376.   [7] *Infra*, p. 20.

and as to what Protestants knew to be the feeling of Catholics. There were many cases of English clergymen becoming Catholic priests. No difficulty on the score of this sort of bigamy was made respecting any convert clergyman who had been married. If Richard Williams had been simply a "married minister," this objection would not have been made about him. It was because his Orders were valid, that his subsequent marriage made a dispensation necessary.

Father Persons' account[8] of this Martyr, though not referring to this point, may well be added here:

I ask then, what crime or wickedness had those seven servants of God committed, whom you slaughtered in London last December? I mean Edmund Genings, Eustace White, and Polydore Plasden, priests, Swithin Wells, and Bryant Lacy, both gentlemen of good family, and two servants. Could you prove anything against them except that they were Catholics, and had heard Mass together? What again of the other priests whom you have executed since with such great cruelty? What of Patenson and Williams, and those many others, whose names, though still unknown to us, are inscribed in the Book of Life? Were they convicted of any other crime beyond that of being priests? Had they joined with the Roman Pontiff and the Catholic King of both Spains in any conspiracy

[8] *Elizabethæ Reginæ Angliæ Edictum, cum responsione ad singula capita.* Per Andream Philopatrum. Rome, 1593, p. 339.

except that of faith and religion, to which you are bitterly hostile?

Of the latter, that is Williams (a man who had once been of your religion), I have heard the following account from an eye-witness of his martyrdom, which took place but few months ago. While, according to his sentence, this servant of God was being dragged along the streets on a hurdle like a felon, he was set at nought by some of your ministers, who were mounted on horseback. Amongst these was a very foolish fellow, and ridiculous preacher, a man of notoriously bad fame, by name David Dee, who often vexed the Martyr, and tried with many shouts to impress upon the people that they must carefully avoid the idea that this man was condemned for cause of religion, since he was suffering for high treason. To whom, however, the Martyr answered nothing, being wrapped in silent meditation on death and heavenly things.

At length he came to the place of martyrdom, where another of your preachers (seeing the sufferer's modesty, constancy, and great patience) adopted a very different line of attack, for he with alternate flattery, praise, and prayer, most earnestly begged him to save his life, which he would certainly promise him, if he would only confess that the Queen was the head of the English Church.

The other listened to him with a smile, and made answer that he had now completed a good part of his journey to Heaven, having already reached the spot where he was to die; and hoped God would not fail to give him strength to complete the rest of his journey. With these words he dismissed the heretical minister, and prepared himself for death, to which he yielded very cheerfully.

In this place it may be well to say that the distinction drawn[9] between William Flower *alias* Way and William Wigges *alias* Way, as two different Martyrs must be withdrawn as untenable. The two dates of martyrdom given, both at Kingston, September 23, and October 1, 1588, do not quite correspond to the diversities of style, but though we cannot decide which of the two is the true date, the doubt expressed by Bishop Yepez whether Way and Flower were two different persons is set at rest by the entry in the prison list,[10] "William Flower *alias* Way, Seminary in the Clink." The diversity of a few days in the date assigned to the martyrdom of Wigges *alias* Way is insufficient ground for making him out to be another person.

Another identification to be found in this book[11] is not without interest. It establishes that the priest who was set free from the Bridewell Prison by the Venerable Margaret Ward, through fear lest his constancy which had broken down once should yield again, was William Watson, who was executed in 1603 with another priest named Clarke for a plot against King James. Of the priest whom the two Venerable Martyrs Margaret Ward and John Roche liberated at the cost of

---

[9] *Troubles* ii. p. 234.
[10] P.R.O., *Dom. Eliz.* ccii. n. 61.   [11] P. 312.

their own lives, Father Christopher Grene wrote,[12] "Sacerdos hic vocabatur Watsonus, qui postea seditiosus fuit, et de vero crimine læsæ majestatis plexus anno 1603." This William Watson, the author of the notorious *Quodlibets*, has not hitherto been identified with the priest for whom Margaret Ward heroically gave her life, through the error of the Christian name in Challoner, who calls him Richard. This mistake Challoner took from Yepez.[13] There is, however, no such person as Richard Watson, while on the other hand the Douay Diary, speaking of his return to England in 1590, calls him William Watson, priest, who had already suffered much in prisons in England.[14]

A curious point in this work is the additions it makes to bibliography. There are various books spoken of[15] in the account of the martyrdom of the Venerable James Duckett, there is also a hitherto unknown first edition of Genings' *Life of Genings*, and there is a puzzle that we have not been able to solve in the title of a book, given as *Verepœum*.

It does not seem to be necessary to draw the reader's attention in any especial manner to the

[12] Stonyhurst MSS. *Collectanea P.* fol. 527.
[13] *Historia*, lib. 5. c. 2, erroneously given by Challoner lib. 2, c. 5.
[14] *Douay Diary*, p. 236.   [15] Pp. 239—246, 216 and 274.

various accounts of the Martyrs. Practically, a full analysis of this volume may be found in the Index under the heading "Martyrs." The headings, "Books," "London," "Manuscripts," may also be found of interest.

The narratives will speak for themselves, and if they are read, they can hardly fail to arouse in the heart of the reader a more earnest devotion and affection to our English Martyrs than he possessed before. But though I need not rehearse the results of the labour of my colleague and friend Father Pollen, I may be allowed to thank him warmly for his excellent work. The book itself, without any echo from me, testifies to his pains in collecting these materials, and to his care in editing them. I have long desired to see a book like this published, for the sake of the Martyrs, whose Cause it is meant to advance; and now that in the Martyrs' name I thank Father Pollen for what he has done, I venture to say that all friends of the Martyrs will look to receive much more at his hands in due time.

JOHN MORRIS, S.J.

31, Farm Street, London, W.
February 3, 1891.

CONTENTS.

	PAGE
PREFACE	v
CHAPTER I.—Blessed Thomas Sherwood	1
,, II.—Blessed Edmund Campion, S.J. . . .	21
,, III.—Venerable John Slade and Venerable John Bodey	49
,, IV.—Venerable Robert Anderton and Venerable William Marsden	66
,, V.—Venerable Roger Dicconson and Venerable Ralph Milner	83
,, VI.—Venerable Edmund Genings and Companions	98
,, VII.—Venerable William Davies	127
,, VIII.—Venerable John Roberts, O.S.B., and Venerable Thomas Somers	143
,, IX.—Venerable John Almond	171
,, X.—Venerable John Thulis and Venerable Roger Wrenno	194
,, XI.—Ten Martyred Laymen.	208
,, XII.—Father Warford's Recollections . . .	249
,, XIII.—Selections from the Westminster Archives .	279
,, XIV.—Selections from Stonyhurst Manuscripts .	298
,, XV.—Papers from Nymphenburg	338
APPENDIX:—	
Decree of equivalent Beatification of 54 Martyrs .	369
Decree of Introduction of the Cause of 261 Venerable Servants of God	376
Table of the Blessed and Venerable English Martyrs .	384
INDEX	385

CHAPTER I.

BLESSED THOMAS SHERWOOD.

Suffered at Tyburn, February 7, 1577–8.

DOCUMENTS.

1. Account by his brother (Stonyhurst MSS. *M.* fol. 157).
2. Contemporary account of his imprisonment (Westminster Archives, vol. ii. p. 75). Latin.
3. Official records of his torture, trial, and execution.
    (i.) Privy Council warrants for his examination and torture (Council Books, Whitehall, vol. vi. pp. 68, 69, 80).
    (ii.) Record of his trial, condemnation, and execution (Coram Rege and Controlment Rolls. P.R.O.). Latin.

---

1. The account of the Blessed Thomas Sherwood, written by one of his brothers, which is here printed from a transcript in Father Christopher Grene's *Collectanea M*, now at Stonyhurst, throws, as might be expected, being composed by one of his own family, much light upon the home influences by which his character was moulded. It is also of special importance as it corrects one of the very few mistakes to be found in Dr. Challoner's *Memoirs*. He represents Sherwood as having been a student at Douay, quoting the College Diary as his authority. The admirable edition of that Diary, published by the late Dr. Knox of the London Oratory, enables

us to say for certain that Challoner is here mistaken. Thomas Sherwood was never a student at Douay, nor was he as young at the time of his death as some have supposed from the application to him of the Latin epithet *juvenis*. He was about twenty-seven years of age.

THOMAS SHERWOOD THE MARTYR.

A Relation written by his Brother for his Nephews.

<small>Henricus Sherwood, pater martyris.</small> Henry Sherwood, born in Nottingham, in his childhood brought up in the chapel of the Earl of Northumberland, and afterwards by the same Earl put to study at Oxford in time of King Henry VIII., where he continued six or seven years, and for that, being to take degree in the schools, he would not take the oath of supremacy, he left the University and being near to thirty years of age, he put himself to a worshipful merchant, dwelling in Watling Street, called Mr. Holt, who employed him into Spain as his factor. Returning to London, he married a virtuous maid called Elizabeth, and used the trade of a woollen draper, although he was free of the Company of Merchant Tailors, as his master was. In thirty years or thereabout which he lived with his said wife, he had by her fourteen children. Three or four of them died very young, all the rest lived to man's and woman's estate, all brought up in the Catholic religion.

After the coming of Queen Elizabeth and change of religion, with consent of his wife he went into Flanders, to enjoy the free use of his religion, and lived for a time at Mechlin, where then the English Nuns of St. Bridget's dwelled. After one year of absence he returned to England, and soon after, both he and his wife being taken at Mass in London, he was committed to prison, where he remained six months. He was delivered thence by means of the Spanish Ambassador, Gusman. Departed from London with his wife and younger children, he went to live at Nottingham, where after some years being called in question for not coming to church, &c., they went to live with one of their sons married in Dorsetshire. That son being molested for the same occasion, they all went to London, where the old man lived wholly retired, attending only to his devotion, &c., and not going out of his lodging.

Shortly after his coming to London, his son Thomas was apprehended (*de quo mox plura*). By this occasion he, together with his other son with whom he lived at London, was forced to depart and travel divers months up and down, none of their friends daring to receive them, till, after the said Thomas was executed, and the fury of the matter was past, he was conveyed to Bristow [Bristol], where his wife had been some time before with [John] her eldest son married there; and where he remained till he died, wholly retired and not going out of his lodging. While he did traffic in the world he was noted to be very wise, discreet, and temperate in his carriage, just in his dealings, frugal but not covetous, much beloved by his neighbours, courteous to all, full of compassion, very liberal to the poor, &c.

For the space of ten years before his death he retired himself wholly from all worldly dealings, and passed his time for the most part in prayer and contemplation, through which by little and little he became voluntarily ignorant and simple in matters of the world. He was of such patience and quietness of mind as for divers years before his death I never saw him subject to any the least passion of choler or other discontentment or grief. Many examples I could set down of his humility, patience, mortification, and true charity, but this may suffice in satisfying your desire. He lived about sixty-six years, rather more than less, in Bristow, in the house of his son, John Sherwood, Doctor of Physick, &c.

Thomas Sherwood, son of the said Henry Sherwood, born in London.

Thomas Sherwood, Martyr, 7 Februarii, 1578.

For some years brought up in learning, but about fifteen years of his age taken from school to serve his father in the trade of a draper, which he did divers years. Afterwards, being more devoted to a religious course of life than to a worldly, he obtained from his parents leave to pass the seas and come to Douay, where, having conferred with certain venerable Fathers, by them he was encouraged to fall again to study; and determining upon that course, it was thought fit he should first return into England, as well to adjustate his accounts with his father, having the best part of his substance in his hands and charge, as also to procure some competent means to maintain him for some time at his study.

Upon which occasion he returned back,. and whiles he travailed in the despatch of his business, he was met one morning in Chancery Lane by one George Marten, son to the Lady Tregonwell in Dorsetshire, which George had seen him divers times at his mother's house in the company of one Mr. Stampe, a priest; and so meeting him and calling for the constable, caused him to be apprehended. He was carried before Mr. Fleetwood, then Recorder of London, who upon the urging of the said Marten, saying he used much the company of priests, and that he had been beyond the seas and conferred with traitors there, did very strictly examine him, and urged him with divers capital questions, as what he thought of the Bull of Pius V., and whether if the Pope had excommunicated the Queen, she were then lawful Queen or no, and divers other such dangerous questions; whereto as he answered plainly according to his conscience, so showed he himself void of all passion or irreverent manner, being of his nature very meek and gentle. As touching the Bull of Pius V., he said he did not know thereof; and touching the excommunication, he answered that if the Pope had indeed excommunicated her (as he did not know whether he had or no), then he thought she could not be lawful Queen.

Of his answers to other questions (as, where he had lived, with whom he had talked beyond seas, &c.), little hold was taken; but for his resolute answer touching the excommunication, the Recorder sent him before the Council, who committed him to the Tower, where he was twice racked, and within three months arraigned, condemned, and rigorously executed, being sensibly alive when he was cut down and opened.

He was of small learning, scarcely understanding the Latin tongue, but had much read books of controversies and devotion, and had used much to converse among Catholic priests, and by reason thereof, having a good wit and judgment, and withal being very devout and religious, he was able to give good counsel, as he did to many of the more ignorant sort, being much esteemed for his virtuous life and humble and modest behaviour: besides, God did give a special grace in his [conversation], whereby together with his good example of life, he much moved and edified others. He was a man of little stature of body, yet of a healthful and good constitution, and very temperate in his diet.

After his first racking in the Tower (which was said to be rigorous), being visited by a certain Catholic gentlewoman, he showed himself of that joyful and comfortable spirit as she was astonished thereat. As also his keeper with compassion giving him warning that he was to be racked again, he was so little moved therewith, as merrily and with a cheerful countenance he said these words: "I am very little, and you are very tall; you may hide me in your great hose and so they shall not find me;" which the keeper did afterwards report to divers, much marvelling at his great fortitude and courage. He was about the age of twenty-seven years when he was martyred.

<small>Elizabetha, mater Thomæ Sherwodi Martyris, obiit in carcere.</small> I think it not amiss to set down a few words touching my mother, your grandmother, who was a very virtuous woman and ever Catholic. She was, as I have said before, in the beginning of the Queen's reign taken at Mass with her husband, and appeared before the High Commissioners, at what time she showed herself very constant in her religion, answering without any fear Dr. Cocks [Cox], then pretended Bishop of Ely, using railing speeches against Catholic priests, and among others saying it was not possible for them to live without women. She, moved with zeal, answered him that if she had the dieting of him three months together, he should confess that it was possible for a priest to live without a woman, but living in pleasure and good cheer, it was no marvel if he held the opinion he uttered.

Many years after she was called for her conscience before the Judges of Assize in Dorchester, and bound to further appearance, at what time also she showed great constancy in her faith. After that, she was taken again at Mass in London (being then a widow) and was imprisoned, and continued for the most part in prison fourteen years together, although by friends she was sometimes gotten out upon sureties, but stayed little out, being still troubled and committed; and in the end died in prison, after she had spent and consumed all her substance.

<small>Joannes Sherwood, Societatis Jesu, frater Martyris Thomæ Sherwodi.</small> My brother John, the younger, being a forward grammarian about the age of fifteen years, was put to serve one Mr. Waferer, a Catholic and counsellor of the law, with whom he continued certain years, profiting well in that course; but being moved by God's grace, he came over to the English College then at Rheims, and afterwards entered into the Society and died in the same, much commended as well for his learning as life.

Finis hujus relationis de Sherwodis.

2. We now give a somewhat fuller account of Blessed Thomas Sherwood's imprisonment from a contemporary document, by an anonymous writer. Though undated, it must have been written before 1582, as it is quoted by Father Persons in his *De Persecutione Anglicana*, which was printed in that year. The introductory paragraphs containing no fresh matter have been omitted.

The brave youth was sent to the Tower and most cruelly confined in a very dark cell near the torture-chamber: meantime the chamber he had in the city was ransacked (according to the custom of those harpies) and all his goods removed, together with about ninety pieces of gold, belonging to other persons, which were owing to his needy and afflicted father, as if the pieces themselves were guilty of high treason and denial of the Supremacy. In the prison Sherwood suffered very grievous things with a constancy worthy of all praise, so as to cause us great regret that they should be noticed so briefly. This, however, was not peculiar to Sherwood; many others also are involved in obscurity, not figuratively only, by the negligence of our writers, but literally also, through the malice of the heretics. Thus the worst tortures are applied in dark dungeons, in order to hide the victory of the Martyrs over their tormentors and their own brutality. Certainly I think that if all the things these illustrious champions of the Catholic faith have suffered in the Tower of London and in the private houses of the magistrates, had been undergone in public, we should see that there were not a few whose noble conflicts equalled those of the early Martyrs. But God wills otherwise, at least for the present. Yet we may well hope that soon, either in our time, or in that of our posterity, there will be very few of these secret doings which shall not be revealed, and what they have done in darkness shall be proclaimed to the glory of those who suffered and to the shame of those who caused their sufferings; but let us return to our Sherwood.

To begin with, the holy youth was harassed by repeated torturings, in order that overcome with pain, he might confess where he had heard Mass, to the intent that any he might name, might be punished with like plunder of goods and bodily injury. But he was brave beyond his years [as one of the Protestants there present confessed[1]]; no racking, no cross-examination could make him name any one. Thus baulked, his barbarous torturers changed their proceedings and cast the Martyr, who had now lost the use of his limbs, into a very dark and fetid dungeon. Here he was left without necessary clothing, in order that the terrors of darkness, the stench, and most of all, the shameful nakedness, might break his resolution, which no torture could move. As to food, it is easy to conjecture of what sort it was, seeing that he was not allowed to buy anything to sustain life. Nay, more, what calls for the utmost commiseration is, that when a certain good man [Mr. Roper, son-in-law to Thomas More[2]], touched by the report of the extreme hunger which the blessed youth was suffering, sent him some money, and by means of a prisoner conveyed it to Sherwood's own keeper (this every one in the Tower has), the keeper returned it the next day, because the Lieutenant would not allow him to have the benefit of any alms. The Martyr's friend asked whether the keeper himself would not expend it for his benefit, but he was told it was impossible. All that the most earnest prayers could effect was to induce him to take sixpence to buy straw for

[1] This is Father Robert Persons' note to this passage.
[2] Father Persons' note.

the youth to lie on, so great was the inhumanity of the Lieutenant towards his starving prisoner.

These things he suffered for six months, without any hope of relief from man, though doubtless Divine consolation did not fail him. At length, after having courageously borne a most cruel imprisonment, chains, hunger, cold, stench, nakedness, and the rack, being hanged and disembowelled, he passed to Heaven on the 7th February, 1578, to receive the reward of his sufferings in mind and body.

Farewell, most holy Martyr, and help with your patronage me, a most unworthy sinner, who am labouring to increase your honour here on earth. Amen.

3. It now remains for us to refer to some of the official documents, which authorized the perpetration of the cruelties just narrated. They are the more important, because Sherwood was the first Catholic who was systematically put to the question; that is to say, who was examined under torture in order to extort admissions that might be used against him on his trial, or avowals that might incriminate other Catholics.

(i.) The first warrant was sent by the Privy Council from Windsor, Nov. 17, 1577.

A letter to the Attorney General signifying unto him that he shall receive the examination of one Thomas Sherwood, lately committed by the High Commissioners, for hearing of a Mass, and since examined by Mr. Recorder of London, which examination, containing matter of high treason against her Majesty's person, their lordships have thought good to require him, after he shall have substantially considered thereof, to acquaint the Lord Chief Justice therein, and presently to give order that the said Sherwood be this term arraigned and proceeded against according to the laws of this realm in that behalf provided, but before they proceed to his arraignment [they are also to examine him on his previous examination, to see whether he can discover any other of his knowledge to be of his opinion, and where he gathered the substance of the arguments of his confession].[3] Wherein perhaps he may bolt out some other matters or persons worthy to be known.

At the same time they sent

A letter to Mr. Lieutenant of the Tower requiring him to receive into his hands of Mr. Recorder of London the person of Thomas Sherwood, and to retain him close prisoner and from conference with any person, until such time as he shall receive order from Mr. Attorney General, who is appointed to examine him upon such matters as he is to be charged withal.

He is required in a postscript, that if the said Sherwood shall not willingly confess such things as shall be demanded of him, he is then required to commit him to the dungeon amongst the rats.

[3] The passages within brackets exactly represent the sense of the original. Complete copies were not allowed to be made.

According to Mr. Jardine,[4] this dungeon "is described as a cell below high water mark and totally dark. As the tide flowed, innumerable rats, which infest the muddy banks of the Thames, were driven through the orifices of the walls into the dungeon. The alarm excited by the irruption of these loathsome creatures in the dark was the least part of the torture which the unfortunate captives had to undergo; instances are related, which humanity would gladly believe to be the exaggerations of Catholic partisans, where the flesh has been torn from the arms and legs of prisoners during sleep by the well-known voracity of these animals."

To return to our Martyr. From the dates given in his indictment, it appears that shortly after the issuing of the above writs by the Privy Council, Gilbert Gerard, the Attorney General, went to Westminster, where Sherwood was then confined, and there obtained again from the Martyr the statements as to the excommunication of the Queen, which Fleetwood had already wormed out of him. According to the iniquity of the times the utterance so obtained was treated as an act of high treason, and for it he finally suffered. As, however, he would not confess the names of any other Catholics, he was sent to the Tower, where his examination was continued under torture, and the next letter from the Lords of the Privy Council abundantly shows how constant was his fidelity to his faith and to his fellow-Catholics. It opens up, however, some points on which we would gladly know more.

Dec. 4, 1577. To the Lieutenant of the Tower, the Attorney General, Solicitor General, Recorder of London, or any of them.

[4] *On the use of Torture in the Criminal Law of England*, p. 26.

That where their Lordships by their letters of the 25th of November, do understand the pains they have taken in the examination of Sherwood in the Tower, for the which their Lordships yield them right hearty thanks, and where they signify that Sherwood doth not only stagger in his first confession, and fain would retract his words in respect he affirmed her Majesty to be an heretic and usurper, and also will in no case be brought to confess or answer such other interrogatories as they have propounded unto him, their Lordships are of opinion that, if he be used thereafter, he can discover other persons as evil affected towards her Majesty as himself. They are, therefore, to assay him at the rack, upon such articles as they shall think meet to minister unto him for the discovering either of the persons or of further matters.

This letter, we say, opens up some points, which we would gladly understand better, though it is improbable that we ever shall. The exact words of the Martyr have not been preserved, and it is clearly unreasonable to place implicit trust in his enemies' insinuations of inconstancy. Of course he would have been glad never to have uttered the words in question about the Queen at all; clearly, too, he never professed them unconditionally, as the Council here falsely represents. His examiners in the Tower informed the Lords of the Council that he "staggered and would fain retract his words." Be this as it may, the letter bears ample witness to his constancy in his religion, in his fidelity to his fellow-Catholics, in short, in all that certainly concerns his faith.

(ii.) We now give the official record of Sherwood's trial from the Coram Rege Roll (20 Eliz. rot. 3). We have translated the record as it stands, omitting only from the second count of the indictment the amplifications, which are repeated exactly as in the first count. Our lay readers will perhaps understand the report better, if they remember that it only professes to recite the legal proceedings, no notice being taken of the pleadings for and against the accused. They should also bear in mind that the Sovereign is supposed to be present in person in the Court of Queen's Bench.

RECORD OF SHERWOOD'S TRIAL.

Middlesex to wit, by indictment Michaelmas, 20 Eliz. Otherwise, to wit, in the term of St. Michael last past, before our Lady the Queen at Westminster, by the oath of twelve jurors, it was presented that Thomas Sherwood, late of London, yeoman, on the 20th day of November, in the 20th year of the Lady Elizabeth, by the grace of God Queen of England, France, and Ireland, Defender of the Faith, &c., in the city of Westminster, in the county of Middlesex, diabolically, maliciously, and traitorously, compassing, imagining, thinking, devising, and intending the deprivation and deposition of the said Lady Queen Elizabeth, from her style, honour, and royal title to the imperial crown of this kingdom of England, did, out of his own perverse and treacherous mind and imagination, maliciously, expressly, advisedly, directly and traitorously in the city of Westminster aforesaid, in the county aforesaid, in the presence and hearing of divers faithful subjects of the said Lady our Queen, utter, answer, publish, and say these false traitorous English words following about the aforesaid Lady our present Queen of England, falsely, maliciously, advisedly, directly and treacherously—to wit "*that for so much as our Queen Elizabeth* (herein intending our said Queen now living) *doth expressly disassent in Religion from the Catholic faith, of which Catholic faith, he sayeth that the Pope Gregory the Thirteenth that now is, is conserver, because he is God's General Vicar in earth: and therefore he affirmeth by express words that our said Queen Elizabeth* (meaning the aforesaid Lady now Queen Elizabeth) *is a schismatic and an heretic:*" to the very great scandal and derogation of the person of our said Lady the Queen, and the subversion of the state of this realm of England, and traitorously and against his due allegiance, and against the form of the statute in this case made and provided in the third Parliament of our said Lady now Queen at Westminster, in the county of Middlesex, in the 13th year of her reign—moreover, also against the peace of our said Lady now Queen, her crown and dignities, &c.

<small>Middlesex to wit, by indictment Michaelmas.</small> Also otherwise, to wit in the term of St. Michael aforesaid, before our Lady the Queen at Westminster, it stands presented by the oath of 12 jurors, that Thomas Sherwood, late of London, yeoman, on the 20th day of November, in the 20th year of the

Lady Elizabeth aforesaid, &c., did diabolically, maliciously, &c., in the city of Westminster, in the county aforesaid, in the presence and hearing of divers faithful subjects of the same Lady the Queen, &c., utter, &c., the following words, namely: *that the Pope hath power and authority to depose any Christian prince or king if he mislike with him, and farther that Queen Elizabeth* (meaning the said Elizabeth now our Queen) *doth expressly disassent in faith from the Catholic faith; and also sayeth that if the Pope had pronounced our Queen* (meaning the said Elizabeth now our Queen) *to be deposed for any matter of Religion, then she* (meaning the said Elizabeth now our Queen) *is deposed, and that then she* (again meaning the aforesaid Elizabeth now our Queen) *is an usurper*, &c., &c.

Whereupon a precept was given to the Sheriff that he should not omit, &c., to take him if, &c., to answer, &c.

And now, to wit, Saturday next after the 18th of St. Hilary in the present term, before the Queen at Westminster, the aforesaid Thomas Sherwood came under ward of Owen Hopton, Knight, Lieutenant of the Tower of our Lady the Queen in London, to whose custody he was before for this same cause and certain other causes committed, in virtue of a brief from our Lady the Queen *de habeas corpus ad subjiciend.* &c. Thereupon he was at once brought to the bar here in his own proper person, and is committed to the aforesaid Lieutenant.

And immediately, questioned separately as to the several premisses alleged against him, how he will acquit himself of them, sayeth that of them he is in nowise guilty: and thereupon for good and evil placeth himself upon his country. The jury, therefore, then came before our Lady the Queen at Westminster, on Monday, the morrow of the Purification of Blessed Mary the Virgin, by whom, &c., and who, &c., to take cognizance, &c., because, &c. The same day is appointed to the aforesaid Thomas Sherwood, committed meanwhile to the custody of the aforesaid Lieutenant.

On which day the aforesaid Thomas Sherwood in his own proper person came before our Lady the Queen at Westminster, under ward of the aforesaid Lieutenant. And the Sheriff returned the names of twelve jurymen, which jurymen having been impanelled and summoned for this, came to say truth about and over the premisses. Who, having been elected, tried, and sworn, say upon their oath that the aforesaid Thomas Sherwood is guilty of the several high treasons aforesaid, laid against him above in the form aforesaid, according to the fashion and form wherein they were charged against him above in the several indictments aforesaid. Also that the self same Thomas Sherwood hath no goods or chattels, lands, or tenements to their knowledge.

Whereupon, Gilbert Gerard, Esquire, Attorney General to our Lady the Queen, begged on behalf our said Lady the Queen, for judgment and execution against the same Thomas Sherwood. Upon this it was asked of the aforesaid Thomas if he had or could say anything for himself, why this Court should not proceed to judgment and execution upon the aforesaid verdict. Who sayeth no otherwise than as he said above. Whereupon the Sheriff, &c., by the Court, having understood all and each of the premisses, the same Gilbert Gerard, the Attorney of our said Lady the Queen, being summoned and present for this purpose, judgment was given that the aforesaid Thomas Sherwood be led by the aforesaid Lieutenant unto the Tower of London, and thence be dragged through the midst of the city of London, directly unto the gallows of Tyburn, and upon the gallows there be hanged, and thrown living to the earth, and that his bowels be taken from his belly, and whilst he is alive be burnt, and that his head be cut off, and that his body be divided into four parts, and that his head and quarters be placed where our Lady the Queen shall please to assign them.

There is no account preserved of the details of Sherwood's conduct at the place of execution. In the Controlment Roll (20 Eliz. rot. 29) may be read the writ addressed to the Lieutenant of the Tower, directing him "on Wednesday, to wit, the seventh day of this instant month of February, to meet the sheriffs of our city of London on Tower Hill, and to deliver there the said Thomas Sherwood to the same sheriffs." Immediately following this comes the writ to the sheriffs, who in turn are directed to meet the

Lieutenant on Tower Hill, to receive Sherwood, and "to do execution upon him according to the form above recited, as is fitting."

Three weeks later, news of the death of this blessed Martyr reached the Seminary at Douay, and is thus entered in their diary.[5]

On the first of March Mr. Lowe returned to us from England, bringing news that a youth, by name [Thomas] Sherwood, had suffered for his confession of the Catholic faith, not only imprisonment, but death itself. Amidst all his torments his exclamation had been, "Lord Jesus, I am not worthy to suffer this for Thee, much less to receive those rewards, which Thou hast promised to those that confess Thee."

[5] *Douay Diaries*, p. 135.

CHAPTER II.

BLESSED EDMUND CAMPION OF THE SOCIETY OF JESUS.

Suffered December 1, 1581.

DOCUMENTS.

1. Metrical life (Bodleian Library, MS. Laud Misc. 755).
2. Notes by Father Thomas Fitzherbert (Westminster Archives, vol. ii. p. 185).
3. Father Walpole's conversion at Campion's martyrdom (Bibliothèque de Bourgogne, n. 2167 and also n. 4554). Latin.
4. Notes by the Ven. Father Walpole on Campion's trial and execution (Archives S.J.). Italian.

Of none of our Martyrs has more been written than of Blessed Edmund, and of none do more ample materials for biography exist. Nor is this to be wondered at. There was something unique in his powers, something electrical in his character that moved and roused men, as few have ever done. His coming, too, raised to its highest pitch the wave of Catholic reaction against Elizabeth's reformation. He came to be regarded as the leader and ideal representative of English priests. It is therefore only natural that much should have been written and much preserved about him. This, however, makes it difficult to select, amongst papers yet inedited, which shall be accounted worthy to represent the life of so great a man. Three documents only have been chosen, the two latter as valuable records of some of Campion's doings, the first as giving a brief outline of the Martyr's life, and much more as letting us see incidentally how strong a hold Campion had won on the sympathies of his fellow-Catholics.

1. The original of the "Brief of the life and death of Sir Edmund Campion" is among Laud's manuscripts in the Bodleian Library, and is written in a minute hand on a small roll of paper. That it was composed at the time of Campion's death, appears from the motive of its author, which is to dispel unfavourable rumours current against the Martyr. These had been set afloat some months before by the cunning of Lord Burleigh, who gave out that various Catholics, imprisoned by him, were arrested because Campion had betrayed their names. But the Martyr's speech from the scaffold and his constancy in death dispelled this cloud on his fame, and though the Catholics of the time were never able to trace the rumour home to its originator as we can now, it was soon discredited. As it seems unlikely that "Light Report" would have been described as she is here, more than six months after Campion's death, the composition can with probability be assigned to the beginning of the year 1582. Its occasional roughness of rhyme and rhythm does not point to a great scholar as its compiler, but it rather enhances the enthusiastic fervour so eminently Elizabethan, in which it is conceived and composed.

A BRIEF OF THE LIFE AND DEATH OF SIR EDMUND CAMPION, PRIEST OF THE BLESSED SOCIETY OF THE NAME OF JESUS.

The Christian Mourner. "And is he dead indeed; is virtue so foreset?
Hath malice clouded humble mind: shall fraud on good men fret?
Is learning now forlorn; hath blood imbrued the ground?
Is no remorse for to be had where virtues all abound?
Do all the muses mourn in losing of their light?
Did pity playne in every heart to see this rueful sight?"

Light Report. As thus amazed I mused, like one with sorrow fed,
Out stept me Light Report, and said, that he indeed is dead:
And that no life was left, where treason did attaint,
But brought himself to wilful wreck, and other to distraint.

Truth. Scant Report had said, but forth there comes in place
A worthy wight, the truest form that ever showed forth face,
All clad in virgin white, of silver pure her gown,
A laurel in her happy hand, and on her head a crown.
Who gravely gave a pause, and after, thus she said,

As far as I remember, came her words, which
   then I weighed.

"Let Light Report go pack: begone," quoth she,
   "with speed.
The noble Sir thou hast belied, he is not dead
   indeed.
Thou rudely dost catch up a tale, at first pursuit,
And seekest to stain the purest bright, with false
   redoubled bruit.
But for this worthy man, with joy he ends his
   plaints:
He liveth still, I say, he lives among the sacred
   saints.
Therefore thou Light Report, thou loudly bruitest
   lies.
Make up thy mouth, and be thou blind where
   truth doth ope her eyes.
This man of mighty mind unto the world I blaze,
What fame, what life, what death he had, which
   time shall never raze.

<small>Born.</small>   In London rose this star, a blessed
   womb him bore,
As good an Edmund for his time, as Thomas was
   before.
Then London herein joy, and hope return from
   sin,
Since thou unto such happy saints a holy nurse
   hast been.
<small>Brought up.</small>   Whilst here with deep desire he did
   the schools frequent,

Even for the muses born he seemed, so forward
    was he bent.
A youngling as he was, he flamed in virtue's love,
That even then the wise did say, this child will
    passing prove.
They were not then deceived that deemed of him
    so true,
He proved in fine their judgment just, as life with
    learning grew.

<small>Sent to Oxford.</small> Now when the city schools had
    yielded all their skill,
And that no more was to be had to feed his
    worthy will,
Then to the learned sort of Oxford was he
    set,
Of virtues rare the fountain clear, and full desire
    to get.
Where as that famous knight the noble Whyte
    did found
A College brave of learned heads built on a happy
    ground.
Here, as a blossom gay, in fresh desire he grew;
He won his praise, in this his prime, of all that
    well him knew,
For memory, for wit, for will, for skill sublime.
He then began for to appear the wonder of his
    time.
In Oxford who him knew, knew well his passing
    praise,
Even then was he a lamp of light to pass in
    virtue's ways.

So fraught with learned lore, so full of fruitful shows,
That every wight that saw him said, lo, there a gallant goes!
What wisdom then he had, what goodly gifts of grace,
They can report that live and know the person, time, and place.
Truth may it boldly speak, Oxford had few before,
And since, for aught mine eye discerns, his peer was seen no more.
I come not to compare, nor to reject the rest,
But that I say, because I know Truth may report it best.
So rare in every art, his words of such a power,
That of the learned of his time he proved the rarest flower.

<small>Proceeded.</small> Saint Mary Church can tell, and all the schools do know,
The walls may yet resound his praise, where he excelled so.
How sharp in science sound, how ripe in skill was he,
How sweet for tongue, how grave for truth, how deep for memory!
How skill'd in antique writs, how rare in every art,
And how the Bible in each point he could repeat by heart.
And that which most appeared, yet rarest for to find,

The more of learning he possessed, more humble
  was his mind.
In travail how expert, in studies grave and long,
How apt for to remember right, and to forget the
  wrong.
No book to him unknown, where learning was
  compact;
The graces waited where he went in every learned
  act.
In English if he wrote, he penned it passing well;
If Tully's tongue he took to speak, he did therein
  excel.
Despite must it report, when she the cause hath
  scanned;
In every part he did surpass, what erst he took in
  hand.
His couched cunning such, as blazeth out his
  name;
His works, that ever more shall live, do well
  declare the same.
Oh, that one day should take, and drive him to
  be gone!
Oh, that so many virtues rare, should so be slain
  in one!

<small>Proctor in the University.</small> In Oxford so beloved, and blazed of
  the best,
That he at last was chosen one to rule above the
  rest.
By due desert obtained, he did the learned guide;
His wisdom did appear therein as in each act
  beside.

Thus reaping earned praise for learning fully tried,
It would have made a youthful head to pitch him-
  self in pride.
And to have launched forth a large desire to seek
Of worldly weal and worship both, a seat among
  the like.
But he by special grace to heaven cast up his
  eyen,
And with a noble courage flamed, he then became
  Divine :
And mounting up his mind above all worldly toys,
He sought for honours uncorrupt, and undistressed
  joys.
He sought the endless realm of the eternal bliss.
What nobler heart, what honour more, what better
  choice than this ?

<small>Travelled.</small>   Now having stayed his time, he
  travelled foreign land,
As ever careful to increase the mean to understand.
And when he did depart, to run a Christian race,
He left a pattern to the house, and praise unto
  the place.
Thus travelled he abroad, possessed with noble
  mind,
As Plato did, that pierced far, the perfect skill
  to find.
What virtues then he had, Prague can report
  it well,
The Universities abroad, the courts of kings
  can tell.

Wherever that he came, his virtues ever shined,
Like as the sun is ever bright, and keeps his course by kind.

Now when eight years were spent, in sacred order set,
When he had lived in passing fame, which no age will forget;
He feared not this world, nor praise wherein he stood,
But ventured life and limb and all, to do his country good.
   Returned. So to his native soil, upon command he came,
Of only love to save the souls, that fell from virtue's frame:
To cure enchanted minds, to end our mortal strife;
What greater love, what faster friend, than to bestow his life?
He came not long to land, but that he taken was.
   Apprehended. What then? to them that love our Lord, nothing amiss doth pass.
I do remember well a sentence that he said:
'I may' (quoth he) 'for Truth be slain, yet not be conquered.'

But first his foes dispute, attempting every way,
Whereby they might entrap the truth, and blessed man betray.
   Imprisoned. The Tower had never man that stood in more defence,

More far from foil, more full of faith, or more
    sincere of sense.
And eke thereto so wise, and of a mind so mild,
Amid the furies of his foes he sweetly always
    smiled.
And when they rail and rave as rages on them
    ran,
It was a wonder to behold the meekness of the
    man.

<small>Disputed.</small> How grave he answers gave, how
    patiently he sat,
That they which hardly wished him well, were
    much amazed thereat.
How wise he silence gave to many words of
    wrath,
An answer best to fond replies, where wisdom
    dwelling hath.
Then say they he was weak, their fautors so they
    feed,
And blear the eyes of yielding imps, that take
    thereof no heed.
But let them lie and limp, let chafing tongues go
    chat,
As they that bark against the sun, and cast their
    cap thereat.
For he in prudent speech did drive them all to
    pause;
In words but few, full sense he gave, well armed
    for his cause.

<small>Allured.</small> When prate could not prevail, nor
    furies him astone,

Then, with attempt of promise fair, the battery
    was begun.
In vain do they allure, preferment to bestow,
With honour high, with seat of lord, with many
    a glory mo.
For neither honours, name, nor threats, nor rope,
    nor rack,
Could move the rock from off his place, nor draw
    the constant back.
    <small>Racked.</small>   Then to the rack they hale, with
    torture they him tear,
That more amazed the lookers on, than put him
    ought in fear.
    <small>Arraigned.</small>   The last assault was made; for, after
    diverse pains,
And torment of the torn limbs, that pierced all
    his veins,
Yet nothing could they win, the fact would
    nothing yield;
He builded was upon the rock, his sufferance got
    the field.
    <small>Condemned.</small>   Then was he threatened death, he is
    condemned to die.
'Judge and discern my cause' (quoth he), 'our
    Lord that sittest on high.'
In modest, wise demands his praise was bruited
    far:
And his prudent speeches were in pleading at the
    bar.
For learning passing rare, for life and learning like,
The banks of Brute possess no peer, if equal there
    she seek.

Of Emperor beloved, and for him princes strive:
And yet not thought a worthy man, among us here to live.
A Solomon for wit, a Solon for his will,
A Cato for his public care, a Tully for his skill.
A Socrates for mind, that feared no loss of breath,
A mirror for his godly life, a martyr for his death.
A Joseph to forgive, a Josua to guide,
As far from malice every way, as prudence is from pride.

Executed. Then to his death he came, where with a constant heart
He did protest he never thought a treason for his part.
As loyal to his prince as any wight beside,
That by his prayer for her life, that by his death he tried.
That every wight might say, with heavy heart that stood,
Here dies a lamb, here spake a saint, here flows the guiltless blood."

When Truth had said all this, now Light Report was bashed
And looked away with blushing brow, to see her dealing dashed.
And ran for to demand the worthy reverent youth,
What was her name. "Forsooth" (quoth she), "my name is called Truth,
By whom the God Eterne takes chief delight on high:

In whom this worthy man did live, for whom he
    chose to die."
This said, now Light Report began away to
    trudge,
As one that had no power of speech where Truth
    did sit as judge.
Then Truth called out for Fame, forthwith Fame
    comes in sight.
"Sound out" (quoth Truth) "thy silver trump,
    of this most worthy wight."
No sooner Truth had said, than [Fame[1]] began
    to sound
With such a blast unto the world as it did large
    rebound.
Which pierced the cheerful skies and made the
    angels glad,
And those were then the words of Fame which
    full in force she had.

His fame after death evermore. "If virtue ever live, if valour never
    die,
If learned arts for ever stand with grace eternally,
If perfect life get fame, if perfect fame endure,
If endless durance make us live, and set our
    honour sure;
If constance earn a crown, if conquest join the
    gain,
If learning armed with godly life do evermore
    remain;
If ardent thirst for souls, if aged acts in youth,
If for to sweat and die the death for the Eternal
    truth,

[1] In MS. "Truth."

If martyrs purchase life, if meekness last in praise,
If charity of highest degree do flourish green always,
If mind invincible do ever blaze and bide,
If all the gifts of manly mind, and virtues therein tried:
Then is not Edmund dead, but gone to bliss before,
He lives among the sacred saints, and reigns for evermore."

When I had heard this Fame that Truth had sounded out,
And that indeed he was not dead: then, being void of doubt,
I cast mine eyes to heaven, I feared none annoy,
I wiped mine eyes, and thanked God, and clapt my hands for joy.

2. Father Thomas Fitzherbert, writer of the following recollections, was a man of note in his time, some account of whose long and busy life may be read in Foley's *Records*, vol. ii. p. 188. Here it will be sufficient to say that he inherited Swynnerton, which he was obliged to leave for conscience' sake. As an exile he was highly trusted by the Court of Spain, as a priest he was selected to represent the English clergy at Rome, and finally, as a Jesuit he was entrusted with important posts of responsibility and authority. The original MS. is in the Westminster Archives, vol. ii. p. 185, and a Latin translation of it (*Ibid.* p. 181) has been corrected by Father Fitzherbert himself, as Father Grene notes.

Mr. Simpson found a paper, apparently similar to this, dated February 1, 1628 (*Edmund Campion*, p. 82). Our paper may have been written sooner, for the use of one of the biographers of Campion, perhaps Bombino, who published his life in 1618.

RECOLLECTIONS OF FATHER CAMPION.
By Father Thomas Fitzherbert.

About the year of our Lord 1567, I knew Father Campion, of blessed memory, in Oxford, who was then Master of Arts (which degree in that University is as much as Doctor *in Artibus* here [in Rome]), and was famed for his eloquence, in which respect he was made Junior of the Act, when he proceeded Master of Art, which place or title is always given to the best orator of those who take degree at that time. And for the opinion and fame which he had for his eloquence, the orations which he made in the University upon occasions then occurring, were diligently copied and greatly desired by all the scholars of the University, whereof I myself saw some copies at that time.

The year after, he was made Proctor of the University (which is the principal office after the Commissary who is head thereof). And although he was not then Catholic, yet he was held for no enemy to Catholics but rather a friend, and was generally esteemed and loved of all men. But after this time he departed Oxford, and I never saw him until he returned into England being of the Society, in the year 1580, together with

Father Persons; at what time I was familiarly acquainted with him. But in this meantime I heard that he was gone over the seas, and not only become Catholic but also of the Society, and that he was so much esteemed for his eloquence, that [Sir Philip Sydney] an heretical ambassador of the Queen of England, being sent to the Emperor, and relating at his return of certain things remarkable and worthy of memory which he had noted in the time of his embassage, recounted for one an eloquent sermon which Father Campion had made before the Emperor in Prague whilst he himself was there, and present at the sermon.

After his return into England he was of singular estimation and fame, no less for his religious virtue and exemplar life than for his learning and rare parts, whereby the Catholics are exceedingly comforted and edified, and particularly by his sermons, wherein he was generally esteemed to have a singular talent.

Shortly after his return into England, he set down in writing the reasons of his return, for the satisfaction as well of heretics as Catholics, concerning his mission thither, as that he was sent by his Superiors for the only good of souls, with express prohibition to deal in matters of State, as it was generally and slanderously given out by the heretics. And by the same occasion he offered to maintain the verity of Catholic Religion by a public disputation if he should be permitted, to which purpose also he published shortly after in print his little book of *Ten Reasons* which moved him to desire and offer a disputation; dedicating the same to the two Universities of Oxford and Cambridge.

And that the same was his own work I can well testify, for Father Persons being his Superior gave it me in written hand to be printed, and told me that it was Father Campion's, and therefore recommended it to me, not only to read but also to examine the places of Fathers alleged therein (because I might have more free recourse to public libraries in London than priests or religious could have). Besides that, after it was printed, Father Campion himself gave me one of the first printed copies as his own work.

Shortly after he had published this book he was taken by the heretics, being betrayed by a false brother, who having been a known Catholic became a secret spy for the heretics, and having gotten a commission from the Council to search for priests and namely for Father Campion, came to the house of a gentleman where he was, not knowing him to be there, and being taken for a Catholic, as he was formerly known to be, was admitted to hear Mass and a sermon of Father Campion's. Whereupon departing, presently after, he went to the next magistrates, and brought them thither to search the house, whereby Father Campion was taken and brought to the Tower of London prisoner.

And albeit I was in London at the same time when he was arraigned and condemned, yet I was not present thereat for divers respects, but understood sufficiently of what passed therein concerning the condemnation of him and divers other secular priests, which were condemned with him under a false pretence of a conspiracy made at Rome and Rheims by them all against the Queen and the state of the realm; whereof the injustice was most notorious, by reason that the manner of the trial of prisoners in England being public, and the witnesses produced before the accused in the presence of all the people, it evidently appeared that neither the prisoners had ever all of them known or seen one another before they came thither to the bar, neither yet the witnesses (as it was here proved by the confession of some of themselves) had ever seen them beyond the seas; yea, and that divers of the accused were in England at the same time when the conspiracy was supposed to be made at Rome and Rheims. And moreover that the particulars alleged and testified by the witnesses against them, did not concern at all Father Campion, nothing at all being testified against him in particular, which he urged notably, to the confusion of the witnesses and the judges. Besides that both he and the other prisoners took such exceptions to the witnesses for their infamy, that it appeared clearly they were suborned and deserved no credit. Finally, Father Campion so substantially pleaded for himself and the rest, that a gentleman of good account, a lawyer, and an earnest Protestant, yet a friend of mine, who was present at the arraignment, told me the day after, that in truth the evidences that were given against Father Campion were so weak, and his answers so sufficient and clear, that he could not persuade himself that he should be condemned, until he heard the chief Judge give the sentence of death. And when I asked him how it could stand with conscience to condemn innocent men, he answered that it was necessary for the State. And the like I heard credibly reported of another of the judges, who being asked afterwards by a familiar friend of his, with what conscience he could condemn Campion and the rest upon that evidence, he answered that he could do no less, for otherwise he should not be taken for a friend to Cæsar.

It was also constantly reported and very famous, that one of the assessors to the chief Judge found his hand spotted with blood at the time of Father Campion's condemnation, and that he showed it to some with great admiration.

As concerning his death I can say nothing but by report of others, because I was not present at it, only I think good to relate that the same day the River of Thames, which daily floweth and ebbeth with the sea, did change his course, ceasing to flow or ebb all that day; which was so notorious that some poets employed their pens to make sonnets thereupon to celebrate the wonder, applying it to the martyrdom of Father Campion. And one of the sonnets was presently after set forth in music by the best musician in England, which I have often seen and heard.

3. An account of one Martyr cannot fail to become additionally interesting when written by another. In this case the interest becomes all the greater, when we remember that the scenes, which Walpole here records, were the very means which converted him to the practice of the Catholic religion. Every action in the tragedy, we may well believe, had its part in preparing his soul to receive the grace of the true faith. How the conversion was finally effected is best shown by the following paper, from the Bibliothèque de Bourgogne at Brussels:

FATHER WALPOLE'S CONVERSION.

The Rev. Father Henry Walpole related of himself to the Rev. Father Ignatius Basselier, that when the body of the Rev. Father Edmund Campion was quartered at the place of execution, he, Father Walpole, then a heretic, stood looking on amongst the rest. As the executioner threw the quarters of the Martyr into a cauldron full of water, a drop of it, mixed with the blood of the Martyr, was splashed out, and fell on Walpole's coat. From a heretic he became a Catholic without delay, from a layman a religious of the Society of Jesus, from a spectator of martyrdoms a most admirable Martyr, the most distinguished among the ten thousand converts said to have been made by Campion's death.

These things, which the aforesaid Father

Ignatius heard from Father Walpole himself, he afterwards related to Father Antony Sucquet.

4. It is to be regretted that in the account we now proceed to give of the martyrdom of Blessed Edmund Campion, Father Walpole only set himself the humble task of filling up the omissions of others in a story, which no one was better fitted to recount than himself. But so it is, and the story has not gained by being only known to us in the Italian version, which was prepared for Father Bartoli as material for the construction of his history. The transcript here used was made by Brother Henry Foley from a MS. volume entitled *Fragmenta Hist. Angl.*, preserved in the Archives of the Society now at Fiesole.

THINGS OMITTED IN THE ACCOUNTS OF FATHER CAMPION'S MARTYRDOM.

By Father Henry Walpole.

I was present during his arraignment in Court and indictment, and stood near him when sentence was passed. The English custom is that the prisoner should not speak, but lift his hand and answer either "guilty" or "not guilty." On the second day he, with seven companions, stood at the bar from eight in the morning till seven in the evening, during all which time the Queen's Solicitor and Attorney kept heaping up odious presumptions against them. A witness deposed, &c. To which Campion replied in his own behalf as well as that of the rest. (As well as I remember Mr. Cottam said: "For the love of God let Campion answer for us all.") Campion's speech was entirely unprepared, yet carefully adapted to meet their calumnies. So complete was his reply that some, who came from curiosity to see what passed, and to set down the speeches of the opposite side, were astonished at his remarkable talent and presence of mind in this predicament. Others, again, considering the merits of the case, were amazed, thinking that one and all, and especially Campion, were innocent, and quite beyond the reach of the law. It was really a wonder that men such as they, who were after all only students, should have made such able answers to arguments on legal subjects, and that, too, with an unassuming grace of manner which reflected much credit on their cause and themselves. Here indeed our Lord's promises were wonderfully fulfilled: "I will give you a mouth and wisdom, which all your adversaries shall not be able to resist and gainsay."[2]

Accordingly, in proof of all this, I may point to the conduct of Lord Chief Justice Wray. He addressed Campion with greater courtesy, calling him Master Campion, and afterwards, taking some one to task for not speaking in his turn or to the point, said: "Look you, imitate the good example of Mr. Campion." In fact he was, like Pilate, desirous of liberating him, but for fear of Cæsar, upon the verdict of the jury, condemned him to death.

[2] St. Luke xxi. 15.

A certain Mr. Hewes, a heretical doctor, who had been engaged by the Earl of Warwick to take notes of everything that happened, promised me a copy of them, if his master would allow of their publication. When the Earl saw the notes, as the aforesaid Hewes told me, he asked him whether Campion really answered as well as he was reported to have done. "Yes, my lord," said he, "and better too, if I could have understood or remembered all." "God's will," replied the Earl, "he is a rare fellow. But let the business die—I undertook it for my own satisfaction."[3]

Thus the whole day passed, and the jury retired to consider whether they should find a verdict of guilty or of not guilty. I asked a lawyer called Strickland, a friend of mine, who stood near me, if he thought they would be condemned, and what he thought of Campion. "As far as he is concerned," was the answer, "he surely cannot be touched, his answers to all that has been laid to his charge have been so excellent. I should say the same of all the rest, except of one or two, who may be found guilty on the insinuations against them." As this man is known to be a heretic, he cannot be suspected of partiality. What the Catholics felt, I can conjecture from my own impressions. Never before or since did I listen to any one with so much pleasure, and I am well assured from the testimony of others that his words and his

[3] The transcript is here defective.

bearing gave strength to the faithful who heard and saw him, and converted many who were not blinded with passion and prejudice.

Now to touch on a few incidents which are still fresh in my mind. In the first place, after he had heard the exaggerations of the Attorney and lawyers endeavouring to please the Government, to maintain heresy, and display their skill—exaggerations which doubtless he never expected—he seemed wonder-stricken; then, lifting his eyes to heaven, and recollecting himself, he began his answer. His innocence, he said, had not looked for such elaborate, earnest accusations, and he asked how they could in conscience utter all that stuff. The answer was, that in this they had done their part in pleading on behalf of the Queen, and now he and the rest must speak for themselves. "Well," said Father Campion, "you have said enough without doubt, but whether justly or no remains to be seen. Reason, moreover, requires that we should have one learned in your law to answer for us, and time to meet such long accusations, especially seeing that it is not only we here present, who are accused at this bar, but also the greatest princes in the world—the Pope, the King of Spain, and all the Catholics in the world. For what you say against myself and these others, about the Northern Rising, the book of Doctor Bristow, and the coming of Doctor Sander to Ireland, does not affect us more than all the rest of our religion. Again, where you call us traitors, you ought to prove, first, that those acts were traitorous, and then that we were their authors. This you have not done, and have therefore arrived at a conclusion without establishing your premisses."

Here one of the Court took him up: "If you want to dispute as though you were in the schools, you are only proving yourself a fool." "I pray God make us both sages," was Campion's reply.

"As for the accusation that we plotted treason at Rheims. Reflect, my lords, how just this charge is. For see; first, we never met there at all; then, many of us have never been at Rheims at all; finally, we were never in our lives all together, except at this bar and in prison." He enlarged a good deal on this point, but I could not hear all, because of the noise, and I do not recollect much.

After Campion had answered clearly the more urgent charges to the general satisfaction, they began to press him with various particulars, &c. After this he treated of the false testimony of Elliot, &c., *ut in libro*.[4] To him Father Campion said: "Why do you tax us with the affair of Mr. Paine? If he is a man of blood, let him answer for himself. Why do you not call him? And, in his absence, why charge us with matters that are not ours? I profess myself free and far removed from all desire of bloodshed; moreover,

[4] The book here alluded to, must be some contemporary account of Campion's trial, not now known.

it is repugnant to the priesthood to undertake such actions. Why do you say such things, except to pre-occupy the popular ear, and prejudice the jury, who, hearing these odious calumnies, may condemn us for that which others have done, or for what is alleged against them in their absence? Moreover, there ought to be a separate accusation against each of us in particular, so that each of us might answer for himself. At present the charge against all in general falls upon me individually, and those which are laid against me affect all without exception."

Answer was made that he had the law, and capable honest men for the jury (though in fact neither the one statement nor the other appeared to be true).

The witnesses being already sworn, Father Campion said: "Pray tell me, Elliot, did I mention the Pope's name in my sermon, or not?"

"I don't remember," was the answer.

"Then, my lords, and you, sirs," said Campion, "I beg you to notice what a conscience this man has, and how he should be trusted in the rest of his story, seeing that after he has sworn that I exhorted him to abandon the Queen and obey the Pope, he now says that he does not remember what I said."

"I told you so," was Elliot's answer. "If you will listen he has a pestilent tongue."

Campion turned to the jury and said: "Sirs, our cause is committed to your hands. Bear in mind that the matter in debate is not an affair of small moment, nor one concerning mere temporal affairs, but it touches the lives of innocent men, an account of whose blood will be demanded of you. It is not our cause only, but that of all Englishmen, and of all Catholics in the world. Let not yourselves be deceived, but imagine it were the case of a single man, accused of stealing a sheep, or something similar. You would not condemn him without good proof and evidence. If it were given in evidence that a sheep was stolen in his absence, that his father used to be suspected of sheep-stealing, that he liked mutton, and therefore (it was concluded) had stolen the sheep, would you on this account condemn him without mercy, unless other evidence appeared to prove that he had stolen the sheep at such a time and place?[5] Much more in this our case, where so many are accused of the crime of treachery and treason, and that, too, on slight presumption, some of us on no presumptions at all, surely you ought to be cautious lest you condemn the innocent, and become guilty of shedding their blood."

Such words, and more to the same effect, did

---

[5] The meaning of the Italian, when compared with the report of Campion's trial given by Simpson (p. 287), is evidently as above, though the transcript is defective. A more spirited version of this passage is given by Father Fitzherbert in his *Apology* (pp. 18, seq.): "If a sheep were stolen, and a whole family called in question for the same, were it good manner of proceeding for the accusers to say, 'Your great-grandfathers and fathers, and sisters and kinsfolk, all loved mutton, *ergo* you have stolen the sheep.'"

Father Campion use, but notwithstanding all, after consulting for half an hour, or rather without any consultation at all, the jury found the fatal verdict against all, proclaiming on their return that all were guilty, to the amazement and horror of every one present.

Father Campion and the rest often protested that if they would make acts of religion the cause of their death, they would die most willingly.

At his martyrdom Father Campion said: "I pray all present who belong to the household of the holy faith to say a *Credo* with me, and that when I am in my agony." This many did bareheaded. The last words which I heard him say in a loud voice, while the rope was round his neck and the cart moving from under him were: "I die a true Catholic."

CHAPTER III.

VENERABLE JOHN SLADE AND VENERABLE JOHN BODEY.

Suffered, the one at Winchester, October 30, the other at Andover, November 2, 1583.

DOCUMENTS.

1. Writ of Privy Council for the arrest of Slade (Lansdowne MSS. 1162, fol. 202).
2. Extract of a letter from the Rev. George Birket to Dr. Allen (Westminster Archives). Latin.
3. Account of their trial (Stonyhurst MSS. *Anglia*, vii. n. 25).
4. Part of a letter of Bodey (*Ibid. Anglia*, i. n. 16).
5. Details of their imprisonment, &c. (Stonyhurst MSS. *M.* 131, by Father Warford, S.J.). Latin.
6. Account of their execution by R. B. (Westminster Archives, vol. ii. p. 341).

1. The lives of these two Martyrs are wonderfully similar. Born at no great distance one from another, they both entered New College, Oxford, where Bodey proceeded Master of Arts, February 1, 1576. Both were expelled for Catholicity, and both went over seas for a time to be able to practise their religion in peace. Again they both apparently wished to follow the law as a profession, but were prevented by the persecution then raging. Slade devoted

himself to the work of education, probably in the capacity of a tutor in some gentleman's family, though in contemporary legal form he is described as a schoolmaster. Bodey was imprisoned about the time of the great increase of persecution which followed the advent of Fathers Persons and Campion. The directions for the arrest of Slade are given in the following extract from the Registers of the Privy Council, under date June 14, 1582.

A letter unto Sir John Horsey, Knight, and George Trenchard, Esq., for the apprehending and sending up of one Selad [Slade], a very dangerous Papist lurking within the county of Dorset, and all such superstitious ornaments and trumpery as they can by diligent search find out, together with the said Slade. And by like authority of their Lordships' letters to make search and apprehend from time to time any Jesuit or Seminary priest, that they shall hereafter know or understand to be within the said county, &c.

2. Slade was arrested in due course and confined with Bodey in Winchester gaol, and sometimes they were shut up together in one cell. On the 11th of January, 1583, a search was made in the prison by Sir Richard Norton knight, William Wright, and Thomas Fleming, esquires, and the following Catholic books were found in their chamber: *Allen of Purgatory, A Christian Exercise, A Treatise of the Church, Smyth of the Mass.*[1]

[1] P.R.O. *Dom. Eliz.* vol. clviii. n. 19.

Shortly after this they were put on their trials, and from a letter[2] of the Reverend George Birket, afterwards Archpriest, to Dr. Allen from London in April, 1583, it would seem that their conduct had made a considerable stir in the country.

Bodey and Slade [he writes], two most valiant soldiers of Christ, have been condemned to death at Winchester, but have not yet suffered. At the bar they pleaded the cause of Catholic religion with answers so apposite, and a zeal so fervent, that they have recalled well nigh the larger part of Hampshire from frequenting the Protestant churches. Many gentlemen of position in that county were indeed Catholic before, but now not only the greater number of these, but even the country folk flock to us from all sides.

3. By some piece of legal chicanery, or freak of persecution overriding all law, these Martyrs were twice tried and twice condemned. The date of Dr. Birket's letter shows that it refers to their first trial, which took place at Winchester. It does not appear whether the next document from the Stonyhurst manuscripts belongs to the spring or the autumn Sessions held at Andover, where they were sentenced for the second time.

John Bodey and John Slade were arraigned at the Assizes holden at Andover upon the Supremacy. Amongst the rest were present Dr. Humphrey, who used persuasions to convert

[2] Printed by F. Knox, in the *Douay Diaries*, p. 353.

them, and vouched a place out of Eusebius, that Constantine the Great did call the Nicene Council upon his own authority as he says, whereby he concluded that the Emperor's authority was above the Pope's; and urged upon the place in this sort. "*Constantinus vocavit concilium.*" Mr. Bodey answered, "Indeed *Constantinus vocavit concilium, sed ex sententia sacerdotis,*" and that these were the words of the author, whereof the one said yea, the other nay.

"Will you pawn your consideration thereon," said the Doctor.

"Yea, and my life and all that I am worth," said Mr. Bodey, "if you will pawn your credit," and so demurred upon that issue.

The book that night was sent for. Next day when judgment was to be given, the Judge according to the course, asked:

"How sayest thou, Bodey, what canst thou say for thyself why thou shouldst not have judgment to die?"

Slade answered, "What! is the matter come thereto? where is Mr. Doctor?" and Mr. Bodey drew out the book from under his cloak, and opened it, and pointed to the place where the words were as he had said. One of the Judges plucked a pamphlet out of his bosom, which the doctor had left with them and cast it unto them, for the doctor had gone away overnight. . . .

The dispute with Dr. Humphrey seems to have excited much interest, and a gentleman named John

Hardy got into serious trouble with the local Dogberry, for saying that Bodey had the better of the argument. A Protestant minister was present at the dinner-table where the remark was made and laid the matter before the Justices. Thereupon all the guests were had up and examined, and the examinations forwarded to the Privy Council.

These papers have been preserved,[3] and from them we learn that there was "a conference had at Winchester [apparently after the trial] between the Dean of Winchester, the Warden of the College of Winchester aforesaid, and one Slade and Bodey, who were condemned for maintaining the Supremacy of the Bishop of Rome. At which time the said Dean and Warden did urge the said Bodey to show what he had collected or could avouch for the maintenance of his said erroneous opinion. Whereupon the said Bodey did pull a paper out of his bosom, with notes collected out of the story of Eusebius touching a Council holden at Nice in the time of the Emperor Constantine, by which the said Bodey would have proved that the Bishop of Rome was above the Emperor. Whereunto the said Warden did make answer," &c.

The answer of Dr. Humphrey has not been preserved, but the paper which Bodey pulled out of his bosom at the dispute, or a similar (if not the same) one which he gave to the Sheriff at the time of his execution, is still to be seen in the Public Record Office.[4] As it contains no further information concerning the Martyr's life, it has not been reproduced here. The substance of the argument is accurately stated by the writer of the Stonyhurst document just quoted.

[3] P.R.O. *Dom. Eliz.* vol. clxvii. n. 15.   [4] *Ibid.* vol. clxii. n. 8.

4. After their second condemnation Bodey wrote a letter to some friends at Rheims, a copy of a part of which is preserved at Stonyhurst. This seems to have been made for transmission to Rome, and is endorsed by Dr. Barrett :

A PART OF A LETTER WRITTEN BY MR. JOHN BODEY, OUT OF PRISON, TO MR. D. ELIE AND MR. REYNOLDS, A LITTLE BEFORE HIS MARTYRDOM, IN THE BEHALF OF HIS BROTHER [GILBERT], NOW AT RHEIMS.

I hope it shall not hinder him in this point that he was taken with a blessed Martyr, Mr. Briant, in London, lying in one chamber together, for whose sake he was piteously scourged in Bridewell, and afterwards imprisoned in one of the Counters. Since which time, being then enlarged upon bond of appearance at a call within a limited time, which long ago is expired, and he never called, he hath kept himself secret, not daring to come into the view of the world for fear of another apprehension; and now he hopeth to be there, where he may live in some quietness of serving God without fear. I beseech you, therefore, and either of you, even for charity sake and for the love of God, that he may have your lawful furtherance either by your letters or as you shall think good.

As for my own part, here I live twice condemned, which perhaps may seem strange unto you, and not once dead. I have not wanted, I thank God, anything necessary for me except the full service of God [*i.e.* Mass] for the space of these three years, and somewhat more since I was first imprisoned. I am now cunning, I thank God, in wearing of iron shackles, and can take heed of interfering. I have been now twice clogged with them. The first time was from the 5th of September, 1581, as well night as day, until the 28th of April next following; at which time my keeper (not the first, for he is deceased, but another) was grievously reprehended for showing such favour, and commanded to lay irons upon me and Mr. Slade again, with strait charge to keep us one from the other and to see that no access might be to us. But we consider that iron for this cause borne on earth shall surmount gold and precious stones in Heaven. That is our mark, that is our desire. In the mean season we are threatened daily, and do look still when the hurdle shall be brought to the door. I beseech you, for God's sake, that we want not the good prayers of you all for our strength, our joy, and our perseverance unto the end. And thus with my commendations to yourselves and others which know me, I commit us all to the grace and mercy of the Blessed Trinity. From our school of patience, the 16th Sept., 1583.

Yours, as you know,
JOHN BODEY.

5. Father Warford's " Relation of Martyrs whom he had known" gives us a little incident which befel one of our two Martyrs on his way to execution.

Mr. John Bodey and Mr. John Slade. Expelled from New College, Oxford, by Horne, the pseudo-bishop. Afterwards in Winchester gaol, they distinguished themselves by their edifying lives and zeal for souls. On this account Cowper, the Superintendent, brought about their death, which they underwent with admirable constancy. Facilities for escaping were oftentimes afforded them, even by the keepers themselves, of whom one or two were converted by them to the Catholic faith.

One of these two, Bodey, I think, as trustworthy Catholics relate, saw in a dream the night before his death, two bulls attacking him very furiously, but without at all hurting him, at which he was much astonished. The next day two hangmen came down from London to execute him, and as they walked on either side of him, he chanced to ask their names, and as they one after the other answered that they were called Bull,[5] he at once remembering his dream, said: "Blessed be God; you are then those two bulls who gave me such trouble last night in my dream, and yet did me no harm." He then joyfully composed himself for death.

6. We conclude with an account of their deaths, from the Westminster Archives, which is probably the same as that printed in London by Richard Jones, in 1583,[6] of which no printed copy is extant.

[5] Bull is called "the hangman of Newgate" in the account quoted by Challoner of the martyrdom of B. John Paine.

[6] *Concertatio*, p. 293.

It may be noted that though the Martyrs are described throughout as traitors, the report is in other respects not unsympathetic. May it not be that while written by a Catholic, this half transparent device was adopted in order to allow of its publication in England? The initials would suit Robert Barnes, who was condemned in 1598 to be hanged for felony, because he had harboured the Martyr John Jones, *alias* Buckley, O.S.F.

THE SEVERAL EXECUTIONS AND CONFESSIONS OF JOHN SLADE AND JOHN BODEY, TWO OBSTINATE AND NOTORIOUS TRAITORS, THE ONE DRAWN, HANGED, AND QUARTERED AT WINCHESTER ON WEDNESDAY THE XXXTH DAY OF OCTOBER, 1583, AND THE OTHER AT ANDOVER ON THE SATURDAY FOLLOWING, BEING THE SECOND DAY OF NOVEMBER. SET DOWN AS IT WAS SENT IN WRITING TO A WORSHIPFUL GENTLEMAN, BY ONE THAT WAS THERE PRESENT AT BOTH EXECUTIONS UPON SPECIAL OCCASIONS.

To the worshipful and his very good friend, Mr. H. G.

Whereas your worship, at my last being with you, desired me to let you have knowledge of the manner of the end and confessions of Bodey and Slade, two notorious traitors, I have, according to my promise, sent you the true discourse thereof. For I being present thereat (as you know) upon some especial occasions have set down, so near as memory would serve me, the certainty thereof, which you may be bold to declare to your friends for a very truth, notwithstanding the sundry flying tales, rumoured abroad by the Papists, according to their accustomed manner, as their affection serveth them. I have sent you the truth and nothing but the truth, and thereof you may assuredly persuade yourself. Thus with continual desire of your welfare with all yours, I commit you to the heavenly protection.

From Winchester, by your friend to use,

R. B.

These Gentlemen and Justices of Peace were present at these executions:

Mr. Robert White, High Sheriff of the Shire.
Sir Wm. Kingsmell, Knight.
Mr. Tho. Fisher, Justice of Peace.
Mr. Wm. St. John, Justice of Peace.
Mr. Thomas West, son to the Lord Delaware.
Mr. Francis Coke, Justice of Peace.
Mr. William Wright, Justice of Peace.
Mr. Benjamin Tichburne, Justice of Peace.

Besides many other gentlemen of countenance and credit.

THE EXECUTION AND CONFESSION OF JOHN SLADE, AN OBSTINATE AND NOTORIOUS TRAITOR, WHO WAS DRAWN, HANGED, AND QUARTERED, FOR HIGH TREASON AGAINST HER MAJESTY, AT WINCHESTER, ON WEDNESDAY, THE XXXTH DAY OF OCTOBER, 1583.

On Wednesday, being the 30th of October, John Slade, sometime a schoolmaster, was drawn upon a hurdle from the prison at Winchester to the market-place, where the execution was appointed. Being come to the aforesaid place, and taken off the hurdle, he came and kneeled down by the gallows, making a cross with one of his hands upon the posts thereof, and kissed it, using silent prayers in Latin to himself. Afterwards, being come upon the ladder, he began in this manner:

"I am come hither this day to suffer death for my faith. What faith? No rare faith, but even the faith that hath continued from all posterities."

Whereupon, Sir William Kingsmell spoke to him as thus:

"Slade, do not thus delude the people with plausible speeches. You are come hither to suffer death for high treason against her Majesty. You have been lawfully and sufficiently convicted thereof, and therefore you are brought to endure the punishment that law hath assigned you. You have denied her Majesty to have any Supremacy over the Church of Christ in England, both in causes ecclesiastical and temporal, which fact is high treason. And therefore you are worthy to suffer death in that you will not give her Majesty her duty and your allegiance."

"O Sir William," quoth he, "I will give her Majesty as much as has been given to any prince in this realm, and will show her as much duty, as he that is her most obedient subject."

"That you do not," answered Sir William Kingsmell. "For you rob her of her ecclesiastical and temporal government, which all princes have enjoyed and you traitorously take from her. Therefore, how do you give her as much as any Prince hath had, and how do you show yourself a subject in this unnatural dealing, to prefer a foreign government before your own lawful Queen?"

"Sir," said Slade, "the Supremacy hath and doth belong to the Pope by right [derived][7] from Peter, and the Pope hath received it as by divine providence. Therefore, we must not give those things belonging to God to any other than him alone. And because I will not do otherwise, I may say with the three children in the fiery oven, and the first of the widow's seven sons in the Machabees:[8] *Parati sumus mori magis quam patrias Dei leges prævaricari.*"

Then Mr. Thomas White, High Sheriff of the Shire, said to him that he showed himself very undutiful to her Majesty, and therefore willed him to ask her forgiveness.

"Oh, Mr. Sheriff," quoth he, "if Paul and Peter would have obeyed their Princes, they had not suffered death."

At these words, Mr. Dr. Bennet, one of the chaplains to the right honourable the Lord Treasurer, came to him and said, "Slade, do not abuse the people thus with these words. Paul and Peter were put to death for Religion, they were commanded not to preach in the name of Jesus. Are you commanded any such thing?"

[7] Wanting in MS.   [8] 2 Mach. vii. 2.

"Oh, sir," answered Slade, "I would wish you to behave after the manner of a truant, whose nature is to forget. And so would I have you to forget your wicked life and begin a new."

"Slade," said Mr. Bennet, "I come as one that wisheth well to thy soul. Thou art now at the pit's brink, consider how highly thou offendest God, and likewise how thou hast transgressed against her Majesty. I desire thee in the bowels of Christ, be not so wilful, lose not that so lightly, which He hath bought with His precious blood. And if my words may not prevail with thee, yet for the love of thine own soul, forsake this damnable opinion. Let not that unworthy Priest be preferred before thine own natural Princess, who is the lawful supreme head of the Church next under Christ. Thou knowest how he hath deprived her of her government by his excommunication, and wilt thou be so wicked as lean to him, and forsake her?"

"Sir," answered Slade, "you are very busy in words: if the Pope hath done so, I think he hath done no more than he may, and than he ought to do. I will acknowledge no other head of the Church, but only the Pope: and her Majesty hath no authority in temporal causes likewise, but only what he shall think good to allow her."

At these words the people cried, "Away with the traitor. Hang him. Hang him."

Mr. Sheriff willed him again to ask her Majesty forgiveness.

"Why should I ask her forgiveness?" quoth he. "Wherein have I offended her?"

Then Mr. Bennet desired him to commend his soul to God, and desire the people to pray for him: but he said they and he were not of one faith, and therefore they should not pray for him, "and I desire all blessed people," quoth he, "to pray for me, and all the saints and blessed company of Heaven."

So, after he had stayed so long as pleased himself, and had mumbled a many Latin prayer silently to himself, he was cast beside the ladder, and afterwards was cut down and quartered according to his judgment.

THE EXECUTION AND CONFESSION OF ANOTHER NOTORIOUS TRAITOR, NAMED JOHN BODEY, SOMETIME A MASTER OF ART IN OXFORD, WHO WAS LIKEWISE FOR HIGH TREASON AGAINST HER MAJESTY, DRAWN, HANGED, AND QUARTERED AT ANDOVER ON SATURDAY THE SECOND OF NOVEMBER, 1583.

John Bodey, a Master of Art sometime in Oxford, and companion to this Slade was carried from Winchester to Andover, a town ten miles from Winchester, where the Assizes were holden and where they were condemned. There was he on the Saturday following drawn on a hurdle to the place of execution, and being laid on the hurdle he said thus, "Oh, sweet bed, the happiest bed that ever man lay on! Thou art welcome to me." Then, being taken from the hurdle, he spake to Mr. Sheriff as concerning a disputation which had passed between him and Doctor Humphrey about Constantine the Emperor. He had writ in a sheet of paper certain articles in answer to Doctor Humphrey, which he would have read before the people, but because the time was short he could not read them, but gave them to Mr. High Sheriff, that Doctor Humphrey might see them.

When the hangman put the halter about his neck, he said, "Oh, blessed chain, the sweetest chain and richest that ever came about any man's neck!" And so kissing it, he suffered the hangman to put it about his neck. There was also present Mr. Bennet, who laboured very godly and earnestly to dissuade him from his evil opinion, but all was in vain, he was so obstinate and wilful. He likewise appealed upon his faith, which he said was the cause of his death. But Sir William Kingsmell told him he died for high treason against her Majesty, whereof he had been sufficiently convicted.

"Indeed," quoth he, "I have been sufficiently convicted, for I have been condemned twice. And you may make the hearing of a blessed Mass treason or the saying of an *Ave Maria* treason, but I have committed no treason, although indeed I suffer the punishment due to treason."

"Why," quoth Mr. High Sheriff, "you know the Pope hath excommunicated her Majesty, and you forsake her and cleave to him. What say you to this? You deny her spiritual[9] authority, and will not acknowledge her for your lawful Queen."

"Yes," quoth he, "in those cases that appertain unto her I acknowledge her my lawful Sovereign and Queen. But for the spiritual[9] cause I will abide a thousand deaths before I consent to it. And if the Pope have done well, let him answer it; and if he have done ill, let him likewise answer it. I acknowledge her my lawful Queen in all temporal causes and none other."

"You shall do well then," said Sir William, "to satisfy the people in the cause of your death, because otherwise they may be deluded by your fair speeches."

"You shall understand," quoth he, "good people all, that I suffer death for not granting her Majesty to be Supreme Head in Christ's Church in England, which I may not, nor will not, grant."

"Well then," quoth Mr. Sheriff, "ask her Majesty forgiveness, and then desire the people to pray for you."

"In truth," quoth he," I must needs ask her Majesty forgiveness, for I have offended her many ways, as in using unlawful games, excess in apparel, and other offences to her laws, but in this matter you shall pardon me. And for the people, because they and I are different in religion, I will not have them pray for me, but I pray God

[9] "Special" in MS.

long to preserve her Majesty in tranquillity over you, even Queen Elizabeth, your Queen and mine, and I desire you to obey none other."

At length saying, *Jesu, Jesu, esto mihi Jesu*, three times, he was put beside the ladder, and quartered according to his judgment.

CHAPTER IV.

VENERABLE ROBERT ANDERTON AND VENERABLE WILLIAM MARSDEN.

Suffered in the Isle of Wight, April 25, 1586.

DOCUMENTS.

1. Father Warford's relation (Stonyhurst MSS. *M.* fol. 134). Latin.
2. Privy Council warrants for their examination (Council Registers, Whitehall, vol. vi. fols. 23, 28, 51, 77).
3. Royal Proclamation read at their execution (Brit. Mus. Grenville Library. Proclamations of Queen Elizabeth).

---

1. A charming account of these two martyrs is given in Father William Warford's recollections of martyrs whom he had known, a manuscript at Stonyhurst from which we have already quoted.

FATHER WILLIAM WARFORD'S REMINISCENCES.

Mr. Robert Anderton and Mr. William Marsden were both Lancastrians, of whom is truly said what the Church sings of the Holy Apostles: *Gloriosi principes terræ, quomodo in vita sua,* &c.[1]

[1] "Glorious princes of the land, as in their life they have loved one another, so in death they are not divided" (Antiphon at Lauds within the Octave of SS. Peter and Paul).

From their early youth to the time of their death, they cherished for one another a chaste and holy friendship, approved by God and man. Both young and both learned, they were well matched in virtue, piety, and letters; by birth, indeed, Anderton would have had the precedence, for he was sprung from the distinguished family of the name, though his parents were not wealthy. Both again were educated, if I am not mistaken, at Oxford, for I knew Anderton intimately at St. Mary Hall; and Marsden, unless my memory deceives me, was at Brasenose. They came a little before me to Rheims, where they both received me most kindly on my arrival, and I knew them both familiarly. Moreover, Anderton taught me Hebrew, and afterwards went through the Psalms of David with me privately, pretending that he would like me in return to teach him Greek, lest I the elder should be ashamed to learn of him without remuneration. He taught extremely well, and quickly, and was very proficient in the sacred language [Hebrew], chiefly on account of his intimacy with Gregory Martin and William Reynold, both well skilled in that tongue. He took great pains in helping the latter while he was writing his books, especially against Whitaker. He was skilful in controversies, and not deficient in scholastic learning.

Anderton was also an excellent preacher, so that, when in 1583, one had to be selected out of the whole College to deliver a solemn oration before a very learned and noble assembly of

Frenchmen, whom Allen, the President of the College, had invited to a public entertainment, he was chosen out of all, as in the general opinion best fitted for the purpose, and accomplished the task with the highest applause, and even to the astonishment of the whole audience.[2] He was somewhat disposed to blush on account of a certain virginal modesty, but in other respects he was very calm in preaching both in voice and manner. When it was determined to establish a junior school for those who were not fit for theology, these two were chosen as examples and patterns of virtue, to be prefects over the boys. This office they discharged for a long time, until God called them both (for they were never divided either in affection or occupation) to set out for the harvest in England. Every one in the Seminary regretted their departure, but great things were hoped from their labours.

They travelled straight to the French coast, where embarking on ship-board, so severe a storm arose in mid-channel, that the sailors gave themselves up for lost, and were ready to abandon themselves and all they had to the sport of the

[2] This sermon is still preserved in the Westminster Archives, and is headed, "Ad Præcipuos Prælatos et Canonicos Ecclesiæ Rhemensis, Primariosque civitatis viros. Oratio habita Cal. Aprilis 1583 in Refectorio Collegii Anglorum." It begins, "Coetera beneficia vestra, ornatissimi viri," and ends, "corona vestra futuri sumus." It covers two and a half sides of folio; expresses the thanks of the English to the clergy of Rheims, but contains nothing historical. It has been thrice endorsed, by Cardinal Allen, Father Persons, and Father Christopher Grene, and it is presumably in the Martyr's own handwriting.

waves. They, meanwhile, threw themselves on
their knees, and lifting most devoutly their hands
and eyes to heaven, made this prayer together:
"O Lord, Thy will be done! But if we are to
die, suffer us to die for Thy cause in our own
country. We do not pray against death, but
against the manner of it. Let us not, we beseech
Thee, be remembered as the first of the Seminarists, who have perished in the waters." (For
it is to be remarked that none of the priests who,
during so many years, went from the Seminaries
to England, perished at sea.) "Spare us, O Lord,
and hear our prayer! Let us be taken on the
English coast, let us be dragged to death, but
excuse us from being swallowed up in the waves."

So they prayed, and lo! quickly driven by the
wind far across the sea, the ship reached the
Isle of Wight in safety, and anchored in port,
contrary to every expectation of the sailors;
indeed not without a miracle. There they found
men and fellow-citizens more-cruel than the
waves and rocks they had left behind them; for
the island is full of heretics, and in no place in
the kingdom are Catholics fewer. So that immediately they came into the town, they were
examined, recognized, and taken, and at once
cast into prison. But when the Sessions came
on, they were brought before the Court, and
bearing themselves with great constancy were
subjected to a long examination. Tried by
threats, entreaties, and offers of reward, they
accounted as nothing all that was offered to

induce them to abandon their faith. The Justices of the whole county were there, nearly all the gentry and two principal Judges, one of whom, Anderson by name, was the Chief Justice of the whole kingdom; and that such a tragedy should not take place in the absence of a false prophet, Cowper, the pseudo-bishop of Winchester, another Caiphas, a well-known crafty old fox, a persecutor, captious and cruel, was also present.

Casting a look on the two young men, whose beards were naturally slight, he began at first in a flippant way to test the courage, learning, and abilities of each. Finding them better instructed and cleverer than he had supposed, he attacked them somewhat sharply, raising many objections; but the Martyrs answered so much to the point that Cowper hardly escaped the open laughter of the audience in the lower benches. Many, struck by noticing in such youths such remarkable prudence and learning, began to waver. All listened with wonderful attention, captivated by the speech and answers of the priests. The discussion turned chiefly on the power of the Pope, for defending which all the orthodox are condemned in England. When therefore the arguments of the Superintendent failed, he betook himself, as the heretics are wont to do, to abuse; he taunted the priests with the foulness of Pope Joan, and dilated on that fable with many words. The audience listened with eager ears for what the Martyrs would answer, and Anderton said:

"Although it is very easy to refute this fable,

being only the foul fabrication of heretics long since exploded, yet if it were true, surely, my lord, it was not for you to propound so absurd a contumely." "Why?" asked the other. "Because," said Anderton, "the basis of your faith, the citadel of your religion, is this, that you profess a woman to be the Head of your Church. Surely whether we call her Pope Joan or Pope Elizabeth matters little. With what face, then, can you object that to us as an infamy, which is your special glory? How taunt the Roman See with that which you proudly regard as the bulwark of your religion?"

The pseudo-bishop being silenced, and not daring to utter a word in reply, was the laughing-stock of all. Then breaking off the discussion, he turned to the Judges, and said:

"You see what egregious traitors these fellows are, not being ashamed to insult the Queen's Majesty in the presence of the Court. Their condemnation, surely, should not be deferred. They alone are enough to pervert many thousands." But Anderson the Judge, though he consented to their being declared guilty of high treason, would not pronounce the capital sentence, saying that the Queen would not have any Seminarists condemned to death without her knowledge and special authority. (This may have been so, or perhaps he had a mind to spare such good holy priests, whom he saw to be guiltless of any crime.) Cowper was thus silenced, and the Martyrs were sent back to prison.

But he, not unlike a lioness deprived of her cubs, raging and breathing threats and slaughter, because he could have them put at once to death, prevailed by his importunity on the exceedingly timid Judge, that these priests should accompany him to London; and this was done at his cost, so exceedingly did this wolf thirst for the blood of these lambs. The old man set off for London to his great inconvenience and cost, obtained an interview with the Queen, and told her the whole story. From her he obtained licence for their execution, and then carried the Martyrs bound hand and foot as before, back to the Isle of Wight.

2. We here interrupt Father Warford's story to add some details from other sources. Challoner records that during their trial the Martyrs urged in their defence the plea that they had not yet been in England the number of days requisite to constitute a breach of the law as it then stood. The Registers of the Privy Council also throw a new light upon some of the proceedings. Father Warford represents the Protestant Bishop as moving the Queen to obtain their execution, and speaks as though this was done immediately, without the intervention of officials. In point of fact, however, the whole business passed through the hands of the Privy Council, and the Bishop, whatever may have been his influence, is nowhere named in the warrants.[3]

[3] See infra p. 88, the account of the Martyrs Roger Dicconson and Ralph Milner, where the opposite happens, the Council warrants showing the same Bishop as the prime mover in the prosecution, while the Catholic reports do not name him.

From them we learn that the letters were "written by the Justices of Assize signifying their [the Martyrs'] conformity to her Majesty in civil causes." Thereupon they were on the 10th of March brought up to London by the Sheriff of Southampton, and sent to the Marshalsea. On the 16th letters were issued to the Master of St. Catherine's, and Dr. Hamond:

To examine William Marsden and Robert Anderton, Seminary priests, concerning their obedience and subject-like duty to her Majesty and the Estate, and if they find that they remain constant in the faithful protestations they did use before the Justices of the Assizes at the time of their arraignment, to cause them to set down the same in writing, and subscribe thereunto, that thereupon her Majesty may be moved to extend mercy unto them, &c.

The London inquisitors were more skilful than their provincial brethren in extracting confessions of treason from their victims, and they succeeded in eliciting several treasonable statements. What these were the reader will see immediately in the Royal Proclamation, issued at the time of their death. Meanwhile they were handed over to Thomas Taylor, "one of the Knight Marshal's men," who, "with three of his fellows ... and a guide," conveyed them to Winchester,[4] where they were handed over

[4] P.R.O. Enrolled Accounts. Treasurer of the Chamber, 21—38, Eliz. rot. 80. Taylor received on his return the sum of £9 for "horsecheer, diets, watches, and other charges." He had also been furnished with a "placard" from the Council "to receive aid and assistance" on his way if he required it. From

to the Sheriff of Southampton on the 21st of April. The Lords of the Council also sent the following letter to Sir George Carey:

April 10, 1586. To Sir Geo. Carey.

That whereas for some special considerations (as shall appear to him from the enclosed) the execution of William Marsden and Robert Anderton, Seminary priests, who by his care were apprehended in the Isle of Wight (for the which their Lordships yield him, as well in her Majesty's behalf as in their own, right hearty thanks), hath been respited; and now order given to the Sheriffs of that county to see them executed according to the judgment upon the late statute given against them at the last Assizes at Winchester. Forasmuch as it is thought meet by their Lordships to have the execution there within that Isle where they were apprehended, either in the place of their landing, or in some other fit place or places within the said Isle as to him shall seem convenient, their Lordships have appointed the under-sheriffs of that county to resort to him to understand his opinion and determination of the place. . . . And at such time as they shall be executed their Lordships think it meet that the declaration herein enclosed be publicly read and published, that the people

this grant and another ordered to be made to the Sheriff of Southampton for bringing them to London, it would seem that Father Warford's statement, that the Bishop paid for their journey to and from London, is incorrect. He may, of course, have advanced the money in the first instance.

may understand the cause and reason of their reprieval, and what hath moved her Majesty to suffer the judgment of the laws to be executed upon them, &c.

3. The proclamation which was enclosed in the above letter, is also entered in the Council Registers, and a copy of the printed form is preserved in the British Museum, and runs as follows:

A DECLARATION OF THE QUEEN'S MAJESTY'S MOST GRACIOUS DEALING WITH WILLIAM MARSDEN AND ROBERT ANDERTON, SEMINARY PRIESTS, SINCE THE TIME OF THEIR JUST CONDEMNATION, BEING CONVICTED ACCORDING TO THE LAWS, AND OF THEIR OBSTINACY IN REFUSING TO ACKNOWLEDGE THEIR DUTY AND ALLEGIANCE TO HER MAJESTY.

1586.

Whereas at the last session of Parliament, among other good and necessary laws and ordinances established for the maintenance, continuance and preservation of her Majesty's most happy and quiet Government, and for the preventing and avoiding of treasons and practices traitorously attempted by certain of her Majesty's evil affected subjects, being Jesuits and Seminary priests, made and created at Rome and Rheims, and other places beyond the seas, who at the instigation of the Pope and others favouring his pretended tyrannous authority over the Crown of England, and envying the happy and blessed estate of her Majesty's said Government, come daily into the realm to pervert and seduce her Majesty's good subjects under colour of religion, to draw them from their due and natural obedience towards her Majesty and her Crown, and to prepare their minds and bodies to assist such foreign invasion as was certainly discovered to be intended by the said Pope and his adherents, as by sundry effects and proofs hath manifestly appeared : namely, by the late rebellion in the North, the invasion attempted in Ireland, and by the discovery of sundry late plots and purposes of treason, as well against her Majesty's sacred person, as against the common quiet of the realm ; there was for these considerations an Act made against the said Jesuits and Seminary priests, by the which their access into the realm for the like seditious and traitorous purposes was prohibited, and ordered to be punished as in cases of Treason.

Contrary to which Act of Parliament, one William Marsden and Robert Anderton, Seminary priests (being reconciled at Douay in Artois by a Jesuit called Father Columbine, and made priests by the Cardinal of Guise at Rheims, arriving secretly out of France, lately, at the Isle of Wight, where they were apprehended), have confessed their purpose of coming into the realm to have been to win souls (as they term it), being in effect (as is before mentioned) to persuade her Majesty's subjects, under colour of maintenance of Popery, to rebellion. For the which they, having been by the due and orderly course of her Majesty's laws tried and convicted at the last Assizes holden at Winchester in the county of Southampton upon the Statute aforesaid, were nevertheless by the Judges of that circuit (knowing the merciful mind and gracious dispositions of the Queen's Majesty towards all her subjects) conferred withal, concerning their meaning towards her Majesty's person and the realm. At which time they pretended in words and exterior show to acknowledge her Majesty to be rightful Queen of this realm, and to vow and protest that they would at all times adventure their lives in defence of her Majesty and her realm against the Pope, or any foreign power whatsoever, that should attempt to invade the realm with force, and that they would not meddle or persuade with any in matter of religion, but only keep their own consciences to themselves.[5] Whereupon they were stayed from their execution, her Majesty minding nothing less, than that any of her subjects, though disagreeing from her in Religion, should die for the same, as by them and their companions hath been most falsely and slanderously published and affirmed.

Upon report whereof made by the said Judges to the Lords and others of her Majesty's most

[5] As will be seen immediately, the Martyrs until the last declared that they never made any such promise. In truth, falsifications of their victims' words are of frequent occurrence in the utterances of the persecutors, and ought to make us very cautious in receiving their statements. That these were made openly by no means shows that the accused could reply.

honourable Privy Council, they, following the mild and temperate course of her Majesty's Government, caused the said Marsden and Anderton to be stayed from execution, and to be removed from Winchester to London. There they were further conferred withal, and examined concerning their obedience and duty towards her Majesty for civil causes, only to prove whether they would remain constant in their protestations in that behalf made to the Judges at their arraignment and conviction, that her Majesty might thereupon have been moved to extend her mercy towards them.

The said Marsden and Anderton, being accordingly examined by two principal persons thereunto appointed by her Majesty's Privy Council, were put in remembrance of their former show of duty made before the Justices of Assize, and advised to confirm the hope conceived of their reformation in matters of their allegiance to her Majesty, to the end they might thereby move her Majesty to show mercy unto them. Whereupon, first the said Anderton, being required to explain his true meaning in his protestation of her Majesty's right to the Crown, and of his allegiance, and particularly whether he did acknowledge her Majesty to be lawful Queen, notwithstanding any sentence which the Pope either had given, or could give against her, and whether he meant that it was his duty and the duties of all her Majesty's subjects, to withstand the Pope, not only if his invasion were for temporal respects, as to make conquest of the realm, but also if he would attempt such an invasion by force, to reduce the realm to his obedience by colour of Religion: he answered that they be questions wherewith he doth not deal, and required to be respited for his answer until such cases should happen, adding by way of abusion that in the meantime he may possibly become a Protestant, and so then become of other opinion than he is now of.

William Marsden, to the same questions before propounded to Anderton, answered, that he acknowledged her Majesty to be lawful Queen of this realm, and of other her dominions; and that he took himself bound to obey her Majesty, so far as his obedience impeached not his duties to God and to the Church (meaning the Church of Rome): requiring that he might not be asked his opinion any further, until such case of sentence given by the Pope should happen: and further saith, that in case the Pope would send any forces into the realm, to reduce the same to the Catholic Religion (meaning Popery) he would then do the duty of a priest, that is, he would pray that right might take place.

And whereas they had both promised before the Justices of Assize, that they would not meddle in persuading of any person in matter of Religion, but only keep their own conscience to themselves, they now in their examination deny that ever they promised not to deal with her Majesty's subjects to persuade them in matter of Religion. Anderton saying, that he taketh such as be out of the

Unity of the Church of Rome, to stand in state of damnation, and that therefore he is bound in conscience to do what he can to reclaim them. And Marsden saith, he may not promise not to deal with any of her Majesty's subjects in matters of Religion, for that he coming into the realm to persuade the Catholic Religion (meaning Popery), he cannot bind himself not to do that duty.

Hereby may appear to all her Majesty's loving and true hearted subjects, the traitorous purpose of these two Seminary priests, being born subjects of the realm, who, though in general terms and speeches they seemed and made show, to the Justices of Assize, of true and dutiful allegiance to the Queen's Majesty, their natural Sovereign, yet when endeavour is used to uncover their masked and feigned protestations, they cannot hide their malice and treasonable intentions, even to their own confusions. Which appearing thus manifestly to the Queen's most excellent Majesty, having subscribed these former answers with their own hands, whereas she was much inclined, upon the report of the said Justices, to afford them grace and pardon if they would have persisted in their former protestations, finding them now unworthy thereof, hath left them to the punishment appointed by the law, to be inflicted upon them for their just offence.

God save the Queen.

Imprinted at London by Christopher Baker, Printer to the Queen's most excellent Majesty.

This proclamation is a sample of the "mild and temperate course" used by the Government to justify a procedure, the manifest iniquity of which might easily cause grave discontent among the people. Two priests are condemned simply and solely for their sacred character, and after this they are questioned about private opinions, of which the law cannot take cognizance. They answer by protesting that they are perfectly loyal, and refuse to discuss opinions, hypotheses, and theories. A skilful appeal to a prejudiced people based upon such a refusal will easily raise some show of odium, and then the execution under the persecuting statute may proceed according to the sentence previously passed.

We may now give the death-scene from Father Warford's narrative.

There on some high ground in sight of the moaning sea the scaffold was erected, and, as in many other cases, their life was promised them with pardon, yea and honour too, and every sort of advantage if they would recant, but in vain; the nearer virtue comes to its triumph the more courageous it grows. The Martyrs, having fulfilled with great piety and constancy the duties of their priestly function, underwent the extreme penalty, being hanged, disembowelled, and mangled. It is said that from that time the Catholic faith was much discussed, and a notable occasion offered to that people of learning the truth. In fine, many returned to their homes striking their breasts, and now there is great hope that a plentiful harvest of souls will arise from such pure and holy seed.⁶ . . .

Anderton was of moderate height but somewhat less then Marsden; the latter had always a pale complexion, Anderton had a more manly countenance, but had evidently suffered from sickness when a child. Both had black eyes, beards slight, which would have been brown when fully grown. Both of them were most unassuming but full of life and spirits, and they were remarkable for their piety and zeal for sacred things.

---

⁶ Father Warford here indulges himself in an elegant rhapsody, "Taceant omnes Thesei et Perithei, Pylades et Orestes sileant," &c., which we spare the English reader.

CHAPTER V.

VENERABLE ROGER DICCONSON AND VENERABLE RALPH MILNER.

Executed at Winchester, July 7, 1591.

DOCUMENTS.

1. Examination (P.R.O. *Domestic Eliz.* vol. clxvii. n. 59).
2. Extract from Father Stanney's narrative respecting Milner (Challoner's translation). Latin.
3. Privy Council Warrants (Council Registers, Whitehall, vol. ix. pp. 79, 328).
4. Account of Dicconson's trial and death (Stonyhurst MSS. *M*. fol. 146).
5. Shorter accounts:
    (i.) Account of Winchester Martyrs (Stonyhurst MSS. *Anglia*, vii. n. 25).
    (ii.) Relation by a Priest in England (Stonyhurst MSS. *M*. fol. 195).
    (iii.) Extract from a letter of John Cecil (Westminster Archives, iv. p. 321. *Collectanea B*. 65).

---

1. Of the Venerable Roger Dicconson very few particulars have yet been published. Challoner's diligence could only gather some dozen lines, and other writers have hardly anything more to add. The additional information about him given here show him to have been one whose character will well bear more detailed study and inspection.

As to his birth we know only this, that he was a native of the diocese of Lincoln, and of his early life no more than that he was at one time a frequenter of Protestant churches. On April the 2nd, 1582, he came to the English Seminary at Rheims, and after a short course of studies was ordained priest, and returned to England in the May of 1583. He seems to have laboured with success in Hampshire, and to have there met with Milner, his future companion in martyrdom. But he was soon arrested, sent to Bridewell, where he was very barbarously used, and on December the 11th, subjected to one of those terrible examinations, the answers to which might prove the subject-matter for a capital charge. Though this examination is lost, some notes of almost greater value have survived, for they show us what were considered its most incriminating points. These had been picked out in order that legal advice might be taken upon them with a view to further proceedings, and they are as follows:

EXTRACT FROM ROGER DICCONSON'S EXAMINATIONS.

A. He was made priest, and took the oath of the Pope's Supremacy at Rheims.
B. He is not bound in conscience to name his associates that came over with him.
C. Is sorry that he went so long to the church.
D. Hath been conversant with Thomas Hall.

The result of these confessions was that on the 19th of January following, Roger Dicconson was sent to the Gatehouse, by command of the Privy Council, "for religion,"[1] and was only freed after a year or so

[1] P.R.O. *Dom. Eliz.* vol. clxix. n. 24.

by being exiled for life, and transported out of the kingdom. But Dicconson was not the man to be thereby frightened from his duty. He returned at once, and took up his abode in Worcestershire, where he was little known. The incidents which led to his finally settling at Winchester belong to the life of Ralph Milner, who was from henceforth to become his companion until the end.

Ralph Miller, or as Challoner calls him Milner, was a husbandman living near Winchester. Though born before the changes of religion, he was not constant to his faith from the first, but submitted, like the rest of his neighbours, to the different alterations in belief, which were imposed by law. Father Thomas Stanney, a Jesuit Father, who was in later days his confessor and afterwards his biographer, tells us that his conversion was effected by comparing the self-indulgence of Protestants, especially that of the unworthy ministers intruded by Elizabeth, with the more devoted lives of Catholics. The contrast affected him deeply, he applied to a Catholic priest for instruction and was soon reconciled to the Church of his baptism. Nor was he long before he found what need the Catholics had to cultivate that self-abnegation, which had originally charmed him. On the very day that he made his General Confession and received absolution and Holy Communion, he was arrested and thrown into gaol.

Gaol treatment was a very variable quantity in those days. Sometimes the prisoners were used with the most horrible barbarity, sometimes under a sympathetic keeper they enjoyed considerable liberty. Milner succeeded in winning his gaoler's confidence, and was often allowed to leave the prison on no other security than his own promise to return. Nay, from time to time, even the prison keys were left in his possession. He was thus able to do much good, making himself a sort of guide to Father Stanney, whom he led to many houses, to complete the work of conversions, of which he himself had laid the foundations.

2. Once [says Father Stanney] he came to me, desiring that I would take a journey with him to preach and administer the sacraments according to our custom. I was obliged of necessity to answer that I had been in those parts not long since, and was very much fatigued with preaching, hearing confessions, and administering the sacraments: the more because I was obliged to watch whole nights and to celebrate Mass twice a day, so that I had not as yet been able to recover myself.

"Well but, master," said he, for so he used to call me, "we have still a great many hungry souls that want bread, and there is no one to give it them, we have many also that would be glad to shake off the yoke of bondage and embrace the Catholic faith, but I can find no one to help them, or receive them into the Church. What then am I to say to them?"

"I tell you, Ralph, the very truth," said I, "I want not good-will, but strength; wherefore I beg they will have a little patience, and in a short time, by the grace of God, I purpose entirely to satisfy their good desires."

"But what shall I do," said Ralph, "if your Reverence's health will not permit you to come amongst us?"

I replied that I had been desirous of a long time to have another priest who might be able to serve those parts; and that, if he could find a proper place for him, I would endeavour to procure them a proper priest.

"That I will do with all my heart," said Ralph, "and I hope to be able in a short time to provide him all necessaries."

Soon after this our Superior [Father Henry Garnet] with another priest happened to come to me, and I consulted him what I was to do. He bade me ask Ralph if he would be willing to have for their priest Mr. Roger Dicconson, whom he was very well acquainted with. On my asking him, Ralph immediately answered, "With all my heart. I would be glad to live and die with that good man above all others." This was what afterwards happened.[2]

Milner soon completed his arrangements, and in a few weeks the future Martyr came down to take up his abode in or near Winchester. He laboured chiefly among the poor and the prisoners, and had, like all other priests, many strange escapes. Once he was arrested and sent up to London, but his keepers got drunk on the way and he made his escape.

[2] Quoted by Challoner, vol. i. Appendix, p. 231. His copy is at Oscott, in Alban Butler's Collections, p. 389. The St. Omers MS. from which it was taken is now in the *Archives d'Etat* at Brussels.

In Hampshire [so wrote a priest[3] from England at the time of the Martyr's death] Roger Dicconson continued for three or four years, taking great pains both by day and night, to comfort his old flock by preaching and ministering the sacraments, and by reconciling unto the Church no small number of all sorts of people, for reward of which in the end he was taken with twelve others lay people. He was betrayed by one that counterfeited to be reconciled, but his drift was to get certain land from his brother, who was then in company with this priest. Presently afterwards they were all imprisoned in the common prison, from whence this priest with the poor man called Ralph Milner was conveyed to London to be there further examined.

3. Dicconson was at this time passing under the *alias* of Richard Johnson, and his arrest, as we learn from the Council Registers, was due to the pastoral diligence of Thomas Cowper, Bishop of Winchester, of whom we heard before in the accounts of the Martyrs Marsden and Anderton. It is worth remembering that, whereas in that case the Catholic account laid great stress on Cowper's conduct, while the Council Registers appear to ignore him, in this case the positions are reversed, the Catholics know nothing of Cowper's action, which is plainly described in the records of the Council. Thus they write to him on January 24, 1591:

[3] The rest of this relation will be found later, p. 96.

To the Bishop of Winton.

Their Lordships having perceived his care and diligence in the apprehending of Richard Johnson the Seminary priest and the rest taken at Mass, &c., wherein he doth deserve their Lordships' thanks, they have thought good to pray and require him to cause the said Johnson together with Ralf Miller, of Slackstead [a] (who, as they likewise perceive from his letters, is a very dangerous and ill-affected member in those parts), to be presently sent hither by the bearer, a messenger of her Majesty's Chamber, assisted by such as his lordship shall think fit for the more safe and speedy bringing of them hither, in such order as in his discretion shall seem convenient. And the rest taken with the Seminary priest as is abovesaid, they pray him to give strict order that they be forthcoming, as the rest of that disposition, in the gaol there, &c.

To advertise their Lordships of the priest's examinations, &c.

To London they accordingly came, where Dicconson was sent to the Marshalsea, and Milner probably to Bridewell. "Thomas Beddam, servant to the Bishop of Winchester," having seen his prisoners safe in their respective gaols, received, "upon the Council's warrant dated at Richmond 8 Feb. [1591], for the charges and pains of himself and seven others with their horses in bringing up from Winchester to the Star Chamber one Richard Johnson, a Seminary priest, and Ralph Miller, a recusant, and returning

[a] Slackstead, not as Challoner prints it, Flacstead.

back again," the sum of eight pounds from the Treasurer of the Chamber.[5]

Father Stanney, whom we have quoted before, says that the Martyrs were subjected to divers tortures during their stay in London, which lasted for five or six months. By that time the inquisitors of the Council, one of whom was Lord Burleigh, and another will surely have been Topcliffe, then at the zenith of his power, had done their work, and on the 14th of June another order was issued to the Knight Marshal, ordering him "to send them both down to the Sheriff" of Southampton, "with a sufficient guard of your servants, and to cause the said prisoners to be delivered into the hands of the said Sheriff or his under-sheriff, by them to be committed to the common gaol, to the end they may receive their trial according to the law at the next Assizes there to be holden."

4. Father Grene has made some long extracts from a contemporary account of Dicconson's trial, respecting which we have no information. The parts enclosed in square brackets are his abbreviations.

THE ARRAIGNMENT OF MR. DICKENSON, EXECUTED AT WINTON, 1591.

First, as the order is, they said, "Johnson, thou art here indicted by the name of Johnson," &c., and read the indictment, which in effect was, that he, made priest beyond the seas, came to this realm against the statute, and said Mass, &c.

Answer. He answered that he was not acquainted

[5] P.R.O. Accounts of Treasurer of Chamber, 1590-1, rot. 155 *b*.

with any such statute, and "no man can prove that ever I said Mass."

Demand. "Art thou guilty, or not guilty?"

Ans. "Not guilty."

Dem. "By whom wilt thou be tried?"

Ans. "By God and the country."

Dem. "If he had ever said Mass in Widow White's house, or no?"

Ans. "Let any man prove it, my lord."

Dem. "If he had ever heard confessions there, or no?"

Ans. "Let any man accuse me."

Then there was a green silly youth brought for a witness that he had heard his confession [and he contradicted himself often and plainly. I omit other things concerning this boy, they cannot be read]. They said, "Fie, Johnson, that thou wilt persuade poor souls from God's religion," &c.

Ans. "I never did anything but to use my office, and that, I hope, was no offence."

Dem. "Thou art made a priest beyond the sea according to the Church of Rome."

Ans. "I was made a priest as other priests are, and have been before me."

Dem. "Are you a Yorkshireman?"

Ans. "Aye, my lord."

[Here is added in the margin: "I think this is a mistake, for he told me that he was a Lincolnshire man."]

The Judge demanded, "What can you say more that you should not receive judgment for these treasons?"

Ans. "Truly, my lord, I can say no more than I have said. I came into the realm, my native country, to give myself to study, to prayer, and devotion, and use my function, and that, I hope, is no treason."

Then they said, "Well, Johnson, it is too evidently proved against thee. Notwithstanding, call to God for grace, for that thou hast seduced the people," &c.

His answer was nothing but an humble beck. [To many other frivolous things that were said, the Martyr gave almost the same answers as before.]

The manner of his execution. First, as he was drawn upon the hurdle, they rested twice by the way, once without the town-gate, the other at the place of execution, where he rested on the hurdle all the time while five felons were hanged, and his fellow-martyr was put to death named Ralph Miller, a husbandman. All this time the ministers were very busy about him. He said, "If you were in my case, you would be loth to be troubled, and therefore I pray you let me alone." They said that if he would recant his religion, he might have mercy, which he stoutly refused. One said, "Acknowledge the Queen to be your Sovereign." As much as I could hear, he said he did.

Then the Sheriff's men unloosed him from the hurdle, and led him to the gallows. Then the Sheriff and gentlemen of the shire talked with him, whilst he himself put off his doublet, his band, his hose and shoes, all persuading him to recant and he might have mercy, which he always stoutly refused. Then they had him to the ladder, which, without altering countenance, he went up, and turned his back to the ladder, and said, "God bless you all, God give us all the Kingdom of Heaven." Then the halter being put about his neck, he said it was [too tight],[6] and with his own hand made it wider. Then he said: "I confess myself to be a Seminary priest. I came into the realm to give myself to prayer and devotion, and here I am accused to have seduced the people from their obedience, which I take to my death I never did."

"No?" said the Sheriff. "Look upon the man that is dead (which was the blessed Martyr); you are the cause of his blood, and here is one that will bear witness against you" (which was the silly youth that accused him at his arraignment).

Ans. "I never dealt with him."

Then George Powlett, a new Justice of Peace, said he lived under a merciful Prince, whose laws were good, and "you will not obey them, therefore yet I pray you ask mercy."

Ans. "I never offended her Majesty unless by using of my office, and that I hope is not offensive."

Then the Sheriff said: "If you will deny the Pope and become a good subject, you may yet have mercy."

Ans. "I will never deny my religion" (and

[6] Blank in MS.

this he spoke twice). "But for her Majesty, I have prayed for her, and if I had a thousand days to live I would; and at His house, I pray God, she may both body and soul inherit the Kingdom of Heaven."

Then they being about to speak, he said, "I desire you to give me leave to say some few prayers, for that I have but a little time to live."

Then he most reverently lifted up his hands and eyes to heaven, and prayed softly to himself, and in the end he said, "*In manus tuas, Domine, commendo spiritum meum. Redemisti me, Domine Deus veritatis,* &c.—' Into thy hands, O Lord,' &c. Here I acknowledge my redemption and justification."

They asked him by whom.

Ans. "By Christ."

They said: "And by no other?"

Ans. "Yea, only by Christ."

They said, "What say you to the Pope?"

Ans. "He is a man subject to all calamities, &c., as we all are, and can do nothing without Christ."

They said, "Well said, Johnson." Then he said, "I beseech you all to pray for me." And they said, "Well said." Then he said, "I pray you all Catholics to pray for me." Mr. Cotton bid him confess his treasons and ask pardon, and said he was not condemned for being priest, but because he came in against the statute and seduced the people.

Ans. "Pardon me, Mr. Cotton, I have been examined before my Lord Treasurer, my Lord Bishop, and others, and you have nothing to say against me, but a statute of your own making, and God knoweth how unjust it is." Then holding his hands together, and his eyes lifted up to heaven, praying secretly, the hangman pulled his kercher over his eyes, and cast him off the ladder. At his going down, he said, *Domine Jesu, accipe.* The word *accipe* he did scarce speak, because he was almost choked with the halter.

Finis.

5. We may here throw together some brief accounts of these Martyrs. Being independent, they naturally record several fresh particulars.

(i.) From the account of Winchester Martyrs.

Ralph Miller was hanged at Bardich[7] for felony, for that he was in the company of Mr. Dickenson, a Seminary priest, contrary to a statute made felony in that case. Being asked by the Judge why he would not go to church, he said that he was born in the reign of King Henry VIII., and that he would live and die in that faith wherein he was born and christened. At the gallows, his pardon being offered him if he would go to church, he answered, "No, no, I will hang," reached his hand to the ladder and went up.

[7] Bardich, that is the ditch at the Bar or city gate.

(ii.) From the *Relation written by a Priest in England*, already quoted in part. This is his account of their trials and death:

The priest was condemned of treason for re-conciling of malefactors unto the Catholic Church, and this poor man was condemned of felony upon the Statute of Persuasion.

The priest was hanged, drawn, and quartered, all which he endured so cheerfully and constantly and without any change of countenance, that the heretics said, "The villain dieth desperately and feareth not death;" he should have had pardon if he would have yielded in anything unto them. When he was cast off from the ladder, he was heard to say, *In manus*, &c., and turning about, another heard him say softly, *Suscipe spiritum meum*, knocking his breast twice and holding up his hands as close as he could, for that his arms were pinioned.

One of his quarters was taken away, shortly after they were hanged up on the gate, by a maid who was imprisoned for the Catholic faith, but yet made this adventure in the night, and returned to prison again with the quarter under her cloak; for the which afterwards was made great search, but yet it could not be found.

The old man abovesaid was offered his pardon if he would go to church, but he stoutly refused it. Having a wife and children, a Justice of Peace told him that he should have care of them, but he answered that he hoped to do them as much good where he went as if he were with them. Having the halter about his neck, his son asked his blessing, which he gave him in this following manner, "I pray God send thee no worse end than thy father," and so he was cast off the ladder. Before, a Justice said unto this man, "Thou art worse than any Seminary priest," and he answered, "You say truly, for I shall never be so good as they."

(iii.) Finally, we add an extract from the letter of John Cecil, a priest, to Father Robert Persons. It seems to be the original source from which Champney and Ribadeneira derived the whole of Dr. Challoner's story.

At Winchester, Roger Dicconson and Ralph Milner, who, desiring the Judges to be good to his wife and 8 or 9 small children he had, was answered thus: "Go to church, fool, and look to thy children thyself." He replied that the loss of his soul was too high a price to pay for so small and vile a commodity, and so he died blessedly *in Domino*. With them were condemned 8 or 9 young damsels, but not sentenced, the which with open outcries and exclamations urged the Judges most constantly that as they were all culpable of the same crime, viz., of hearing Mass, relieving a priest, confessing their sins, and serving their Saviour after the rite of the Catholic Church, so they might drink all of the same cup, with such fervour and vehemence that they made the whole assembly astonished.

CHAPTER VI.

VENERABLE EDMUND GENINGS AND COMPANIONS.

Executed December 10, 1591.

DOCUMENTS.

1. Relation of James Young, otherwise called Younger (Stonyhurst MSS. *Anglia*, vi. 117).
2. (i.) Writ of Privy Council for the torture of Eustace White and Brian Lacey (Council Registers, Whitehall, vol. x. p. 30).
   (ii.) Letter of the Ven. Eustace White (Stonyhurst MSS. *Anglia*, i. 117).

The following document needs but little introduction, save some words as to its author. Of his adventures very much that is interesting may be found among the State Papers in the Record Office, but they do not specially relate to the English Martyrs, and indeed would not have been mentioned here at all, were it not that it would not be right to let James Young tell his story without a hint of our knowledge of a sad stain on his life.

A native of Durham, and educated at Durham College, he left his birthplace under pretence of going to Cambridge, but really to pass over seas to France. There he was advised to enter the English

Seminary at Rheims, and he was admitted in November, 1581. In March, 1583, he was sent to Rome. Having been there ordained priest in 1587, he went to the newly-founded College at Valladolid in September, 1589. He returned to England in 1591, and was arrested and committed to the Poultry about Easter, 1592. In the following August he began a series of letters addressed to Lord Keeper Puckering, in which he told all that he knew respecting his fellow-priests and Catholic affairs in general. If any one will take the trouble to study his letters carefully, it may yet appear that he played this part more to save his own skin, than out of real ill-will to the people he informed against. However, the fact remains that his letters of information to Lord Keeper Puckering are still extant in the Record Office, and may be followed, in the year 1592, under his various aliases of Dingley and Christopher, through the Calendar of State Papers. Once he even offered to "displace" the very Father Persons, to whom the following letter is addressed. But, as we have said, perhaps some advocate on the other side may show that Young's discoveries were not really of so dangerous a nature as they seem, and that his offer to "displace" Father Persons was only a blind to obtain leave to escape from the country. He thus succeeded in obtaining his liberation, and he soon went abroad. Certainly, after he did get back to Douay in 1593, we hear no more of correspondence with the persecutors at home. His reports to Puckering were unknown to the Catholics, and before 1596 he took the degree of D.D., probably at the University of Douay.

The martyrdoms described by him took place

just before his imprisonment, with the exception of Margaret Ward's and John Neele's, which were before his coming to England, and those of Davys and Cornelius, which happened after he left it. The credibility of the following "relation of Martyrs" is proved by its close correspondence with the full and entirely independent account of these Martyrs, written by Father John Genings, O.S.F., a charming little volume with most interesting plates, published at St. Omers in 1591. This book, with its plates, was reproduced in 1887 by Messrs. Burns and Oates, edited by Father W. Forbes Leith, S.J.

RELATION OF MARTYRS, BY MR. JAMES YOUNGE, PRIEST. WRITTEN FROM DOUAY, FEBRUARY, 1595.[1]

1591. Dominica 1ª Adventus. Edmund [Genings, priest of the College of Rheims, was apprehended in the house of Swithin Wells, gentleman, dwelling in Holborn, and with the said priest were taken many other Catholics men and women, whereof two serving-men [made resistance against the pursuivants breaking into the house, but being enforced to surcease from arms by the multitude, they with all the rest were led to prison. At this time Mr. Wells was not at home, but hearing what had happened he absented himself from his own house, to know in time what would become of his wife now imprisoned with all the others. When, lo! a rumour was made that the priest was not taken, but had escaped privily. Which Swithin Wells hearing, and believing it,

[1] So endorsed by Father Persons, to whom it was sent in Spain.

presently went to Topcliffe, entreating him for his wife's freedom, especially seeing there was no cause to detain her, as he supposed, for "there was no priest," saith he, "in my house." "Yes," said Topcliffe, "thou thyself didst know it well enough." Whereupon presently he sent Mr. Wells to prison.

Within one week he was arraigned at the King's Bench, Westminster Hall, together with many other Catholics and three priests, Mr. Genings, Mr. Plasden, and Mr. White; I myself was present in person and stood fast by Topcliffe next to the Judges. The Chief Judge was the Lord Chief Justice of England, my Lord Wray, now dead; there was also present Anderson, Chief of the Common Pleas, John [Aylmer], the false Bishop of London, Popham, then the Queen's Attorney, now Lord Chief Justice of England, Wade, Clerk of the Council, Mr. Gilbert Garret [Gerard], Master of the Rolls, with divers others, whom I do not now remember. The quest of twelve men was now empanelled, and after evidence was read and avowed by Topcliffe, forthwith was found by the twelve *billa vera*, [true bill], as they speak.

Then they were asked what they could say why the Judge should not pronounce sentence of death against them, according to the verdict of the twelve men. Mr. Plasden began to answer, saying they had not offended against any just law of the realm, wherein they reported themselves to the conscience of all the Bench there, who better knew what was law than twelve simple men, that understood not what it was to be a priest. "They find us guilty," saith he, "of treason for exercising our priestly function, which was in all ages an honourable calling, as you the learned on the Bench have read in your own laws and histories, if yet you dare to speak the truth."

"What," saith Fleetwood, for he also was present, "dost thou talk so, Plasden? Methinks thou wouldst better wind a horn; for I think thy father is an horner dwelling at Fleet Bridge," at which all men laughed.

And then Popham began to show the equity and necessity of the late English statutes, made for the reclaiming of the Queen's subjects in their obedience; wherein he roamed wide. Who having ended, Anderson followed the same point, and showed what commodity had ensued of those statutes; to wit, that many traitors were weeded out of the commonwealth by the practice of those laws, "of which myself," saith he, "can give testimony, having in my time adjudged above sixty of these Papistical traitors to the gallows." Then Topcliffe, avowing so much as had been said, adjoined, moreover, that all priests must needs be traitors. For they all did hold opinion (whatsoever they said otherwise) with Sander, Bristow, and Allen, and forthwith he read out of the *Apology of the Seminaries* that Allen did maintain it lawful for the servant in case of heresy to forsake his master, the son his father, yea, the wife her husband. "Oh, forgive," said he, "all you English hearts, that hears this,[2] I know abhors this doctrine, which maketh married men not to be sure of their wives. But," saith he, "I will make your hair stand upright upon your head, telling what another of them executed of late did hold." Then he drew out a little note-book, some time Mr. Beesley's the Martyr, said *in verbo* "*homicidio*,"[3] that it was lawful for the subject to disobey, yea, to kill his Sovereign in case he be an heretic. "And this all priests do hold," said he, "although peradventure they dare not utter their mind plainly, therefore they are all traitors."

Then John of London began a heretical and a wise speech, I warrant you, speaking in this sort: "Young [fools], so I must needs call you, because you are greatly abused by those whom you call your Superiors; yourselves having no experience, and thus are the sooner deceived. Think now of my counsel, which is to help yourselves, and to acknowledge your fault and error; then doubtless I dare promise you from the Queen's Majesty sure pardon. Poor youths, how greatly do they deceive you who send you hither, with danger of your lives to perform this. You, miserable men, do what in you is, to kill yourselves; which is a damnable thing unless

---

[2] Topcliffe's grammar is always outrageous.

[3] This means that the note-book was arranged under various headings, and that this statement was found "under the word *homicide*." It is extremely improbable that the Martyr's notebook contained anything of the sort.

you now repent. But your blood shall be one day demanded at the hands of [Allen] and Persons who wittingly send you hither, where justice must needs be executed upon you, according to the godly laws of this realm. They dare not come themselves, but by flattery and cosenage, they get you fond men to venture your lives for the Pope. And then if they durst come, we would dispute with them, and I know her Highness would condescend unto it, so all the world should perceive their ignorance and yours, who, because forsooth you are priests, think that her Majesty can not, nor ought not, to control you nor the Pope. But the ancient Fathers were of contrary judgment."

Then he alleged a place out of Tertullian: I do not remember in what book. This I marked, that upon those words, *Omnis anima potestati superiori subdita sit*, he quoted St. John Chrysostom, saying, that every soul should be subject to a prince, yea, even bishops, wherefore (where was the man's wit, think you?) if the Pope has a son, he must needs be subject to some prince. I could not but smile hearing the long-bearded dolt, and Mr. Genings began also to smile; saying that he was but a young student, yet with my lord's leave he would show how vain such allegations were. "Peace," said John of London, "I see you are all wilful. Here I acquit myself before all this audience that I have given you sound counsel. At the latter day when you and I shall all stand before the Judge, this my word now shall then condemn you," and with that the dissembling wretch wept, as it seemed, [and] wiped his eyes trickling down with tears, every one as big as a millstone. "Almighty God pardon your obstinacy. I may not stay to hear the just sentence of blood pronounced against you, because it is not according to my profession." Which said, he presently departed from the Bench. Many silly people commended his great charity and tender heart as I heard them speak.

Then the Lord Wray began, saying that many things had been well urged against the priests by them of the Bench; as that they were men who took part with Spaniards, who by all likelihood would kill the Queen if they possibly could, who solicited the people secretly to rebellion and change of religion, all which are of great moment. "But I at this present am to pronounce sentence against you, for that against the statute made in this behalf, you have been made priests by authority from the See of Rome, and have returned into this country to exercise your priestly functions, as you term them, and have confessed, wherefore you are found guilty of high treason. And therefore you shall return to the place from whence you came, and from thence be drawn," &c.

Which words were no sooner heard, but the catchpoles who guarded the prisoners at the bar, began every one to catch some a hat, some a cloak, others the ruffs and handkerchiefs which the condemned persons had, yea, they pulled their very points from their hose. When, lo! one of the priests spake to the Judge about the cruelty used amongst Christians. "Besides our priesthood, we are freemen born, and yet in the sight of you, Judges of the land, we are thus despoiled and bared, even before we be dead." Which heard, Wray commanded their hats and cloaks should be restored.

Amongst these Catholics there was arraigned one Robert Sydney,[4] sometime a serving-man, taken at Mass with Mr. Genings; he, by the entreaty of the Judge, and of the Lord Anderson, asked pardon of the Queen for his fault, which being done the Judge told him that he had showed himself a good subject, and therefore should have favour at her Majesty's hands. Presently he was unpinioned, every man thinking he should be dismissed; for he was not condemned with the other; but only was singled out as a poor simple man whom they thought would yield easily, and so every one judged of him, because he had craved pardon. The Lord Anderson said unto him, "Sydney, thou must go to my Lord of London, and he will instruct thee in the truth." To whom he answered, "My lord, I would not have you to think that I will deny my faith, although I have asked her Majesty's forgiveness. I will die twenty times first."

Which being heard, forthwith the twelve men were commanded to go upon him, and, I think, before I could have said *Credo* to the end, they

[4] This is the Venerable Sydney Hodgson.

returned and found [him guilty], and anon the Judge pronounced sentence against him as he had done on all the rest.

I will report you their deaths in order, one after another, as they happened. The next day Swithin Wells, a man of good birth and ancient years, his head almost as white as snow, was brought by the Sheriff of London and Topcliffe with many other officers into Grays Inn Fields, where before his own house was erected a gibbet. Many hundred people were there present, myself stood fast by the gibbet, and heard whatsoever was said. Mr. Wells was commanded to go up the ladder, which done, Topcliffe called for a minister. At last a hot-spirited Sir John came, who persuaded Mr. Wells to acknowledge his fact with this reason. Saith he, "It is a point both of Papists', and also of Protestants', religion, that no man can be saved without confession. Papists say to a priest, but we say to the congregation; wherefore, if thou wilt be saved, thou must needs confess that thou hast offended God and her Majesty by following false doctrine and traitorous priests." Swithin Wells, then saying his *Pater noster*, ended, and turning about looked upon the minister. "Although I heard you say somewhat," quoth he, "yet it is but one doctor's opinion, and he also a very young one." With which the beardless minister was so daunted, that he could not reply one word more.

Then Topcliffe bade Mr. Wells look upon the priest Mr. Genings, who lay upon a hurdle at the foot of the gibbet. "I see him well," quoth he, "and I thank God that ever I did know him. Good Father, give me your blessing," which the priest did. "Nay," quoth Topcliffe, "rather reprehend him for having brought you to this shameful end." "I count it honourable," quoth the other. "Dog-bolt Papists!" said Topcliffe, "you follow the Pope and his Bulls; believe me, I think some bulls begot you all." Herewith Mr. Wells was somewhat moved, and replied, "If we have bulls to our fathers, thou hast a cow to thy mother." And anon he corrected himself saying, "Good sir, forgive me. I request all Catholics here to pray for me. At this time, Mr. Topcliffe, you should not use such speeches to drive me to impatience. God pardon you and make you of a Saul a Paul, of a bloody persecutor one of the Catholic Church's children; by your malice I am thus to be executed, but you have done me the greatest benefit that ever I could have had. I heartily forgive you." "This dialogue," said Mr. Topcliffe, "will be talked of hereafter, for I warrant you there are some of thy own profession who hears thee." Anon the ladder was turned, and Mr. Wells was suffered to hang until he was dead, and afterwards was worshipfully by his friends buried in St. Andrew's Churchyard in Holborn. The cause why Mr. Wells was condemned was, because it was proved he had served a priest to Mass some three days before this happened.

Edmund Genings then was taken from the

hurdle, and commanded to put off his doublet, which done he mounted the ladder and kissing the rope turned himself to the people and began to speak. He was bid to confess his fault first, otherwise he could not be suffered to talk. All the people in my hearing much pitied him, for that he was of a comely and gentlemanly countenance, fair and young, of great courage, showing no fear at all of death, but thanking God that he had lived until that time to die for Christ's cause. He was turned off the ladder and presently was cut down, where the hangman taking him yet alive and speaking, he ripped his belly and showed his heart to the people crying, "Thus God grant it may happen to all traitors! God save the Queen!" When scarce one voice was heard amongst all the people to say Amen, at which they much wondered who were the chief executors. His heart and bowels were there burnt. His head and quarters were set upon London Bridge and other gates of the City.

Whiles this was happening, the other Sheriff carried to Tyburn Mr. Brian Lacey, John Mason, and also Robert Sydney, laymen, Mr. Plasden, Mr. Eustace White, priests; and anon Topcliffe hastened to Tyburn, whither I also went to see the execution.

Brian Lacey had sometime, as I think, served Momford Scott, a priest and martyr. He was arraigned before the Lord Mayor of London, called Webb, a salter by occupation, at Sessions House in the Old Bailey. Others who were present I do not now remember, except Young, the arch-persecutor; he was condemned quickly and in such sort, that in truth I thought they but jested with him. Such ridiculous matter was laid to his charge, as also to all the others aforenamed, that in good truth I was persuaded that they would never make so small account of men's lives as to take them away on such slender and childish accusations, as they must needs seem to any man of judgment who heard them. But yet it proved good earnest.

Lacey, now having the rope about his neck, was willed by Topcliffe to confess his treason. "For," saith he, "there are none but traitors who are of thy religion."

"Then," said Lacey, "answer me. You yourself in Queen's Mary's days was a Papist, at least in show. Tell me, were you also a traitor?" At which all the people laughed aloud.

"Well," quoth Topcliffe, "I came not here to answer thy arguments. Thou art to answer me."

"I have said," quoth the other, with smiling and cheerful countenance, and voice as merry as though he had been far from death. Anon the cart was drawn away, and he suffered to hang until he was dead.

Then followed John Mason, servant to Mr. Owen of Oxfordshire, who was condemned at the bar as an aider or abettor of priests. He was first indicted for knowing a Seminary priest, and not revealing him. He answered that the law allowed three days' space, within which time if one did not betray the priest, he is guilty of felony. "As for me, I was taken in his company, and therefore you know not what I would have done, if I had had longer time."

Then a second indictment was framed, in which he was charged to have aided the priests, which was proved thus. When the pursuivant came into the house, this young man met him at the top of a pair of stairs, and clasping with him, tumbled him down to the foot of the stairs, he himself being fastened in the pursuivant's arms, and thus much the young man confessed. Hereupon they proved that he aided the priests, because if there were any window in the house the priests might have escaped. For this he was condemned in my hearing, and executed the morrow after. He was demanded if he were not sorry for the fact. "No," answered he, resolutely, "if it were to do again, I would resist the wicked, that they should not have God's priests, yea, although I were to be punished with twenty deaths." In the same cart was also Sydney of whom I spake before, to whom they never tendered any question, wherefore he prayed all the time secretly, holding his hands towards heaven, and so both, gloriously confessing their faith, they were suffered to hang until they were dead.

Oliver [Polydore] Plasden,[5] priest, born by Fleet Bridge, in London, was next put into the cart,

[5] In Rome, Polydore Plasden was called Oliver Palmer. He signed himself Oliver Plasden in 1586 (Foley, *Records*, vi. p. 508).

who prayed for the Queen and the whole realm, which when Sir Walter Rawlin [Raleigh] heard, "What," said he, "dost thou think as thou prayest?"

"Otherwise," quoth he, "I expect no salvation at God's hands."

"Then thou dost acknowledge her for thy lawful Queen?" said Rawlin.

"I do sincerely."

"Wouldst thou defend her," quoth Rawlin, "against all her foreign and domestical enemies, if so thou wert able?"

"I would," said Plasden, "to the uttermost of my power, and so I would counsel all men who would be persuaded by me."

The people hearing this, began to speak one to another: "There is no cause why this honest man should die. He would never say thus at death, except he thought so in his heart."

Then Rawlin said: "How happened it that yesterday before the Judges thou wouldst not say thus much? Then thou hadst not come thus far. I know, good people," said Rawlin, turning himself, "her Majesty desireth no more at these men's hands, than that which this man hath now confessed. Mr. Sheriff," said he, "I will presently go to the Court, let him be stayed."

Which when Topcliffe heard, "I pray you," saith he, "suffer me to offer him one question, and anon you shall hear that I will convince him to be a traitor." Then he said: "Plasden, in thy conscience, before all this assembly, tell me thy judgment. If the King of Spain or the Pope would come into this country by force for no other end precisely, but by his canonical law," for so he spake, "to establish that faith which thou believest and which thou thinkest to be the true Catholic faith as you call it, tell me, wouldst thou resist them?"

"I am a priest," quoth he, "and therefore may not fight."

"Although thou mayst not fight, wouldst thou give counsel to others who would fight to defend her Majesty?"

"I would," said the priest, "counsel all men to maintain the right of their Prince."

"He saith marvellous well," quoth Rawlin. "No more. I will presently post to the Queen. I know she will be glad of this plain dealing."

"Then," said Topcliffe, "let me say but one word unto him," which was granted. "Thou sayest, Plasden," quoth he, "that thou wouldst counsel all to defend the Queen's right, but tell me, dost thou think that the Queen hath any right to maintain this religion, and to forbid yours?"

"No," said the priest.

"Then thou thinkest not," quoth he, "to defend the Queen against the Pope, if he would come to establish thy religion; speak, what sayest thou to this? I charge thee before God."

"I am a Catholic priest," quoth he, "therefore I would never fight, nor counsel others to fight against my religion, for that were to deny my faith. O Christ," saith he, looking up to heaven and kissing the rope, "I will never deny Thee for a thousand lives."

Then lo! they cried, he was a traitor, and the cart was drawn away, and he, by the word of Rawlin, was suffered to hang until he was dead; then was he drawn and quartered after their custom.

Eustace White was put up into the cart last, who kissing the rope said:

"Christian people, I was yesterday condemned as a traitor for being a priest and coming into this country to reconcile, and use other my priestly functions, all which I confess I have done in sundry places of this realm for some years together. I thank God, that it hath pleased Him to bless my labours with this happy end, when I now am to die for my faith and priesthood; other treasons I have not committed. If I had never so many lives, I would think them very few to bestow upon your Tyburns to defend my religion. I wish I had a great many more than one, you should have them all one after another."

The people cried: "Fie on the obstinate traitor!"

"Confess thy fault," quoth Topcliffe.

"I will say no more," said the glorious Martyr. Lifting his eyes to heaven, and saying, *In manus tuas*, &c., he was presently cut down, and arose from the ground after his fall from the gallows; then they tripped his feet from him and trailed him to the fire, saying, "Sweet Jesu, sweet Jesu." Two men set their feet upon his arms to keep him down till the hangman had taken out his heart. Then they quartered him and Mr. Plasden, sending their members to divers parts of the City. The other Catholic men were buried in a pit made for that purpose by the highway-side.

In the same 1591, on the third Sunday in Advent, after I had seen the tragedy of these my brethren and fellow-priests, I remained in Clerkenwell at that time, in the house of a worshipful gentleman, Mr. Lawrence Mompesson's, and with me was also at that time another priest called William Pattinson, a Yorkshire man, sometime of the College of Rheims, who was come from the country to find some help amongst priests, how he might rid himself from scruples of conscience, wherewith he was much troubled, as sometimes it happens to devout persons. We had both said Mass that Sunday, and before dinner I took the opportunity to explicate out of the English Testament a text fit for the third Sunday of Advent, when lo, there knocked at the door, churchwardens, sidemen, and constables, coming to know who were in that house that did not go to the church. Unawares, a maid of the house let them in, all the other doors of the house were open, and before I could get into a secret place which we had, and draw up Mr. Pattinson after me, the searchers came into the place, and espying his leg to hang out of an hole, they bid him come down, which he did.

I remained in an inner place made for that purpose, if so be the other place should happen to be found. They heard me go over their heads, and calling for a candle they came up. Mr. Pattinson said: "Here are no more but myself." Yet one fellow came up, swearing that the place were able to contain twenty. "Yet," saith he, "here are no more."

Then they asked Mr. Pattinson, what he was. He told them one of the country, who came to that gentlewoman because she had some skill in healing a sore leg, which he also had. But they believed him not, and therefore they carried him to Justice Young, leaving charge in the Queen's name that no person should stir out of the house until they returned. Yet they being all gone, the door was bolted, and I escaped[6] out of the back door, and all the rest forsook the house, leaving all, and losing all they had. Who are also now living in Antwerp, having marvellous greatly well deserved of all Catholic priests.

Mr. Pattinson, being known to be a priest, was condemned at the first Sessions, after Christmas, at the Sessions [House] in the Old Bailey, as I think. Anderson was the Judge. In that little time he was in prison he converted and reconciled three or four thieves, and communicated

[6] In August, 1592, James Young wrote to Lord Keeper Puckering that he "said Mass every Sunday to Mrs. Mompesson, as did Patenson, another priest since executed, to the rest of the household, Mr. Mompesson standing behind the door, to hear and not to be seen by the servants; and at a search, he escaped and went to Mr. Wiseman" (See *Life of Father John Gerard*, 3rd Edit. p. 75).

them before their death. When they came to
the gallows they all confessed their faith, and
that they died Catholics. One only, hoping to
gain pardon, said that that traitorous priest had
dealt with him also to worship idols, but yet he
would never consent, nevertheless he was also
hanged with the rest. Mr. Pattinson was cut
down alive, and spoke unto the hangman even
when he was ripping his bowels; I do not now
remember the words. He was quartered as the
others were.

All this I saw and beheld myself, with great
comfort to see the constancy of my fellows and
acquaintance; more particulars chanced, which
yet I think of no great moment. I recommend
myself heartily unto you, as likewise to all of both
Colleges. I trust you will freely use my labours,
if so be they may be profitable unto you in anything. My dictates came in good season, for
which I still acknowledge myself much indebted
to your mindfulness. These few lines I now write
in haste, you shall hear more at large from me
shortly.

Yours ever most assuredly,
JAMES YOUNG.

Douay, February 9, 1595.

[*Postscript to the above letter.*]

Margaret Ward, gentlewoman, was hanged at
Tyburn, because she brought a rope, enwrapped
in a clean shirt, to one Watson, a priest, being in

Bridewell prison, out of which he escaped by the help of that rope.

John Neele, an Irishman, was also executed with her at Tyburn. He, in a search, was found in that apparel which the priest had on, when he escaped out of prison. Neele, being a serving-man, had given the priest his own clothes the better to get away. He was examined what he was, for at the first they thought he had been Watson the priest, but he confessed that he was a Catholic and had holpen the priest to escape, for which he was executed at Tyburn.

William Davys, priest of the College of Rheims, being about to go into Ireland, was apprehended in Anglesea, and there put to death, anno 1593. Thus much reporteth one Price, a student here in Douay, who saith that assuredly he knows it for a truth.

Anno 1594. John Cornelius was executed at Dorchester, and with him Mr. Thomas Bosgrave, sister's son to Sir John Arundell. Patrick Salmon, also an Irishman, servant to Mr. Cornelius, was also executed at the same time.

Thomas Pormort, priest, was taken in London, anno 1592,[7] upon St. James's day, and after some months' imprisonment escaped, but was taken again presently. Many particulars worth the

---

[7] As the Venerable Thomas Pormort, or Portmore, was taken in August, 1591, when he was committed to the Tower, this first arrest on the 25th of July, from which he escaped after some months' imprisonment, must have been in 1590.

noting are reported of this man, which I cannot write with any certainty. Yet this I know that at his arraignment he pleaded that he came not unto England to reconcile any, for that he had no authority, wherefore he thought the law had not been so rigorous, otherwise he would not have come into England. He requested that he might be banished, but Topcliffe, his sworn enemy, withstood it forcibly. The Judges offered him favour if he would confer. He refused, saying that he doubted of no article of faith. The twelve men found him guilty of treason, and the Judge, Anderson, I think, pronounced sentence of death against him.

Then he would have admitted conference, but the Judge replied that it was too late, nevertheless the false Archbishop sent his chaplains unto him, and commanded also the Sheriff not to execute him before authority had from his Grace. But Topcliffe, hearing of this, went to the Lord Treasurer, and got a mandamus to the Sheriff to execute the priest that self-same day. The cause why Topcliffe laboured his death so vehemently was because Mr. Pormort openly at the bar had charged Topcliffe to have said unto him [something not fit to be written].[8] Mr. Pormort also charged him that he had likewise said that there was not a true Stanley in all England. There were present upon the bench when Mr. Pormort related this, my Lord of Essex, and the

[8] Pormort accused Topcliffe of having boasted to him of indecent familiarities with the Queen.

Lord Strange, after Earl of Derby, now dead. The Earl of Essex frowned much, saying if Topcliffe had said so much of a Devereux, he would have stabbed him. The Lord Strange yet calmly said: "Topcliffe, I trust you know to use noblemen with honour, otherwise you shall understand of it." "My lord," quoth Topcliffe, "believe not a traitor priest, who doth belie me." Yet Mr. Pormort avowed it for truth even unto death. He was enforced to stand in his shirt almost two hours upon the ladder in Lent time, upon a very cold day, when Topcliffe still urged him to deny the words, but he would not.

The gibbet was erected before the door of one Barrows,[9] an haberdasher, dwelling in the west end of Paul's Churchyard in London. This man in his sickness had been reconciled by Mr. Pormort, which was known to Topcliffe, whereof he caused Barrows to accuse the priest, or else he should also be hanged and lose all his goods, by which fear he did so, standing at the gibbet, and confessing that he had offended God and her Majesty by being reconciled by the priest. At last the ladder was turned, and the priest was quartered after their manner.

The same year, the Saturday as I think after *Dominica in Albis*, Richard Williams,[10] priest in

---

[9] Stowe gives this name as Barwys.

[10] The date here given is April 28, 1592. In a letter from Father Garnet to the General of the Society, dated March 27, 1594 he says that the Martyr Pormort was followed by Mr. William, one of the old priests of Catholic times, who was condemned to

Queen Mary's time, was executed, especially being condemned for that he had relieved with money and clothes one Shaw, a relapsed priest, and for that he was reconciled, which you know is treason. They proved it thus: because he had been a married minister sometime, and therefore he could not become a priest again, except he were reconciled. He was hanged, drawn, and quartered at Tyburn, and afterwards his quarters were set upon the gates of the City. He was likewise, as I think, condemned by Judge Anderson in the Sessions House within the Old Bailey in London. More I cannot report of him or the rest.

JAMES YOUNG, Priest.

Your great friend and of ancient acquaintance, Mr. Walker,[11] sendeth you most hearty commendations, saluting you with the good news of your mother's well doing, now again being made Catholic, and remaining in Wales. The gentleman keepeth at his wonted home, you know where, I need not name the place.

2. (i.) As an appendix to the account of this group of Martyrs we may add the directions for the torture

---

death because he left Calvinism—that is, the Church of England—in which he had been acting as a minister, and had joined the Catholic Church and obtained a dispensation from the irregularity of bigamy, caused by his having been married. Nothing more is known of this Martyr.

[11] This may be Father Henry Garnet, who frequently mentions "the old woman," Father Persons' mother, in his letters to Father Persons.

of two of their number, with an account of its infliction told by one of the Martyrs who bore it.

Oct. 25, 1591. Letter to Dr. Fletcher, Richard Brainthwayte, Richard Topcliffe, and Richard Young, Esquires.

Whereas one Eustace White, a Seminary priest, was of late taken, and there was also one Brian Lacey, a disperser and distributor of letters to Papists and evil affected subjects, in like manner apprehended; these shall be therefore (in virtue hereof), to require you to take the confessions of both the said persons and very straitly to examine them upon such articles as you Mr. Topcliffe shall administer unto them. And if they shall not declare their knowledges and answer directly to all such matters as you shall think meet and necessary to be propounded unto them, then shall you by virtue hereof, for the better bolting further of the truth, cause them to be put to the manacles and such other tortures as are used in Bridewell, to the end they may be compelled to utter such things as shall concern her Majesty and the Estate. And their examination so taken, we pray you to send the same to us.

This letter has also been published by Dr. Jessopp, from Jardine's *Use of Torture*, in his very valuable book, *One Generation of a Norfolk House*, p. 241. Dr. Jessopp adds that our Martyr, Brian Lacey, was brother to Richard Lacey, of Brockdish in Norfolk. " He had been *betrayed by his brother*," we learn, "eight years before this horrible torturing, but had apparently managed to escape apprehension." The "confession" of Richard Lacey, to which Dr. Jessopp refers, was taken before Sir William Heydon and William Blenerhaiset, on the 13th of March, 1584.[12] After giving information respecting Momford Scott and other priests, Richard Lacey says that his brother Brian is in the service of Sir John Arundell, and he relates sayings of Robert Hartley and others, that "if Sir William Heydon and Mr. John Stubbes could get hold of Brian Lacey, they would rack him, even till the nails should start from his fingers."

(ii.) Of the treatment the Martyrs went through in consequence of this order, the reader may form some notion from the very modest but most touching letter addressed by the Venerable Eustace White to Father Henry Garnet. It is headed in Father Garnet's hand:

A COPY OF MR. WHITE'S LETTER, LATELY A MARTYR.

23 of November, anno 1591.

Sir,—I presume somewhat rashly to address unto you (as unto a patron of orphans in these miserable days) importing my present calamity, which surely without temporal comfort I am very hardly able long to endure; the time of the year and the hard handling of my torture masters, with the malicious and devilish dealing of my keepers against priests especially and all Catholics generally, growing so fast towards their extremity.

---

[12] P.R.O. *Dom. Eliz.* vol. clxix. n. 19.

This bearer, Mr. N.[13] I think can partly relate unto you mine estate from the mouth of one[14] in prison by me, my dearest friend in bonds. For he hath spared from himself to relieve me with victuals as he could through a little hole, and with other such necessaries as he could by that means do, whom truly I did never see in my life but through a hole. Nothing was too dear unto him that he could convey unto me, for whom as I am bound, so will I daily pray while I live.

I have been close prisoner since the 18th day of September, where of forty-six days together I lay upon a little straw in my boots, my hands continually manacled in irons, for one month together never once taken off. After, they were twice or thrice taken off to shift me, and ease me for a day together. This was all the favour that my keepers did show. The morrow after Simon and Jude's day,[15] I was hanged at the wall from the ground, my manacles fast locked into a staple as high as I could reach upon a stool. The stool taken away, there I hanged from a little after eight o'clock in the morning till after

[13] This has been inserted by Father Garnet, who has cautiously blotted out the words which follow. At present, however, owing to the ink drying in different colours, many of them may be read in whole or part. They are: "Mr. . . . late and last servant unto the good Sir Thomas Fitzherbert (for he attended on him . . . his death in the Tower)."

[14] Here again Father Garnet has substituted "one" for "his good . . ." erased.

[15] October 29, which follows closely on the date of the Privy Council warrant.

four afternoon, without any ease or comfort at all, saving that Topcliffe came unto me, and told me that the Spaniards were come into Southwark by our means: "for lo! do you not hear the drums?" (for then the drums played in honour of the Lord Mayor). The next day after also I was hanged an hour or two, such is the malicious minds and practices of our adversaries.

For my clothes I have no other than my summer weed, wherein I was taken; and then I was rifled of all, of my horse that cost but then £7, of £4 in money, and odd money, with my rings, a silver pipe [16] worth twenty shillings, and many other things. Nothing left, more than on my back, and he that took me had £5 of the Council [17] for his labour, before whom I was, at Basing, a courtier, for a week at her Majesty's charges.

This is mine estate till this hour, in extremity of all worldly comforts. Money may be conveyed more easily unto me than other things whatsoever, though with leave of Justice Young other things also, but it must be done by some Protestant friend. Mr. [18] doth owe me forty shillings for a legacy from his father, which he promised

---

[16] That is, a flute.

[17] This corresponds exactly with the payment made by the Treasurer of the Chamber "to Henry Adis, gent., upon the Council's warrant, dated at Basing 14 Sep. 1591, for the apprehending one Eustace White, a Seminary priest, in Dorsetshire, and bring him from thence to Basing at his own charges:—c. shillings" (Enrolled Accounts, rot. 158).

[18] Blank space in MS.

me this summer in [19] fields. I beseech you, sir, make means unto him, that I may have it, for he will pay it at the first sending. The Catholics in the west country among whom I bestowed my pains, would willingly help me if I could convey unto them ; though others I know would not be unwilling, with them I would be most bold.

I was taken at Blandford in Dorsetshire the 1st of September, and there had disputations two days together with Doctor Souche and divers ministers before people of all sorts, all whose arguments were too too ridiculous. Thus I have showed you my bold rashness with you in troubling you so long, praying to have me excused for the same, beseeching withal, if you can, to work that some honest Protestant may have access unto me, that by him I may be somewhat relieved. And so commending you to our Lord's protection, that can defend you from the mouth of the roaring lion, that goeth about seeking whom he may devour, I take my leave this twenty-third of November, 91.

Your worship's,
[EUSTACE WHITE.]

The letter has no signature.
This holy Martyr suffered at Tyburn on the 10th of December, 1591, seventeen days after the date of this letter.

[19] Blank space in MS.

CHAPTER VII.

VENERABLE WILLIAM DAVIES.

Executed at Beaumaris, July 27, 1593.

DOCUMENTS.

1. Letter of the Martyr (Stonyhurst MSS. *Anglia*, vii. 9).
2. Account of his trial and death (*Ibid. M.* fol. 107 *a*).

The Venerable William Davies was born of good family in North Wales, and came to the Seminary of Rheims in April, 1582, where he studied for the priesthood, was ordained and sent back to his native country in June, 1585. Here he laboured with great success for more than five years, until in March, 1591, while he was arranging for the passage of three students and a boy for the Seminaries of Spain, he was arrested at Holyhead with them, and with Robert ap Hugh, a priest. Whether through the connivance or the blundering of Hugh ap Robert, High Constable of Llynon, or some of his inferiors, Robert ap Hugh escaped the hands of Fulk Thomas, to whose "diligence" the arrest was attributed. The Council was very angry at this negligence, and sent down stringent orders to the Bishop of Bangor on the 25th of March to inquire into the matter and examine the prisoners, and on the 9th of July further orders to the Justices of Assize to try the High Constable, the Bailiff and his men on Fulk Thomas' evidence, and to proceed against the priest and his companions " at the next Assizes, according to the quality of their several offences." [1]

1. The Martyr's letter which we now give was probably written shortly after this. He is so reticent about the sufferings he had already undergone, that it is necessary to inform the reader that he had already been confined more than a month in one of the worst dungeons of Beaumaris Castle. Father Garnet has written on the back of this document: " Mr. Davies the priest's letter, I know not whether of his own hand." It does not seem a far-fetched suggestion to suppose that the "faithful brother," to whom it was addressed, was the same Robert ap Hugh, the priest, who was in Davies' company when he was arrested and managed somehow to escape. Whoever the "brother" was to whom the letter was addressed, the Martyr thought that he had tried to obtain for him some means of escape from prison and from martyrdom, and it is touching to see that he calls this " a hindrance to his preferment."

LETTER OF THE VENERABLE WILLIAM DAVIES AFTER HIS TRIAL.

Though you have been in some part a hindrance to my preferment (faithful brother), but mine own unworthiness most of all, yet nevertheless do I acknowledge myself more bound unto you for your care and travail in the behalf of me and my

[1] *Council Registers*, vol. x. pp. 282, 469.

children than I can express in words or writing, much less discharge in deed. Wherefore, giving you hearty thanks, I refer the rewarding thereof unto Almighty God, Who is able to do it, for the which I daily pray unto Him, as I am bound.

You long, I am sure, to know how we have sped in our suit. To declare every circumstance would be too long, wherefore I think good only at this time to touch the principalest matters which I judge convenient to certify unto you; and if you will be desirous to know particulars more at large, send us word and you shall be certified hereafter as occasion shall serve. Many enemies we have had, which I construed for my part and in my sense to be indeed my greatest friends (I thank God Who helped me to keep that mind always), so that I was nothing afraid of them. For if they had prevailed, I hoped (by the help of God) to obtain my chief desire; if they missed of their purpose, I was to have that, which I was content withal in respect of myself, and wished in respect of my children and friends.

The means you wrought for us took great effect as we do now think; they would have taken greater, if we had been so well acquainted with them in time, as after the time was past. Our other friend did his part to further your means and in removing all impediments, so that nothing lacked but that we were not thoroughly acquainted with your travail in our behalf, that accordingly we might have done somewhat for our parts. This (I suppose) happened through the simplicity of a messenger that undertook to make us acquainted therewith. But I hope it was for the best.

But to let you understand somewhat more particular. First, ministers and preachers being sent by the Ordinary, as they said, pretending also good-will, flocked about me, having one Burgess to be their principal, which laid hard siege to me for the space of four or five days together, at last they gave me over. The man of Bangor[2] was sent for by the Justices. He came and spake with them and departed immediately, seeming as though he had no mind to deal with us. One Tuesday, the head Sheriff came in the afternoon, to bring me solemnly to Justice Leighton's chamber, where was also Justice Philips, Sir Richard Fowler, and others. Justice Leighton asked me some questions, as where and when I was priested, upon what intent I came to England, &c. Then he wished me to be conformable and promising mercy, then he disputed a little about the Sacrament very civilly, at last he said he was no divine, and bade Burgess, which [was present][3] to speak. After some reasoning, Justice Philips stood, saying, I should consider between that and the next morrow, and declaring the danger of the law. Fowler asked me the question of the Supremacy. Philips said they would give me time till the next morrow to

---

[2] This is evidently Hugh Ballot, Bishop of Bangor, to whom the letters of the Privy Council had been sent.
[3] MS. torn.

consider of that question, so the Sheriff took me away. Wednesday morning the said Burgess came to us, declaring that now he was to deal with us in principalest matter indeed which concerned our lives, being sent of purpose by the Justices, for they were to deal with us touching the Supremacy in the afternoon. I told him for my part I was determined what to answer, and that I would not be taught by him. He desired I would give him leave to declare his mind in the matter to the rest of my companions. I answered, if he would needs preach I would depart; if I were stayed by force, I would answer every falsehood. So seeing it would not be, he departed.

After noon I was brought to Justice Philips' chamber, where were Sir Ric. Bulkley, Tho. Moston, the Chancellor of Bangor, two or three besides. Justice Leighton and Fowler came not. Fowler had received by this time letters to stay him a little. Justice Philips gave very fair words, wishing me to look to myself, saying it was come to that now, that a thread divided between my life and death. I said I never made other account of my life.

After many persuasions he began to examine me, the Register of Bangor writing my examination, not requiring any oath at all. When I had acknowledged my going over seas, my coming back and my intent, "Alas," said he, "you have spoken so much against yourself." I said, I would not go from that I had spoken.

Sir Richard said I was but a simple man. Mr. Gruff, of Carnarvon, desired leave to ask some question. The Justice granted. He asked who had received me and maintained me since I came to England. I said I would not answer to such question. The gentleman was moved[4] with that answer. Then the Justice said it was in vain to ask such question, and that I had been asked often enough before, but would not answer.

Then the Sheriff and the Chancellor took me up sharply because I would not answer, they being called by authority to demand. I being then somewhat moved, told them that they knew not what they said, and that I was not bound to answer them, but what I thought meet, being a spiritual man, whereas they were but laymen, and that by right they had no authority to examine me.

"What," said Mr. Sheriff, "do you not know whose person Mr. Justice doth represent?"

"So I do," said I, "yet he is but a temporal man, yet I yield to the time."

The Justice said nothing, but proceeded mildly, and from that time they asked me no such question.

The Justice bade me read the examination and put out what I thought good. I read it, and said I would stand to it, and so put my name to it.

Then was I brought away, and Roger called to

[4] "Moved," that is, to anger.

be examined, whom the Justice used courteously. The Register moved the Justice to examine him upon the Supremacy. He said he would defer it unto the next morrow. The Register urged still. At last the Justice was fain to say he could go no further than his commission, and so this quest was no more moved to any.

With the boy they kept great stir, threatening to whip him, to set him on the pillory, to cut off his ears and nose. Sometimes they spake him fair, promising liberty and many other fair promises; at last, if he would then but say he would go to the church, he should presently go from that place whither he would. But no persuasion would serve.

Thursday in the afternoon we were brought solemnly with the felons, guarded with halberts and bills, to the bar. The Grand Jury having been called to give their verdict, my bill of indictment was read, I being called and bidden to hold my hand. Then Justice Leighton stood up and took to him the statute book, and turned to the statute according to the which the bill was made, and sent to me bidding me read the statute myself. I said it needed not, but yet he would have me to read it. Then I took up the book and read it. Then he asked me what I would say for myself. I answered that I acknowledged that I had gone out of the realm and was made priest, according to the Order of the Church of Rome, which is the Catholic Church, and came after to England to minister the sacraments according to the use of that Church, contrary to this statute, "but for the satisfying of my mind I have this saying of St. Augustine: *Principes quandoque sunt in errore*——" There he interrupted me, saying there was more skill at the making of that law, than all the Papists in the world had.

After their bills were read, then everybody looked for sentence to be pronounced against me the next day. So did I myself think, but I thank God I was nothing dismayed, and I pray God I may be resolute when the time come indeed. My children were in great sorrow and heaviness; Robert wept bitterly from the time the indictment was read at the bar, the space of two hours, so did all the rest after they were brought to the prison for anything I could say unto them. [They][5] spent all that night in weeping and praying. The next morning, when the time came that we should be brought to the bar, the deputy sheriff came for them, saying I should not be brought at that time to the bar, but the morrow after, when the Justices were to depart, I should be brought to have sentence pronounced.

When they came to the bar, they found Justice Leighton sitting alone, for Justice Philips sat in another place, hearing of matters belonging to the town. Then were they somewhat comforted, for they hoped they should die with me, for Justice Leighton seemed to be more sharp with us. But it proved to be contrary, and at first he

[5] MS. torn.

said the boy should go. Then the Sheriff said it was not well to let him go without bonds to appear the next Assizes. The Justice said, "Then let him be bailed."

John and Roger moved the Justice for their money which the Sheriff had. The Justice said they ought to have it: but the Sheriff answered they should have none, for they were indebted to the Queen, and that they lived too well; he would look better unto them, and they should wear irons. The Justice said that for their debt to the Queen he was to make inquiry for lands and goods, and gave order that he should allow 3d. towards every meal as long as the money lasted; but they doubt whether they shall have any.

My children do hope, if you continue your suit for us, that we all may be delivered the next Assizes; they have no mind to be released without I might also.

The statute whereupon I was indicted was an old one made in the first year of her Majesty's reign, which appointeth certain time for such as would not conform themselves to the statute to depart the realm. The Justice bade me read the statute and say what I could for myself. Seeing he dealed with us so favourable where we expected no favour, it made me to think that if I had pleaded ignorance of the statute at my going out and coming into the realm, I might have obtained banishment, alleging also the example of divers in my case which have had that favour.

My children would needs have me to let you understand of this to have your advice.

Also some colour must be devised for their releasement, other than that some gentlemen would beg Thomas and John, in respect of their qualities, or some better than their own bonds being strangers in the country. Roger may be released on his own bonds, the boy without a bond.

I have not time to write as [fully as I could wish. It would]⁶ be very good to see my brother William to confer further touching these matters. I pray you commend us heartily to your [friend],⁷ oft letting him understand we forget not his faithfulness and travail for us. Commend us also to all the rest of our friends in his house. God reward you for your goodness towards us, and make us worthy to be heard for you, as our duty is to pray. Commend me, I pray, to all other good friends as you shall have occasion to see them; and lastly, committing you to God, I commend myself to your prayers.

2. A year passed away between the writing of this letter and the final scene, which we are about to describe. During that time the Martyr was first hurried about from one prison to another, paraded in the streets in the company of criminals, and confined in the undrained, unlighted dungeons into which, according to the barbarous practice of our forefathers, condemned prisoners were thrust previous to execution. At last he was sent back to

⁶ MS. much torn. ⁷ Some word is wanting.

Beaumaris Castle, where he rejoined his young companions, whom he loved to call his children. The pleasure of such a meeting can well be imagined, and to their intense delight they were henceforth allowed to live together, and occupy themselves as they liked. They accordingly devoted themselves entirely to prayer, study, and spiritual exercises, making their prison into a sort of religious house. "This manner of life they led for six months, and seemed to all men to be dwelling, not amid the miseries of prison, but in the joys of Heaven."

The following account of the trial and death of this Martyr is taken from a transcript with abbreviations, made by Father Grene, who, without stating whence he copied, heads it,

THE MARTYRDOM OF MR. DAY, OR DAVIES, PRIEST, IN ANGLESEA, 27 JULY, 1593.

The Sessions being at Beaumaris in the county of Anglesea, Mr. William Davies, priest and prisoner, was called to the bar upon Wednesday morning, being St. Symphorosa her day [July 18]. The bill of the indictment, framed upon a statute made in the 23rd year, as I think, of the Queen, being read, Justice Leighton asked what he had to say why he ought not to die.

"Sir," quoth Mr. William, "I acknowledge the contents of the bill to be true, which is no more, as I understand, than that I am a priest; but for the statute whereupon this was framed, I was never acquainted therewith, and therefore

I trust I shall have mercy and the favour of the law, as others have had being in my case."

"It is true," said the Justice, "that some priests have been banished, but the most part executed, which thou dost well deserve, because thou art so stubborn, that thou wouldst not reveal, for anything what was done unto thee, either the parties or the places wherein thou didst use thy trade, nor anything else to her Majesty's commodity." And so gave judgment that he should be executed, as in case of high treason, to the uttermost, commanding the Sheriff to look to his office at time convenient. Then said Mr. William *Te Deum Laudamus*, going forward. Wherewith the Justice bid take him away, saying there were better learned in that place than he was. His countenance and behaviour at the time of his condemnation all that [were] sober and wise did admire, and do continually as yet talk of.

Immediately after his condemnation he was put in a place of the Castle called *the black alley*, a dark, loathsome aisle between two walls, where he gave himself wholly to prayer and meditation, and omitted none of his daily wonted exercises until that very morning he was brought forth to be executed. All his friends that came to visit him, he did so replenish with comfort, that howsoever they came to him, they returned merrily. For such as were Catholics, he hoped he should meet with them merrily again; for his own father, or such as were not, nor yet would not be Catholics, he bid them farewell for ever.

When any would tell him that he hoped he should be reprieved, he would wax very sad and heavy; as contrariwise, when he were told that he must be executed, he would be most merry and pleasant.

A preacher was with him to have him recant and swear to the Supremacy, and he should be reprieved, whom he sore checked, and bid get him away thence. There could not be found an executioner in all the country; but at length the Sheriff was forced to send to Westchester, forty-two miles off, for a poor butcher, and a hangman that was in prison for thievery. These two were brought to the country and hired for four or five pounds; and because they could have no lodging in the town, they were hid in a barn, and there kept like hungry dogs until the day appointed, with stolen scraps and meat secretly conveyed to them. The deputy sheriff had much ado to provide necessaries for execution. The best man there and the townsmen denied the Sheriff of a place to set the gallows upon [in] any of their grounds. He was fain to make a new gallows, and to set it within the liberties of the Castle, out of the liberties of the town. The word is about the country, that the Sheriff was fain to send to his own house for a pan, but the truth is that an old covetous woman in the town, that would not be known of it, lent her pan, and gave a few faggots withal to the deputy sheriff for eight shillings of money.

That day morning being St. Pantaleon's day

[July 27]⁸, wherein he was executed, the blessed Father delivered, through a crevice in the wall, tokens to his children and brethren abroad for a remembrance to persist in the Catholic faith. So having done, he said, "Now let them come when they will; I am ready for them." Thereupon the sheriffs, bailiffs, and servant calling him forth, bound his arms with a cord and set him upon a cart, which they themselves were fain to drive the horse to draw forward; whereat being ashamed, the deputy sheriff threatened to hang a poor boy that met him on the way, unless he would drive the horse. Whereunto the boy answered, "I am well content to be hanged with this man with all my heart, but drive the horse I will not, do what you will." Then said Mr. William, "You shall not need, Mr. Sheriff, to trouble any more; the horse will go of himself."

Being come to the place, he was permitted a good while to pray upon his knees, which he did very devoutly, until at length a preacher called Burgess had overheard him say, *Ave Maris Stella*, or naming our Blessed Lady, whereat the preacher fretted, and bade despatch him. Here the deputy sheriff (for the head sheriff was not there) asked him what he thought of the Queen. "God give her a long, prosperous reign, and grace to die a member of the Catholic Church." Then caused to climb up the ladder, he said: "This island (meaning the Isle of Anglesea) was called in the

⁸ Challoner says July 21, but he does not take this date from Yepez.

old time the dark island, the which name it never better deserved than at this present. But I beseech God that the blood which I am brought hither innocently to shed, may give a light unto it of that faith which it hath received above a thousand years agone." So being interrupted, he was not suffered to speak more but thrice, *In manus tuas, Domine.* The ladder was turned, whereupon he closed his fists hard, and so kept them till he died, at which time he opened his hands broad. He was pulled by the hangman to die, before he was taken down, the deputy sheriff asking often to break the halter before he was dead, for a colour belike lest he should be complained upon.

After his death, he was bowelled, headed, and quartered; his head set upon the top of his fellow's chimney,[9] and his two quarters in Beaumaris Castle, one other in Conway, the fourth in Caers.[10] One or two [were] put in prison in Conway, because they would not climb nor meddle with the quarter that came thither.

Note by Father Grene.—This relation was sent to Father Persons, as it seemeth, by two or three words written thereon by him.

Of "his children," our histories only inform us that one was entrusted by the judges to a school-

---

Presumably the chimney over the cell where his youthful companions were confined.

[10] Perhaps Caerwys.

master, "with orders to whip him if he did not come to the Protestant church on every festival-day. But he finding himself at liberty, found means to escape to Ireland." . . . Here he fell in with another young gentleman, a Protestant, whom he instructed in the faith, and brought to a priest to be reconciled. Finally, "both finding themselves animated with a desire to go to the Seminary of Valladolid, they betook themselves thither, and are now living there with great edification to all, whilst I write this, which is in the 2nd of July, 1598." Such are the concluding words of Bishop Yepez,[11] in his History of this venerable Martyr, an account which, he tells us, was furnished him by the youth himself. The whole of the story as told by Yepez deserves a closer translation than that given by Challoner, who omits several graphic particulars. For instance, we learn that the Martyr's cassock and other clothes were brought by the hangman to the prison, to sell them to his companions, and they were laid, running with blood, on the table on which the Martyr used to say Mass. The clothes were divided amongst Catholics, and "the cassock, stained with blood, was kept in a certain part of the kingdom, that priests might with much devotion wear it under their priestly vestments, when they said Mass."

[11] *Historia*, &c., p. 666.

CHAPTER VIII.

VENERABLE JOHN ROBERTS, O.S.B., AND VENERABLE THOMAS SOMERS, SECULAR PRIEST.

Suffered at Tyburn, December 10, 1610.

DOCUMENT.

Trial and execution of these Martyrs (Stonyhurst MSS. *Anglia,* iii. n. 102). Italian.

The history of the trial and death of the Venerable John Roberts shows us enough of his vigorous, manly character to make us regret that we know so little of his adventurous life. Challoner suggests that he may be the Cambridge student of the same name, who came to Douay while still a Protestant, was subsequently converted, and, after several years' study at the English College, Rome, passed on to Valladolid, where our Martyr certainly was a few years later. But the Cambridge scholar seems to have been also a native of that place, while the Martyr's name in Religion, Father John de Mervinia, is said to point to Merionethshire as his birthplace. Moreover, the first was certainly ordained in Rome in 1587, while the date of the latter's ordination in Spain is given as 1600.

We know, however, that he was at one time an alumnus of the English College at Valladolid, and thence joined the Spanish congregation of the Venerable Order of St. Benedict, was professed in the Abbey of St. Martin of Compostella, and after his ordination in 1600, was sent to England. There the ancient Order still lived on at least in the person of Dom Sigebert Buckley, and there, too, others, such as the Venerable Mark Barkworth, had obtained admission to its privileges; but Father Roberts is said to have been the first, who left a Benedictine monastery, to labour on that dangerous mission.

In England he displayed a devotion and constancy worthy of his Order. With the examples of the great Benedictine missionaries who first converted this nation ever before his eyes, he strove heroically to emulate their virtues. Four times was he arrested, imprisoned, and banished, and he returned as often to post of danger; nor was he more chary of exposing his life to danger when a severe outbreak of the "plague" devastated London. His success was commensurate with his labours and sufferings, which were becomingly closed by his apprehension in the act of celebrating Mass, when a trial on the charge of priesthood and a death bravely faced, were turned, as only a skilful missioner could turn them, into a notable occasion of bearing witness to the Faith.

Of Thomas Somers, *alias* Wilson, his companion in martyrdom, Dr. Challoner tells us that he was for some time a schoolmaster in his native county of Westmoreland, and that he so discharged his duties as to do great service to religion. After his ordination in 1606 he laboured chiefly in London, where his diligence and zeal were such that he was commonly called *the* parish priest of that city. Imprisonment and exile, the common fate of so many priests at that time, had their part in preparing him for the final struggle.

The following account of these two Martyrs, dated May 16, 1611, is evidently translated from one of the various narratives of such heroic deaths, which the Catholics in England used to send to their friends abroad. One such paper, sent to him from St. Omers, has been used by Challoner in his account of the death scene, and a comparison of the two shows that, whilst they are independent sources of information, they strongly corroborate each other's fidelity.

THE ARRAIGNMENT AND CONDEMNATION OF FATHER JOHN ROBERTS, O.S.B., AND OF THOMAS SOMERS, SECULAR PRIEST.

Holden in the Justice Hall, Newgate, in the presence of the Bishop of London, the Lord Chief Justice, and other Justices, and Royal Officials. December 5, 1610.

Related by one present thereat.

The two prisoners having been removed from Newgate prison and brought into the presence of the aforesaid Court, Mr. Somers was first asked by the pseudo-bishop if he would take the new oath of allegiance. He replied briefly but pointedly, that he would not take it in the form in which it was entered on the statute book. Then the Bishop rose to his feet, and holding in his hand a bundle of writings (containing the examination of several Catholics, and amongst them that of Father John, who usually passed by the name of Roberts), said,

"Mr. Roberts, you know how often you have been brought before me, what trouble I have taken for you, and with what kindness I have treated you, and all in order to persuade you to become a good subject to the King's Majesty, who has shown you so much mercy. Hitherto you have only been punished with exile on several occasions, though you have been captured and recaptured time after time. And even still, in spite of your contempt for his laws and ordinances, notwithstanding your return contrary to his express command and will, still, I say, he desires to make one more trial of your loyalty and good disposition in his regard, and to grant you favour. It is, therefore, my duty to offer you the oath of allegiance made and ordained expressly by both Houses of Parliament, in order to discover the loyalty and obedience of the recusant Papists and priests, who are subjects of his Majesty. Now what say you, Mr. Roberts? Will you take this oath or not?"

"Sir," answered the other, "you know very well what I think about this oath; I have told you before. I have not refused, nor shall I ever refuse to take any oath of allegiance offered me, which shall in truth be only such; but this oath contains other matter besides allegiance. I have before offered to prove this to you, and to point out what part concerns matters of faith. If these parts be expunged,

I was willing then, as I am now, to swear to the rest, which only concerns allegiance to my sovereign. At that time your Lordship promised me a hearing, but as yet you have never given me one. I therefore now again humbly beg that I may now be heard by this Court."

"No, no, Mr. Roberts," said the Bishop, "it is not seemly to discuss further what has been legally decreed and established by both Houses of Parliament, nor is it in my power to give such a leave, seeing that the Houses have ordained it, and that it cannot be altered. Wherefore you must simply answer whether you will take it or not."

"No," said Father Roberts, "I will not take it otherwise than as I have said."

"Then we," said the Bishop, "shall deal with you in a different manner."

"In God's name," replied Father Roberts, "do as you will."

The Recorder, too, tried a long while to persuade Father Roberts to take the oath, but he always gave the same answer.

The accusation against them was next called for, the jury were picked and called over, and then the indictment against Mr. Somers was read. This was founded solely on the statute prohibiting priests made according to the Roman rite. Asked if he were guilty or not, he answered that as regards his priesthood he was guilty, "for priest I am," said he, "but no traitor for all that."

"That will do," said the Recorder, and turning to the jury: "you have heard that he confesses he is a priest, and this is enough for you to find him guilty."

They next read the indictment against Father Roberts, and then asked him if he were guilty or not. He answered that this was for them to prove.

"Ah," said the Lord Chief Justice, "I can see that this is a cunning fellow. But speak plainly, do you deny that you are a priest?"

Father Roberts answered, "Sir, are you my judge or my accuser? Both offices cannot be united in the same person."

Then the Bishop of London said, "Surely, my lords, we shall find this man is of a different temper from his fellow." And getting up he spoke as follows:

"Mr. Roberts, I am astonished that you want to raise such difficulties for yourself and this Bench. You cannot now be ignorant that I know you to be a monk of the Order of St. Benedict, and, in fact, the Provincial of the monks of that Order in England."

"How is it proved, my lord," said Father Roberts, "that I know that you are acquainted with these things? If this is so, and has been confessed to you, pray read it out openly here in the presence of all."

The pseudo-bishop then handed him two sheets of paper covered all over with writing, and after Father Roberts had looked at them carefully for awhile,

"Perhaps you recognize the handwriting?" said the Bishop.

"Yea, my lord," said Father Roberts, "I know it well, and if it please you, pray have it read."

This was done, but first the Bishop made a long address to the assembly, purporting to give an account of its contents, but adding that Father Roberts was a person of high standing and very dangerous to the State, and that he had been found on the very day of the Powder Treason in the house of the wife of its author and contriver. He concluded by saying, "Now you see, gentlemen, what sort of man this is, and from all these circumstances you can infer how dangerous he is to the King and country."

Father Roberts replied: "It would be better for you to say no more about the Plot, as no one knows better than you do how entirely I established my innocence at the time before the lords of his Majesty's Privy Council. So clearly was I justified that they declared me to be a man of good repute, and in liberating me testified that no imputation whatever rested on me. They could not have done this if they had considered that I was in any way cognizant of or consenting to that conspiracy, nor should I be here to-day before this tribunal."

"No, Mr. Roberts," replied the Bishop, "I do not intend to charge you with the guilt of the Plot, I only say it by way of induction, but by your leave I will pass on."

"Say anything you like," was the answer, "but do not say what is not the truth."

The Bishop then began a long discourse as to Father Roberts' first leaving England, in which country he had lived, as well as in Flanders, France, Spain, and Rome, also as to the time he spent in studies, his progress, and the degrees he had taken in the schools. Also that he had lived at the Benedictine Monastery of St. James of Compostella in Spain, and then returned to England, the length of time he had remained in England, and the mischief he had worked among the subjects of his Majesty.

Then the aforesaid two sheets of writing were read containing the substance of his examination, most of the facts in which the Bishop had stated; but there was no word directly proving that he was a priest.

"What is the use of all this, my lord?" said Father Roberts; "your lordship wants to prove me a priest by an induction similar to that whereby you tried to prove me guilty of the Powder Plot, for there is no proof in this writing that I am even the person referred to."

The Bishop then caused to be read a mandate from the late Archbishop of Canterbury ordering some of his officers and the keeper of the Gatehouse prison to bring before him one John Roberts, priest and seminarist, a Benedictine monk and scandalous and dangerous person, who had recently escaped from prison.

To this Father Roberts answered, "What is

there in this mandate to prove that I am a priest? The Archbishop can call me what he chooses, but no one can maintain that that is sufficient proof in this case, which is a matter of life and death."

"Well, then," said the Bishop, "we will go a little further," and ordered them to read out a report of what passed in the examination of a certain Mr. William Jennison, a Catholic gentleman, and at Father Roberts' second examination.

The Father hearing this, and finding himself already weary owing to a weakness brought on by many sufferings and a sickness which he had, said freely and cheerfully,

"My lord, I will spare you this trouble; I can see very well what you want; and I, too, wish you to have your desire. I say it not to you only, but to all the Court, and I acknowledge that I am a priest and a monk of the Order of St. Benedict, and you can take any advantage you like of that."

"Ah," said Justice Crook,[1] "now you confess at last what you are so much ashamed of."

"No, my lords," quickly answered the Father, "I am not ashamed of acknowledging either my faith or my religious profession. I am here to do so, and (putting his hand on his heart) if my one life were ten thousand lives, and every life ten thousand times more dear to me than mine is, I would give them all in this cause."

[1] In MS. Crocche.

"And yet," said the Recorder, "you will not die for your faith, but for treason; as it is not for being ordained priest, but for returning to this country to exercise your office of priest against the order of the law that you have been declared guilty."

"Sir," said Father Roberts, "I am bound by my priesthood to do the duty of a priest, and the reason I have returned to this country is to work for the salvation of souls, as I have done, and should continue to do were I to live longer."

"No," said the Bishop, "you disturb the people, you have come to deceive the subjects of his Majesty, and seduce them from their loyalty and obedience, and this is the reason of your coming back."

"No, my lord," said Father Roberts, "I do not deceive, but try to lead back to the right path those poor wandering souls whom you and your foolish and ignorant ministers have led astray, and infected with a thousand deceits and heresies. If I deceive, then were our ancestors deceived by Blessed St. Augustine, the Apostle of the English, who was sent here by the Pope of Rome, St. Gregory the Great, and who converted this country from error to the Christian and Roman Catholic faith. This same faith which he professed I now teach. Nay, I am of the same religious order, and have been professed of the same rule as St. Augustine, and I am sent here by the same Apostolic See that sent him before me."

Upon this he was ordered to be silent, but he replied,

"I must speak, as my mission is from Heaven. St. Matthew says, chap. xxviii., 'Go ye and teach all nations, baptizing them and teaching them to observe all things whatsoever I have commanded you.' Your ministers do not do this, because they do not fulfil in their lives and actions the command of Christ: they do not administer the Sacrament of Penance or of Extreme Unction. I do, and withal I teach obedience to princes as a matter of conscience against the false doctrine of Luther and his companions. All this I can prove to you."

Then turning to the Bishop, he continued, "For you indeed, sir, there is no time more suitable than now. Your lordship professes to be a man of learning, and you are considered a bishop amongst the rest. I am here to speak in defence of my faith, my profession, and my religious rule, and I demand to be heard."

"No, no, my good sir," said the Chief Justice, "you are not come here to preach sermons, we will find you another place for that."

"Yea, my lord," was the answer. "I know what that means, and I expected nothing else, for I know right well that that must be the end of the business."

And thus did the Bishop decline the offer of disputation.

Notwithstanding that Father Roberts had acknowledged that he was a priest, the Bishop now had the confession of Mr. Gienison [Jennison] read, as well as that of Father Roberts. In these mention was made of certain Indulgences obtained by the Father for that gentleman and his wife, when they were received by him into the confraternity attached to the Benedictine Order. There were also specified certain prayers, fastings, confessions and communions, as well as blessings and privileges for the living.

The Judges on the bench took occasion to laugh and jeer at these details, and the pseudo-bishop said that Roberts had been Superior of the Benedictine Order in England, and had himself ordained priests.

"You, my lords, and all you of the Bench," answered Father Roberts, "take occasion to jeer at the ordinances and Indulgences of the Church of Christ. But do you choose one or more persons, and if I cannot clearly prove myself in all this to be in exact conformity with the ancient use and practice of the Catholic Church, then consider me a reprobate." Then turning to the Bishop, "Sir, you are quite mistaken, I am not Superior of the Benedictines, nor did I ever confer Orders, nor have I power to confer them."

The Bishop said he was not there at that time to dispute, but to act as a magistrate, and to fulfil his duty to his King as a minister of justice.

"Well, then," said Father Roberts, "if that is so, allow me to ask you a question."

"Ask what you like," replied the Bishop.

"You, sir," said Father Roberts, "take to yourself the name of bishop, and make profession of religion and learning. Have you the boldness to offer a single instance, before these our miserable times, which you have read of, written of, or heard of, where a Catholic Bishop has seated himself among secular judges in a capital case? Certainly you are not able to bring forward one. You would have done much better, my lord, to remain in your palace and in your church and chapter reforming the dissolute conduct of your clergy, than to come and sit on this Bench, while matters of life and death are being decided."

"I am not come here," the Bishop answered, "to give an account to you of the duty and service I owe to the King my master in business of this kind."

"Well," said Father Roberts, "I wish to ask you and the other magistrates one more thing. These twelve men, who have to give a verdict in this case, are ignorant persons, unable to discern or judge of the difference between the priesthood and treason. You strive to do an impossible thing, when you wish to make it appear, that to be a priest is to be a traitor. That would make Christ Himself a traitor, and all His Apostles—St. Augustine also, the Apostle of England, and all the priests and bishops, who have succeeded him to this day, would also be esteemed traitors, and you would condemn them if they were brought before you. I therefore say that it is impossible that being a priest should make one a traitor."

Here there were general murmurs, and before Father Roberts could explain, several of those on the Bench began to look at him and say, "Impossible for a priest to be a traitor?" They went on repeating these words until Father Roberts explained.

"A priest as such, and in regard to his office as priest, which is sacred and holy, cannot be a traitor. But if a priest commit treason, I am not so ignorant as not to know that the *man* is a traitor, but not by reason of his being a priest or in consequence of exercising his priestly office. With this I was going to conclude before. However, as these are simple and ignorant men, I humbly beg the members of this Court to decide the case in their stead, so that these poor men may not be responsible for our blood."

To this the Recorder answered: "We cannot do this. You must be content to let the law take its course, and you should be satisfied that your case is decided by twelve of your own countrymen. Where are the jury?"

"Yes," added the Bishop, "these men are quite competent to judge rightly in your case."

"Well," said Father Roberts, "the account of our blood will be demanded of you and not of these poor men."

Then the twelve men retired together and returned after a short time and pronounced them guilty of high treason. The holy men heard the verdict with joy as was apparent in their smiling faces; they prayed God to pardon those poor men who knew not what they did. They were then taken back to Newgate till the Saturday following.

WHAT PASSED AT THEIR CONDEMNATION.

On Saturday the 8th of December, and the Feast of the Conception of the most Holy Virgin, Father Roberts and Mr. Somers were taken back to the Court to hear their sentence. When they arrived and had been placed with the other criminals in the place set apart for those about to be sentenced to death, silence was proclaimed and the Recorder addressed them as follows:

"You know that on Wednesday last you were brought up to trial, accused, convicted, and found guilty by twelve jurymen of the offence of high treason, and you also know that for the same reason you are now called to appear before this honourable Bench. If you have anything to say to show reason why I (by virtue of my office), should not pronounce sentence on you, say it now, for hereafter you cannot expect to be heard."

Father Roberts then demanded a hearing, and silence being again ordered, he spoke as follows:

"Most honourable Bench and you my dear countrymen,—You will not have forgotten—for I persuade myself many of you who are here now were here then—how three days ago when I was examined, I demonstrated my innocence, and how I defended myself against the charges brought against me. The Bench simply sought to convict me of being a priest, saying that that of itself was high treason. I acknowledged then, as I do now, that I am a priest and a monk of the holy Order of St. Benedict, as were also St. Augustine, St. Laurence, St. Paulinus, St. Mellitus, and St. Justus; and as these monks converted our country from unbelief, so I have done what little I could to liberate it from heresy. I leave it to you, Mr. Recorder and the rest of you, to judge whether this is high treason.

"But suppose I had really offended against the State and were worthy of death, I ought not even then to be judged by you, Mr. Recorder, nor by this Court, nor by these twelve men, they not being men of my condition or quality, since it has been decreed by the Councils of the Church and the Popes, the Vicars of Christ on earth, that priests should not be brought before secular judges to be examined, but if their crimes are grave and merit death, that they must be first examined and found guilty by the ecclesiastical judges and be degraded by them, and when all their ecclesiastical privileges are taken from them, then they can be handed over to the secular arm to be dealt with as the laws of God and man decree. This being the case, I do not see, Mr. Recorder, that you are competent to pronounce sentence against me."

The Recorder at this only smiled, and said, "Have you anything else to say?" To which he answered, "I have said enough, you can do what you please."

The Recorder then said, "God have mercy on you," and then went on to make a violent attack on them, especially on Father Roberts, pointing him out to the people as the most turbulent and dangerous priest in England, who had seduced and drawn the people from their allegiance, and had reconciled more subjects of his Majesty to the Pope, than any other priest for many years. He was Superior of the Benedictines in England, had been taken for the Gunpowder Plot, and had broken out of prison. And after having received much grace and mercy from his Majesty, he had repaid nothing but ingratitude, by returning straightway to England contrary to his Majesty's express will and order."

After that, he pronounced sentence on each in turn, in the usual way for those convicted of high treason. When this was done Father Roberts asked again to speak. This the Recorder opposed, saying it was too late to say anything in his own defence, nor did the law permit it. But Father Roberts in a loud voice said:

"Dear countrymen, do not believe what this man has said, because I clearly showed my innocence the other day before all the Judges." Turning to the Recorder, "I pray God to pardon you and all who have plotted to shed my blood. I pardon you all with my whole heart. May God protect the King, the Queen, the Prince, and all the family of his Majesty, and give them grace to serve Him faithfully. I shall pray, as long as my life lasts, for his Majesty and for all his, and for the conversion of our country, and I hope that after my death I shall have better opportunity of doing so. May God grant us strength and patience!"

The Recorder took off his hat and said, "I congratulate you on making such a good end." Their hands were then bound and they were taken back to the prison, Father Roberts remarking that of all the days of his life this day had been the happiest and most joyful.

WHAT PASSED ON THE DAY OF THEIR EXECUTION.

Early in the morning of the 10th December a hurdle made of osiers was brought dragging at a horse's tail to the gate of Newgate Prison. On it was bound Father John Roberts, and at his left hand Mr. Somers. In this condition they were drawn slowly along to Tyburn, the place of public execution, about two miles from the town.

When they came within about sixteen yards of the gallows, they stopped for about half an hour, while sixteen criminals who had been conveyed thither on two carts, were fastened to the crossbeam by the hangman. During this time, and during the whole route, many friends and acquaintances gathered round the two holy men, partly to show them reverence and also to profit by their last prayers and blessings. There was also, as is usual, a great crowd attracted by curiosity.

Father Roberts after a time asked if the malefactors had all been executed—for he could see nothing, being on the ground fastened to the hurdle and unable to see by reason of the crowd. They said, "Yes."

"Then," said he, "we shall die without company."

"No," said a bystander, "be of good cheer, gentlemen; they are not really dead, and you will die amongst thieves, as your Lord did."

These words consoled the holy men very much, especially as they were said by a Protestant. After waiting a good half-hour, the executioner wanted to drag them nearer and bring them if possible under the gibbet, but could not owing to the dense crowd, so they had to be unbound and taken on foot.

Father Roberts came first, wearing a cassock, and with a calm and smiling face. He tried to climb upon one of the carts where eight of the criminals were standing with ropes round their necks, but owing to his weakness and long illness, and the two hours of suffering on the hurdle, he could not get up until the hangman helped him. No sooner had he climbed in, than turning himself to the criminals and stretching out his hand to bless them, he spoke as follows:

"Here we are all going to die, nor have we any hope of escape, but if you die in that religion now professed and established in this country, without any doubt you will be condemned to the eternal fire of Hell. For the love then of our

Blessed Saviour, I earnestly pray you to return from the evil path, so that we may all die in one and the same true faith, and to show this, say with me the following words: *I believe in the Holy Catholic Church, and I desire to die a member of that Church. I repent and am sorry for having led so naughty and wicked a life, and that I have so grievously offended my sweet and merciful Saviour.* If you say these words truly and from your hearts I will absolve you, and then my soul for yours."

At these words, spoken with so much love and unction, one of the poor wretches was so affected that he burst into tears. The Father then exhorted him specially, and prayed silently to God for him, covering his face with his hand, then again spoke to him in a low voice. In the end the poor creature publicly professed that he died a Catholic. What further occurred, it is not possible to be certain of.

All this took place in the presence of a Protestant minister, who was there, as is usual, to talk to the criminals, the better to prepare their souls for hell-fire. But when Father Roberts appeared, he stood aside and, so far from opposing himself to anything Father Roberts said, seemed to yield to the dignity of the holy man and to the doctrine he taught. Father Roberts then turned to the other cart where were the eight other condemned men, and began to exhort them with many loving words, but a churlish officer interrupted him and prevented his speaking. Then he fell on his knees, and making the sign of the Cross on the gibbet he kissed it, and, as he had before worked with so much love and pity for the eternal salvation of others, he now for a short time gave himself up to thinking of his own soul. Then rising again and looking at the people with great joy and cheerfulness, he blessed them, and particularly saluted and blessed his own friends, of whom many were present, taking care to do this quietly towards those, who in the presence of the great crowd, were not afraid to show themselves openly Catholics by asking his blessing.

Meantime Mr. Somers was taken to the same cart, and Father Roberts giving him his hand, helped him to climb up, and said, "Welcome, dearest brother," and so they saluted and embraced each other. The executioner then began to strip off Father Roberts' clothes to prepare him for execution, and a friend gave him some *aqua vitæ* to refresh and strengthen him, in regard of his weakness. Having drunk a little, he asked leave of the Sheriff to speak to the people. There was a murmur of assent, and the Sheriff replied that he might say what he liked. He then raising himself up on the cart began to speak, but was interrupted by the minister and some of the criminals behind him singing hymns made up from the Psalms according to the fashion of Geneva. Turning therefore towards them, he said, "I pray you, cease that noise: it wearies me, and does you no good," and then turning to the

Sheriff, he said very mildly, "In courtesy, sir, remember I cannot be heard through that singing."

The Sheriff upon this commanded silence, and Father Roberts began, *Audite cœli quæ loquor, audiat terra verba oris mei.* Having spoken on these holy words and wishing to continue, he was again interrupted by the aforesaid churlish officer as before, but several gentlemen of condition interfered and reproved his insolence and presumption. The Father then continued:

"Dearly beloved friends, I am here to die in the presence of God and His angels and of the saints of Paradise, because being a priest, I returned to this country in spite of a statute passed in the 27th year of the late Queen's reign which declared this to be high treason. I have committed no fault except this, if this indeed be a fault, nor have I even been charged with any other offence. I die therefore for my faith and for my faith only, that same faith, I say, which St. Augustine, the Apostle of England, preached when he converted this country from idolatry. The vows of my Order, and the habit I wear, are the same as his, and I observe the same Rule, and live in the same Religious Order as he did. I teach the same faith that he taught. As he delivered you from paganism, so I have tried to deliver you from heresy. I affirmed this before the Judges at my trial, and I repeat it to you now in this place where I am about to seal my testimony with my blood."

While he was thus exhorting the people, the executioners were busy preparing Mr. Somers for his death, as they had already been with Father Roberts, who after he had remained a few minutes silent, returned, as well as he was able, with his hand or by bowing the salutations of those who were showing him compassion and reverence. He then again broke forth into these words, *Memorare novissima tua*—" Let every man remember his end." And reasoning on that said, *Quia nos omnes manifestari oportet ante tribunal Christi*—" We must all appear before the judgment-seat of Christ there to render an account of our faith and of our deeds. Those who have done well will have eternal life, and those who have done evil will suffer eternal torments." Having said this, and taken breath, he exclaimed loudly, *Extra ecclesiam nulla est salus*—" Outside the true Church of Christ there is no salvation."

The rude officer again tried to silence him, saying that he ought not to be allowed to speak to the people in that way. But the Sheriff said that as long as nothing was said against the King or the State, that he saw no reason why the Father should not say what he wished. The churl answered that he ought not to be allowed to mislead the King's subjects with such words.

Then the good Father replied, "I have never said, nor will I ever say, any evil against the King. On the contrary, I pray God to bless him and the Queen and their children, and those of his Council, also those of the Bench that condemned me, and likewise all you who are here present, and all the other subjects of the King. It is not the King who is the cause of my death, but heresy—heresy desires my death, and is the cause of it."

He then again bowed, and said a last farewell to his friends and those who saluted him; and, to be the sooner ready to receive the reward of his labours, began to unbutton his doublet and to loosen the strings of his shoes, and distributed these and other small things that he had to some intimate and zealous friends who begged to have them.

He then covered his eyes with his hand, and prayed silently until they told him that Mr. Somers was ready. Then he arose, and looking at the fire that was already burning to consume their bowels, said, "Here's a hot breakfast ready, despite the cold weather." A bystander, thinking he must feel cold after standing so long with his clothes loose, offered him a nightcap to cover his head, but he said with a smile, "Do not trouble yourself about that, sir, I am not afraid that hereafter I shall ever suffer from headache."

Mr. Somers, who had had irons on his hands up till now, said in a loud and cheerful voice, *Benedicat nos omnipotens Deus, Pater et Filius et Spiritus Sanctus*, and added: "Father Roberts has told you the reason why we are to suffer death, and so it is not necessary that I should repeat more than one thing. I did not refuse to take the oath because I refused any sort of allegiance that his Majesty the King could justly demand of me. I refused on account of the matters of faith included in that oath, and that is why it has been forbidden by His Holiness the Pope, whom all of us who are sheep of Christ are bound to obey in matters of faith. I pray you all therefore and exhort you to be obedient to the chief Shepherd of the Church of God." He concluded with the same words as Father Roberts, "Out of the Church there is no salvation."

At last Father Roberts turned to the people and asked them to excuse his speaking any more as his strength failed him, but he begged those who were Catholics to pray for him; then turning to his dear companion, Mr. Somers, they embraced and blessed one another, and then spoke for a short time in a low voice (no doubt confessing) until they were told that the moment had come when they must die.

Both together once more as well as they could blessed the people again, and, while they waited with great constancy and cheerfulness for the cart to be driven away, they used the following words. Father Roberts said, *Omnes Sancti et Sanctæ Dei, intercedite pro nobis*, and Mr. Somers said, *In manus tuas, Domine, commendo spiritum meum;* when on a sudden the two carts were pulled away at the same moment, and the two Martyrs in the midst of the sixteen criminals were left hanging, and quietly rendered their souls into the hands of the Holy Angels. They were allowed to remain until they were quite dead, a special mercy which it was not usual to extend to Catholics.

It was already late, and nearly an hour after mid-day when the executioner cut the rope and took down the body of Father Roberts; it was first disembowelled, and the bowels thrown into a large fire. Then he cut off the head, and divided the trunk into four quarters. The same thing was done to Mr. Somers. But here a remarkable thing happened. It is usual for the hangman when he disembowels those executed for high treason, to take out the heart, and holding it up, to say, "This is the heart of a traitor," and the people answer, "Long live the King." In this case when the hangman said the words, not one person answered, but all remained silent as if struck dumb.

About one hundred paces from the gibbet on the high-road a large trench was dug, into which the quarters of the two Martyrs were cast, and over them were thrown the bodies of the sixteen criminals. This was done with the intention that, as they had been persecuted and ill-used by wicked heretics during their lives, so their dead bodies should rest with those of evil-doers. But God did not permit this further outrage, for several religious and other Catholics (knowing what a pious act it was always considered in the early Church to give due honour and sacred burial to the remains of holy Martyrs cruelly treated and buried with ignominy by barbarous pagans or heretics), went by night and with great trouble removed the bodies of the holy Martyrs to religious houses and churches on the Continent, where they might be treated with honour, instead of leaving them in a common ditch by the public road, a fit place only for the burial of treacherous heretics and criminals.

Dr. Challoner adds that the Catholics who recovered the relics met the watch as they returned to London, and that one of them, in his endeavours to escape, let fall one of the quarters of Father Roberts, which was afterwards by command of Archbishop Abbot buried in the Church of St. Saviour, "to hinder the Catholics from recovering it. The rest of the relics were carried to Douay to the Convent of the English Benedictines there. But one of Father Roberts' arms was sent into Spain, to the Abbey of St. Martin at Compostella."

Some of these relics are still preserved in England. One is in the possession of the Cardinal Archbishop of Westminster, marked " Ex digito B. Somers, M.," and another at the convent of Our Lady of Dolours, of the Third Order of St. Francis at Taunton, marked "Joannis Mervin. digitus, Ordinis Sti. Benedicti, Sacerdotis et Martyris in Anglia." Joannes de Mervinia, it will be remembered, is the name which Father John Roberts bore in his Order.

In conclusion, we may be permitted to remind the reader of the wonderfully beautiful account of the last evening on earth of these Venerable Servants of God, recorded in the *Life of Luisa de Carvajal*.[2] Twenty confessors of the faith supped together in

[2] *Life of Luisa de Carvajal.* By Lady Georgiana Fullerton. 1873, p. 220.

the prison, with Donna Luisa at the head of the table, and on her right hand and her left the holy Martyrs elect. It would be hard to find, in the Acts of the Martyrs of any age or place, anything more beautiful than the question of Father Roberts to her, "Do you not think I may be causing dis-edification by my great glee? Would it not be better to retire into a corner and give myself up to prayer?" "No, certainly not," Luisa answered. "You cannot be better employed than by letting them all see with what cheerful courage you are about to die for Christ."

CHAPTER IX.

VENERABLE JOHN ALMOND.

Executed at Tyburn, December 5, 1612.

DOCUMENTS.

1. Introductory paper (Stonyhurst MSS. *Anglia*, iii. 121). Italian.
2. Letter written by the Martyr to Father Persons, April 16, 1604 (Stonyhurst MSS. *Anglia*, iii. 43).
3. His examination before the Bishop of London. Extract. Printed by Challoner.
4. Letter from a priest in Newgate with the Martyr (Stonyhurst MSS. *Anglia*, iii. 113).
5. An anonymous letter (*Ibid.* 114).
6. Narrative of the martyrdom (*Ibid.* 120).

---

1. The Venerable John Almond was born at Allerton (then also called South Allerton), near Liverpool. There and at Much-Woolton he remained till he was eight, when he was taken to Ireland, and thence passed, when twenty years of age, to the English College at Rome. His early life is summarized in the following document.

Father John Almond, student of the English College at Rome, studied there for the space of seven years,[1] and having successfully completed his philosophy and theology, he publicly defended theses on the whole course in the Roman College with general applause. The disputation was under the patronage of Cardinal Baronius, and when it was over that man of holy memory, as though foreseeing the still more glorious defence of the faith he was going to make in English dungeons and on the scaffold, embraced him many times and kissed his tonsure and that blessed brow, which was so soon to be encircled with the heavenly and eternal crown of a most glorious martyrdom. Cardinal Tarugi, who was also present, did the same.

He was an exemplary and holy priest, as well as a learned man, and, like a good husbandman, as soon as he arrived in England, he began at once to work and labour in that vineyard, in order to sow the Divine Word in a soil which is hardened beyond measure by the perfidious obstinacy of heretics.

When the news of the great good he was doing came to the ears of the King's ministers, [they were seized] with anger and ill-will against the holy priest, and therefore sent out cunning spies to catch him. He was taken prisoner, loaded with chains, and thrown into a very dark prison called Newgate, where for some years he, together with some Jesuits and other priests, bore with

---

[1] This is not quite accurate. The College Registers give March 30, 1597, as the date of his arrival, and September 16, 1602, as the day of his departure (Foley, *Records*, v. p. 201).

unbroken patience incredible pains and discomforts, not only from the darkness of the place, which was like an underground cavern, lit with no other light than that of a lamp, but also from the badness of their fare, for the King's officers provided no other provisions but black barley bread, such as one might throw to a dog, and some cold dirty water.

Though thus maltreated, he often had to dispute with heretical ministers, who came away so confused as not to know what to say. Finally, on the 3rd of December,[2] a day so many years before consecrated and immortalized by a similar defence of the faith in the same city of London by Father Edmund Campion of the Society of Jesus with six other blessed priests, he was brought to the bar at the Sessions House, which is the place for the public trial of malefactors.

This document is a rough draft with corrections, intended apparently to serve as an introduction to a fuller narrative in the same volume.

2. Among the treasures of the Stonyhurst muniment-room is an autograph letter of the Martyr, written before his arrest to his old Rector at the English College at Rome.

THE VENERABLE JOHN ALMOND TO FATHER PERSONS.

Reverend Father,—This bearer, upon other occasion of business being resolved to travel so

[2] There is an error of date here.

far as the place where you remain, thought also to defer his resolution in matters of religion until he came thither. But being touched afterwards with the uncertainty of his arrival, and certain danger of his soul, if death should have prevented his designment, he altered his resolution and is become Catholic and a member of God His Church here, nothing doubting but God Almighty will afterwards water with His heavenly grace and give increase there, to that which is already planted here. The time of his conversion he himself can declare, but that he is already converted and a Catholic I give you sure testimony, because it pleased God to make me the instrument of his reconciliation. Your charity I know will show him that favour and kind entertainment which usually you do to strangers of his quality and condition; but something more (much I dare not desire because my deserts are few or none) I hope he shall find at my request, and I shall not fail to remain thankful.

Concerning my brother I have made much inquiry, but can hear no certainty whether he be in Spain or Italy, religious or as before; no, not so much as whether he be dead or living. I heard he was bitten by a mad dog in his return from Compostella, but as yet I cannot learn any more. Good Father, let me humbly request you to certify me concerning him as soon as you possibly can find the means. I remain about London. Mr. Blunt well knoweth the place of my abode.

Thus humbly recommending myself to your Reverence, with great desire to be made partaker in the prayers of that virtuous company, I leave to trouble you any further.

London, this 16th of April, A.D. 1604.
Your assured and dutiful child,
JOHN ALMOND.

The "virtuous company" to whom our Martyr commends himself must have been the community at the English College, and the elder brother whom he inquires about, was Oliver, some sixteen years his senior. It is perhaps worth while pointing out that Challoner has fallen into one of his extremely rare errors in not distinguishing them, though in truth there is little wonder in this, seeing that the Douay Diary, which he followed, does not give their Christian names. This Oliver must have been a man of some worth, for he was recalled by Cardinal Allen from England and stationed at Genoa with the duty, an important one in those days, of forwarding letters and the like from England to Rome.[3] How long he remained there does not appear, nor where he was at the time of this letter, but the last record of him is a touching one.

Father Grene,[4] notes that at the time of his writing —this is in the year 1666—there was preserved at the English College a chalice valued above all others, with this inscription in Latin: "Oliver Almond, once student of this College, in bonds for the faith, consecrated and gave this chalice in honour of the Holy Trinity, Blessed Mary, and St. Thomas of Canterbury, Bishop and Martyr, A.D. 1620."

[3] Foley, *Records*, vol. iv. p. 576. [4] *Collectanea N.* vol. i. p. 73.

3. The document first quoted stated generally that our Martyr was arrested and confined in Newgate. It appears, however, that he was really twice arrested, and moved to different prisons. Father Richard Blount, whom the Martyr alludes to in his letter as one who knew his place of abode, writes to Father Persons, February 20, 1607 :[5]—

"While I am writing this, one telleth me that the Bishop's pursuivants, searching a house in Holborn of one Cook, have found his secret place, and therein a priest called Almond, a young man. The times were never so bad as now."

In July, 1608, he was in the Gatehouse, having the honour of taking the place of the Venerable Father Thomas Garnet, S.J., who had lately been martyred,[6] and then he disappears again from our sight until he is re-arrested in March or May, 1612, when he was carried before Dr. John King, Bishop of London. Challoner has given long extracts from his examination, from an account of it written by the Martyr himself.[7] The conclusion is as follows.

Bishop. "Will you take the oath of allegiance?"

[5] Whether this date is reckoned in the Old style or the New is not stated in Father Grene's quotation (*Collectanea N.* vol. i. p. 49).

[6] "Three priests in the Gatehouse are going on bravely, for now Mr. Molinax, *alias* Almond, takes Mr. Garnet's place." Translated from a Latin letter of Father Michael Walpole to Father Persons, July 26, 1608. Father Grene adds this comment: "I believe he means by *tenet locum* that he succeeded him, not only in place, but in zeal of suffering and refusing the oath of allegiance" (*N.* i. p. 49).

[7] Challoner only gives the parts quoted by Knaresborough (vol. ii. p. 167), whose Collections were purchased by Lord Herries at the sale of the Burton Constable manuscripts. To him I am indebted for the highly valued privilege of consulting them at Everingham.

Almond. "Any oath of allegiance, if it contains nothing but allegiance."

With that the Bishop reaches out his arm for the oath, lying towards the middle of the table, which I perceiving said:

A. "That oath you cannot with good conscience offer."

B. "Yes, that I can; and I thank God, I have taken it myself seven times."

A. "God forbid!"

B. "Why?"

A. "You have been seven times perjured."

B. "Wherein?"

A. "In taking this false clause. *And I do further swear that I do from my heart abhor, detest, and abjure as impious and heretical, this damnable doctrine and position, that Princes excommunicated and deprived by the Pope may be deposed,*" &c.

B. "There is no perjury or falsehood in it."

A. "If in taking it you abjure that position as heretical which is not heretical, then is it perjury and falsehood to take it. But in taking it, you abjure that position as heretical which is not heretical. *Ergo.*"

B. "I grant your *major*, I deny your *minor*."

A. "No position in your grounds can be heretical, unless it is expressly censured for heretical by the Word of God, or the contradictory expressly contained in the Word of God. But this position is not expressly censured for heretical by the Word of God; nor is the contradictory expressly contained in the Word of God. *Ergo* it is not heretical."

B. " It is censured as heretical by the Word."

A. " Allege the text, give us a Bible."

B. " Bring in a Bible."

Then turning with an evil will, he said it was censured in the 13th of the Romans.

A. " You mean those words: '*He that resisteth power, resisteth God's ordinance.*' But I ask, where is this position censured? There is not one word of the position in hand."

Other place he alleged none.

B. " You would have it censured in express words ? "

A. " You are bound to bring a censure in express words. Which because I see you cannot, answer this consequence. *This position is not set down at all in the Bible; ergo it cannot be censured by the Bible.*"

He answered not, but said I was a *proud, arrogant Jack.*

To which I replied, " God forgive you; your words trouble me not." And so two or three times more I prayed God to forgive him, when he miscalled me and abused me in words.

Then leaving the oath, which he was weary of, he asked :

B. " Have you gone to church ? " And added, " I forgot it before, but I go beyond you now."

A. " I have not gone to church."

B. " Will you go ? "

A. " I will not. Is not this plain dealing ? "

B. " Now you deal plainly."

A. " If it would not offend you, I must tell you that you went beyond yourself. For you confessed even now that you should have asked it before, and so go beyond yourself in asking it now."

Much more passed between us before about a disjunctive position, wherein the Bishop needeth not to boast of his logic. At part of this, a certain Dean coming in, after the Bishop was weary, the Dean began to talk of the Pope's power to depose kings, saying it was essential to the Pope and a matter of faith in our doctrine. To whom I replied, that it was not essential to the Pope's power nor any matter of faith: and that (whether the Pope could or could not depose) it was perjury to take the oath in their grounds and ours too. This, I said, I would undertake to demonstrate before all the bishops in England, or else I would lose my hand and my head. The Dean said I was too quick with him, and that my logic would deceive me if I builded so much upon it, wishing me to look to a good conscience. I replied that it was my conscience which I did stand upon, and therefore refused the oath for the reasons alleged. Yet to give satisfaction, this oath I offered that I would swear: "I *do bear in my heart and soul so much allegiance to King James* (whom I pray God to bless now and evermore) *as he, or any Christian king could expect by the law of nature, the law of*

God, or the positive law of the true Church, be it which it will, *yours or ours*."[8]

The Bishop and the Dean said they were fair words, but the Dean added, he knew well which Church I meant.

To this I answered: "Let you and me try that, and then put it out of question." But he was deaf on that ear.

Then the Bishop bade me put my hand to my examination. I first perused it, and in the end of it where the Register had set down: "Being asked whether he would take the oath of allegiance, he answered he could not without perjury." I bade him add also, as I had said: "I could not in their grounds nor ours." The Bishop would not suffer him to add that, but said I should have another time. Upon that I put my hand to it, though I said he had put it in by halves. Thus ended the pageant, saving that I said publicly (giving the honour to God) that I had not sworn any oath, no, not so much as "in faith" in sixteen year before, and therefore they needed not wonder that I now refused an oath with falsehood and perjury in it.

4. He was then sent to Newgate, and what he suffered there may be gathered from the following letter of his fellow-prisoner, Henry Cooper, a priest, addressed:

---

[8] An oath very similar to this had been proffered by the Venerable Thomas Garnet (Foley, *Records*, vol. ii. p. 490).

To his assured kind friend, Mr. Richard ——[9]

+

Good sir,—I am sure you have heard of the inhuman dealing of our new keeper with us, putting us all into Justice hall without commodity of lodging; forcing divers of us to sit up night by night, and yet exacting money for beds, debarring all access of friends, suffering the pursuivants to seize such as come unto our grate, yea, vexing even Protestants themselves that come unto us. Neither can we have any remedy against him, such is the malice of the B[ishop], who maintaineth all injuries done unto us. Our keeper's pride [is] in that excess, as overruled with passion he will admit of no reason, insomuch as we are wholly ignorant of what course to take whereby we may best redeem our vexations. Our comfort only is, that the cause for which we suffer is good and honourable, being for God Himself; and these our miseries are infallible signs of His love towards us, according to that of the Apostle: *Quem diligit Dominus castigat, flagellat autem omnem filium quem recipit.* This, I say, is our comfort; in this, I hope, we shall overcome.

In the meantime I would desire your good prayers for us, that we may so endure these our troubles, as they may turn to God's greater honour and glory, and our souls' comfort. And so remembering my duty to yourself and a kind

[9] This name has been blotted out.

remembrance to the rest of our good friends, I humbly take my leave this 10 November, 1612, though never leave to be
Yours,
HEN. COOPER.

Four of our company are fallen sick of late, whereof Fr. Corneford is one, and not in least danger, as Dr. Foster hath delivered his opinion of him. If our keeper continue as he has begun, we shall all fall into extreme misery.

5. Another paper from the Stonyhurst collections, endorsed "Advices," and headed "November, 1612," continues the story.

Seven Catholic priests escaped of late out of Newgate; their names are Cornford, Young, Mayler, Yates, *alias* Boulton, Greene, Parr, Cooper. Much search hath been made for them, but none taken. The occasion of their escaping was the hard usage without compassion or mercy, whereupon they refused to give their words to be true prisoners, but told their keeper that as long as they were used so hardly, they would give no such word, but would escape if they could, and within few days after they got away. And as those seven went away, they might all have gone, to the number of twenty, but they refused it, choosing rather to stay. Those that remained in prison have ever since been cast into the dungeon with fetters and gyves.

Addressed, For Marke, merchant at Florence.[10]

The paper is endorsed in Latin, "Of the flight of the priests from Newgate. Almund remained in prison, as appears from the Douay Catalogue of Martyrs, published in 1614."

6. This time he did not lie in his dungeon for long, but was quickly brought to trial. Here it is provoking to have to state, that the record of these proceedings is lost, though the cover which once contained it is preserved in the muniment-room of the Guildhall. On the fly-sheet of this is a list of the prisoners presented from Newgate at the gaol delivery, amongst whom we find "Francis Lathom" (one name by which the Martyr was known, Molineux being another) *pro proditione*, with the marginal note *jud*[*icatus*]. Probably the record, as in other cases of treason, was separately filed, then got separated, and so lost.

Happily there are several Catholic accounts of the proceedings, and from them we learn that he was indicted on the statute of 27 Elizabeth, which made it treason for a priest ordained according to the Catholic rite to live in England. He refused to put himself upon the jury, but was nevertheless found guilty and sentenced. Letters[11] written at the time of his death inform us that he was "arraigned and condemned upon a question demanded of him by his keeper's wife, whether if one should kill the King he might absolve him." For thereupon "his enemy Mr. Price, the keeper, deposed against him, that he

[10] This was an address often used for Father Persons, but when this was written, he had been dead two years.

[11] Stonyhurst MSS. *Anglia*, iii. nn. 118, 119. The second is unsigned, the first is signed William Bartlet, and addressed "to my assured good friend, Mr. Luke, merchant att Venice." Both names are probably aliases.

heard him say that he had power to absolve one, though he should kill the King. But Mr. Almond upon his oath denied this, and said that he only had said, 'Through true repentance Ravalliac might be saved.'"

The Martyr disputed with the Bishop in court with the same fearlessness and vigour which he had shown in their private meetings. The Bishop was silenced for the time, but afterwards persuaded King James to allow the execution to take place, "promising him that it would be very profitable to their cause, for that the priest was both timorous and unlearned, which when the King heard to be otherwise he raged exceedingly, and said he would execute no more." [12]

✠

A RELATION OF THE DEATH AND EXECUTION OF MR. JOHN ALMOND, *alias* MOLINEUX, THE 20TH DAY OF DECEMBER, 1612.

As he was drawn all the way from the prison to Tyburn, he remained with his hands closed and erected [up towards] Heaven, and so continued in silence, prayer, and meditation all the way, except that sometime he spake to those that were about him, but could not well be heard because none were suffered to come near him but those that guarded him.

Being come to Tyburn and raised up into a cart right underneath the gallows, with a cheerful

[12] *Anglia*, iii. 119, ut supra. Brother Foley (*Records*, vol. vii. p. 1377) has printed a re-translation of a full account of the trial, of which a copy in the original English may be found in the Stonyhurst MSS. *Anglia*, iii. n. 117.

countenance signing himself with the sign of the Cross, and saying *In nomine Patris*, &c., he desired the Sheriff to give him leave to speak, protesting he would not speak any one word either against his Majesty or the State. This the Sheriff did yield unto, but first would have had him put off his clothes, and speak in his shirt, which he was unwilling to do, urging that he could not speak so well with his clothes off, desiring he might have them on and he would be very brief; which at length was granted him. Then kneeling upon his knees and saying some private prayers to himself, which when he had done, he rose up and making again the sign of the Cross, he said : *Domine, labia mea aperies*, &c. And then began his speech thus, as near as could be gathered :

He said he was born in Lancashire, the town's name was South Allerton, where he was brought up until he was about eight years old, at which time he was carried over into Ireland, where he remained until he was at man's state. And when he was last taken, which was on the 22nd of May a year since, no man knew whether he was an Englishman or no. He then being carried before a Justice of Peace, "which here," he said, "he would [not name, to avoid] offence," was by him examined whether he was a priest or no.[18] He did not confess to him that he was. Whereupon the Justice offered him the oath (which he called of allegiance), which by him was refused, in

[18] He seems to mean Dr. John King, Bishop of London.

respect that in conscience it could not be taken without danger of perjury, both to his Majesty and to him that shall take it.

Then he, kneeling on his knees, said he took God to witness, and as he hoped to be saved by the Death and Passion of our Saviour, that this which he spake, he spake from his heart, without any manner of dissimulation, that his Majesty was sole and lawful King of this realm, and that he bare so true and loyal a mind to him, as either the King of Spain, or King of France, or any other Catholic prince whatsoever could desire, either by the laws of God, nature, or nations, of their subjects. He protested also that never in all his lifetime any jot or least thought of treason did enter into his heart, neither directly or indirectly, by commission or otherwise; and if he should have heard of any intended against his Majesty, he would have revealed it by all means possible.

Then a preacher standing by did ask him whether he held the King to have sufficient power to make laws or no. Before he could answer him, another preacher asked him another question. What it was I know not, but by his answer it seemed to belong to the former question, for he desired him to hold him excused, till he had answered the first, and then he would speak to him.

Then turning to the former he answered his question thus: that the King had as sufficient power to make laws in England, as the King of

France, Spain, Turkey, or any other prince whatsoever had to make laws in their own realms. "But as the King of Spain, France, and all other princes have power to make laws over their own subjects, so likewise both the Kings of England, Spain, France, and all other princes whatsoever are subject to our Saviour Christ Jesus. And though the kings and other princes have sufficient power to do this, yet they have no power to make any one law against the law of God, which I hope you will not deny," speaking to him that first moved the question.

Then turning to the second he answered him in this manner, alleging a place out of St. Matthew, the sixth or seventh verse, saith he (as I remember), "our Saviour being with His disciples, said to them, *All power which is given in Heaven and in earth is given Me from on high. Therefore go you and preach throughout the world,* &c.,[14] this he said to them breathing on them His breath." Thus out of St. Matthew he proved that our Saviour, having power, gave it to His disciples and they to others, "and by tradition, it hath come down from one to another even to this Pope, which is now living. And so consecrated priests have it from Him, and at His commandment do go through the world to preach the Gospel. This being the law and commandment of the Pope, who is the substitute of Almighty God, to go and preach throughout

---

[14] There seems to be some confusion here between St. Matt. xxviii. 18, and some similar text, perhaps St. John xix. 11.

the world, the priests in England are no traitors in coming into England to preach the faith."

This was his answer to the second question, which I think was grounded upon the first, that if the King had power to make laws, and that those laws were good and ought to be kept, he making a law that no priest receiving Holy Orders beyond sea should come into England to persuade or pervert his subjects under pain of treason, why did he and such others come into England, contrary to these laws of his Majesty made, &c.?

The first preacher told him he was not executed as a traitor, but as an heretic. But he said again, Why was he hanged then and not burned, which is the death of an heretic? The minister hereupon was silent, and he went on with his speech as afore.

He told that he was brought from the Justice of Peace that first examined him and committed to Newgate, where he remained until about ten days since, when seven of the prisoners made an escape out of prison, at which time on Sunday morning he was taken out of his chamber with all the rest that remained, put into a dungeon, filthy and loathsome. The Sheriff said that he did malign the State therein. Whereupon he said, " Good Mr. Sheriff, I do not and will not. For I thought that was done by the keeper, and not by the State." Then going on with his speech, that being cast into that loathsome dungeon where he had scarce meat and drink to sustain nature, or keep him alive, he there was kept till the time that he was brought forth to his arraignment, where he was indicted of two several points. What they were I have forgotten, but as I remember one of them was for denying the oath of allegiance, which he told them he had answered before, that in conscience he could not take it, and being condemned he was now brought to shed his blood, for our Saviour Jesus Christ His sake, Who was crucified and shed His Blood for his sins.

At which words, he being suddenly interrupted by one of the preachers, who told him that he held it no sin to kill the King, he utterly denied that, and did abjure all such thoughts, and held them as most wicked and abominable sins. The minister answered again, "But if a man should determine to kill the King, the Pope would forgive him that sin." He denied that also, and said that the Pope neither would nor could do it, but if a man had committed a sin, after hearty repentance, contrition, and satisfaction, &c. At which word *satisfaction* he took exception again, and asked him what satisfaction would be made for killing of a king. He answered that every venial sin was great, and no satisfaction was sufficient for it without the Death and Passion of our Saviour. "Neither is His Death and Passion sufficient without repentance and contrition of heart. But if any man had committed a sin and was truly penitent, the Pope both might and would forgive him. And so for the killing of a king, if a madman killed a king, and were heartily sorry and repentant for it, God forbid that you and I should then deny that his sin might be forgiven him." Then asking him how he thought of it, the minister answered that he must confess, that if any man had committed a sin, and were truly repentant for it, he held his sin might be forgiven him. But although it were true doctrine, yet it was an ill instance, and dangerous to speak before a community: and so that argument ended.

Then he went on with his speech, that he was come hither to shed his blood for our Saviour's sake, Who shed His for his sins. In which respect he wished that every drop of blood that he should shed might be a thousand, wishing to have there St. Laurence his gridiron to be broiled on, St. Peter's cross to be hanged on, St. Stephen's stones to be stoned with, to be ript, ript, ript, and ript again. Desiring to have a thousand lives to suffer so many deaths for Jesus Christ His sake, through Whose Death and Passion, and this of his, he made no doubt but to enjoy the Kingdom of Heaven.

Then putting his hand into his pocket he took forth ten shillings, and gave it to the Sheriff, desiring him to distribute it among those men that took pains with him and went afoot with him through the dirt, which were those that guarded him with halberts. Then he hurled forth by handfuls among the people to the quantity of 8 or 9*l.* Then he gave to the Sheriff an handkerchief, and to the hangman an angel in gold, which, he said, he gave him, not to spare him, but to execute his office as he should do.

Then one of the preachers urged an argument of faith unto him. That the Catholic Church did teach that good works did justify without faith. He answered that he believed the Catholic Church, for it did teach that faith and good works did justify together. The minister said that faith alone justified. He asked what faith an infant could have ere he had the use of reason? The minister left that question and reason, and talked of something else.

Then he desired the Sheriff leave to pray for the King, and kneeling down he prayed for the King, Queen, and Prince, and all his royal progeny, and said there were two princes, but now there is but one. He protested he loved the King, the Queen, the Prince, and all his progeny, and wished them as well as to his own soul, wishing to God that the King had many more children, especially of the male kind, which when he had said, he rose up.

Presently one of the preachers bade him pray for himself, for that he prayed for others, but never a word for himself, as thinking he was no sinner. He said he would not pray for himself at his bidding, but to give the people satisfaction that he had no such thought, he acknowledged himself to be a great and grievous sinner, and did ask God heartily forgiveness for his sins, not doubting but that his intercession and blood that he should shed that day would be a full satisfaction of all his sins, and that he should enjoy thereby life everlasting.

Then he kneeled down and said some prayers in Latin, which when he had done he rose up. Then he hurled from him amongst the people his beads, and another handkerchief, his band he gave away, and all his points he hurled, with his discipline [for those] to get them that would. Then the hangman pulled off his clothes, and he blessed all the people round about him. Then he took a gold ring off his finger, and gave it to the Sheriff, earnestly entreating him to give it to Mr. Muskett in Newgate, for that he gave it him to wear so long as he lived.

The Sheriff told him that he should hang till he was more than half dead. He answered they should rip him up alive as he was, if they pleased, and not hang him at all. So willing he was to endure torment for so good a cause.

Then standing up after a pause he said: " There is a doctor of divinity in this company, that holds opinion that no man can live chaste, which I deny, I myself having lived chaste, pure, and die a maid." Then the hangman put the rope around his neck, and tied a handkerchief before his eyes. With a cheerful and merry countenance he willed him to tell him when he drew away the cart from under him, because he desired to die with the name of Jesus in his mouth. At which speech the minister which had conferred with him all the while in scoffing manner, said to him that there was great virtue in that name sure. For which audacious speech a gentleman standing by took him up very roundly.

Then he signed himself with the sign of the Cross and said: *In manus tuas Domine commendo spiritum meum. Redime me Domine Deus veritatis. Jesus, Jesus, Jesus, esto mihi Jesus*, and so died. Amen.

The Stonyhurst letters, which we have quoted before, add a few details. One says: "He craved no favour to be shown in cutting him up alive. Yea, he wished them if they pleased to begin with his fingers' ends and so go forwards." Another adds: "At his death a Protestant beholding his undaunted courage and bold spirit, full of life and comfort, he concluded in himself that he only was happy for his religion. Thereupon he went from the gallows to the Gatehouse, and desired to speak with a priest. They bringing him to Father Blackfan, he resolved to the best, and was reconciled within few days, for which my Lord of Canterbury clapt up close Mr. Blackfan, where he still remaineth, for at the same Sessions there were between fifty and sixty indicted."

Three days after the martyrdom of this Venerable servant of God, Ussher wrote a letter from London, in which he speaks thus of him: "On Saturday last, Lathom, *alias* Molyneux, one of the learnedest and insolentest of the Popish priests here (for so I might easily discern by the conference which I had with him and his fellows at Newgate), was executad at Tyburn."[15]

[15] Rawlinson, *Letters*, 89, n. 3.

CHAPTER X.

VENERABLE JOHN THULIS AND VENERABLE ROGER WRENNO.

Suffered at Lancaster, March 18, 1616.

DOCUMENTS.

1. Account in verse of their imprisonment and martyrdom.
2. Song written by Thulis.
   Both taken from a manuscript in the British Museum (Add. 15,225, pp. 49 and 44).

---

1. The following account, in a north country dialect, of the Martyrs' imprisonment and death, is taken from a very interesting collection of Catholic poems and songs written in a contemporary hand, preserved in the British Museum. This manuscript contains what seems to be the earliest version of the familiar hymn, "Jerusalem, my happy home,"[1] together with others of the same plaintive, earnest character.

HERE FOLLOWETH THE SONG OF THE DEATH
OF MR. THEWLIS.

To the tune of " Dainty come thou to me."

1. O God above relent,
   And listen to our cry;

[1] This hymn and the "Prisoner's songe" are printed in *The Month* for September, 1871, p. 232.

O Christ our woes prevent,
   Let not thy children die.

2. As at th' Assizes late
   Good proof too much we see,
Thy lambs their lives have left
   Through tyrants crueltie.

3. One Thewlis is the man
   Which makes me call and cry,
Come help me all that can
   Of Christ to beg mercie.

4. His courage mild and meek
   And his most comlie glee,
His answers not to seek
   In middes of miserie.

5. In a dungeon he was cast
   Amongst the thieves to lie,
Of all meats he did taste
   Which came to felons fee.

6. And in th' assizes week
   In Lent arraigned was he,
Where friends and kinsfolk were
   To see his constancie.

7. Best preacher in the land
   By name one parson Lee,
(No better can be found
   Within the counterie).

8. Three several days did tempt
   To try his constancie,
The Judge being present there
   With all his companie.

9. To all things they demand
    He answers cheerfullye,
   His answer there was found
    In all controversie.

10. As they were apt to move
     From point to point trulie,
    He did not them reprove
     But answered quietlie.

11. When they could not prevail
     To wrest his constancie,
    They did him traetor call,
     And said that he should die.

12. Then smilingly he said
     With sweete and pleasant glee,
    No treason I have wrought
     Nor wicked treacherie.

13. No treason I have done
     Against king nor countrie,
    Christ Jesus, God's own Son,
     A witness take for me.

14. It is for His dear sake,
     His Church both meek and free,
    That I do undertake
     A true Catholic to die.

15. It is for His dear sake
     That gave His life for me,
    My crosse I undertake
     His spouse to glorifie.

16. Then gave they him a note,
    Th' effect did signifie,
    That he must take the oath
    Or else prepare to die.

17. Then answered he and said
    For duty temporal,
    I every oath will take
    Whensoe'er you do call.

18. For other oath, quoth he,
    I utterlie denye;
    God save our king and queen
    And send them mikle joy.

19. According to the law
    Death certain then had he,
    And as all people know
    He took it patientlie.

20. On Friday in the morn
    Attempted sore was he,
    They willed him to reform,
    And take the king's mercie.

21. His kinsfolk in like cause
    Did proffer gold and fee,
    If his faith he would refuse
    A Protestant to be.

22. He gave them hearty thanks,
    And told them cheerfullie,
    His life they should not crave
    A Protestant to be.

23. In wresting of his bonds
    Somewhat too hastily,
    They hurt his tender legs
    Whereat they seemed sorrie.

24. Then smilingly he said,
    " Forbear to mourn for me,
    Small hurts do little grieve
    When great ones are so nigh.

25. " I thank my Saviour sweet
    From these bonds I am free,
    So soon I hope I shall
    From all extremitie.

26. " By afflictions God doth prove
    Who His true children be,
    Christ Jesus this can remove
    In the twinkling of an eye."

27. They forced him to the church
    In spite of his bodie,
    When he full mildlie sate
    For all their crueltie.

28. Then did he ask the Sheriffe
    His brethren for to see,
    With them to take his leave
    Before he went to dye.

29. The Sheriffe gave consent,
    He thanked him heartilie,
    He to his brethren went
    With humble curtesie.

30. Then did he friendlie leave
    Of all his brethren take,
  Saying, "Do you not grieve,
    Nor mourn not for my sake.

31. "For it's God's blessed will
    That I must lead the way;
  But be you constant still,
    And I will for you pray."

32. And then with waterie cheeks
    They parted mournfullie;
  His gesture little shrank,
    Such was his constancie.

33. Another constant wight
    Which I had near forgot,
  Was constant day and night,
    And tranquil for his lot.

34. One Wrennol was he called,
    A layman happie he;
  They both prepared themselves
    On hurdle for to lye.

35. And thus these faithful wights
    So mildlie framed the same,
  The father and the son
    Thus both their journey came.

36. My muse begins to faint,
    And grief me overflow:
  But of these martyred saints
    The second part shall show.

THE SECOND PART.

1. As Thewlis passed the way,
    The poorest he did spy,
   He gave what money he had left,
    Their wants for to supply.

2. O God above relent,
    And listen to our cry!
   Sweet Christ thy spouse defend
    From tyrant's crueltie.

3. To th' execution place
    They being thither drawn,
   Present before their face
    Was fire and cruel flame.

4. Then did they them attempt
    Their faith for to deny,
   Saying they must be hanged
    And burned cruelly.

5. Then smiling, Thewlis said,
    "If that the worst may be,
   Our Saviour Christ hath paid
    Far greater pains for me."

6. Then mildly they repaired
    To th' execution place:
   Three felons they did see
    Hanged before their face.

7. And at the ladder foot,
    Where many people stood,
   He held them with dispute,
    While ever they would abyde.

8. Then did they proffer them
    Part of the oath to take,
   And they should not be slain,
    Such friendship they would make.

9. But all could not prevail
    Their minds for to remove,
   Nor once their courage quailed
    So constant was their love.

10. With cross and signs so meek
     The ladder he did take,
    Where many a watery eye
     Appeared for his sake.

11. A hundred pounds was there
     For his life offered free,
    If he would yet consent
     A Protestant to be.

12. Then smilingly he said,
     "That ransom I denye,
    That may no way be paid
     But by death eternally.

13. "I thank you for your loves,
     Your good-will all I see,
    But I must take the cross
     That Christ hath left for me."

14. Then willingly he did
     Himself most ready make,
    He proffered to unbare,
     And his clothes off to take.

15. A cap as white as snow
      Over his face pulled he,
    His hat he threw him froe,
      And purse away gave he.

16. The hangman played his part
      As he did him command,
    Three strokes upon his breast
      He gave with his right hand.

17. The father being gone
      The child did after hye,
    Without all show of moan,
      He suffered willingly.

18. At first the rope did break
      Which parson Lee did see,
    He said it was God's will
      To shew him such mercie.

19. Then proffered him the oath
      Which he did still denye:
    "This night I hope we both
      Shall sup in Heaven high."

20. The people moved and blushed
      Both high and low degree,
    And said they thought no less
      But he should saved be.

21. When that the rope was cut
      And quartered he should be,
    The hangman did denye,
      And then away went he.

22. The Sheriff did him oppress
    With great extremitie,
    And said, " Either thou or I
    Must do this butcherie."

23. When Thewlis was unbared
    A vision there was seen,
    Out of his mouth appeared
    A colour bright and sheene.

24. Most like the glorious sun,
    Shining in clearest skye,
    Downe over his bodie run
    And vanish from their eye.

25. The butcher played his part,
    His bodie he did gore,
    And sure the hardest hart
    Did much his death deplore.

26. A hundred handkerchiefs
    With his sweet blood was dight,
    As relics for to wear
    For this said blessed wight.

27. Then were his quarters set
    Upon the castle high
    Where hapt as strange a thing
    As ever man did see.

28. A flight of ravens came
    And picked flesh from bones,
    In the churchyard they did light
    And scraped there deep holes.

29. O Christian hearts relent,
    Prepare your souls to save,
  When feathered fowls shall help
    For us to make a grave.

30. O happy martyred saints,
    To you I call and cry,
  To help us in our wants,
    And beg for us mercie.

31. O Christ that suffered death,
    Thy spouse for to defend,
  Like constancie till death,
    And in Heaven be our end.

Finis.

2. In the same volume is found another piece about this Martyr. It is headed,

HERE FOLLOWETH THE SONG WHICH MR. THULIS
WRIT FOR HIMSELF.

To the tune of[2]

1. True Christian heart cease to lament,
    For grief it is in vain;
  For Christ you know was well content
    To suffer bitter pain.
  That we may come to Heaven bliss,
    There joyfully to sing,
  Who doth believe, shall never miss
    To have a joyful rising.

[2] Blank in MS.

2. But England hear, My heart is sad,
    For thy great crueltie,
And loss of faith, which once thou had,
    Of Christianitye.
In thee false doctrine doth appear
    Abundantly to spring,
Which is the cause I greatlie fear
    Thou lose thy happie rising.

3. As for myself I am not afraid
    To suffer constantlie,
For why due debt must needs be paid
    Unto sweet God on high.
Saint Paul he being firm of faith,
    Hoping with saints to sing,
Most patientlie did suffer death.
    Lord send us happie rising!

The fifth verse is curious, as seeming to indicate that the power of giving Confirmation was entrusted by the Holy See to some English priests. At least it is difficult to see what other meaning the third line can have. The "mighty power" is probably that of exorcism.

5. I have said Mass and Matins both,
    And true instructions taught,
Confirmed by the Holie Ghost,
    And mighty power wrought:
The holie Communion also
    With manna ever living;
The holie Sacraments I taught:
    Lord send us happie rising!

The writer then goes on to dwell on his own labours, and the sufferings of several Saints and Martyrs, and continues thus:

13. And many saints and martyrs moe,
      Which were too long to write,
    Have suffered cruel death, you know,
      As Scripture doth recite.
    They now with Christ above do reign,
      And joyfully do sing,
    That we may all God's love attain.
      Christ send us happie rising!

14. And then why should I be afraid
      To suffer constantlie,
    Sith in this cause so many saints
      Did suffer patientlie,
    And left examples for us all,
      That we with them may sing.
    God grant we may for mercie call,
      And have a happie rising.

15. O you poor prisoners dread not death,
      Though you have done amiss,
    But pray to God with faithful hearts
      To bring you unto bliss.
    Confess your sins with contrite hearts
      Unto your heavenlie King,
    For He is merciful indeed:
      Christ send us happie rising.

16. The saints also did suffer death,
      And martyrs, as you hear,

      And I myself am now at hand,
         And death I do not fear.
      Then have I trust of greater grace
         Unto my soul will bring,
      Where we shall meet both face to face
         Before our heavenly King.

17. No hurdle hard, nor hempen rope
         Can make me once afraid.
      No tyrant's knife against my life
         Shall make me dismayed.
      Though flesh and bones be broken and torn
         My soul I trust will sing,
      Amongst the glorious companie
         With Christ our heavenly King.

18. Thus I, your friend John Thewlis,
         Have made my latest end,
      Desiring God when His will is
         Us all to Heaven send.
      Where neither strange nor damned crewe
         Can grief unto us bring.
      And now I bid my last adieu :
         Christ send us happy rising!

19. God grant you grace still in your hearts
         False doctrine to refrain,
      And hold the true Catholic faith,
         Which Christ did once ordain.
      All honour be to God of hosts,
         All glory to His Son,
      All praise be to the Holy Ghost,
         Three Persons all in one.

Finis.

CHAPTER XI.

TEN MARTYRED LAYMEN.

DOCUMENTS.

1. Relation of Frances Salisbury about her father Blessed John Felton (Westminster Archives, vol. ii. p. 3).
2. Narrative of the imprisonment of James Layburne, by an eye-witness (Stonyhurst MSS. *Collectanea M*. fol. 168.)
3. Father Warford's account of John Jetter (*Ibid. M.* fol. 133). Latin.
4. Father Grene's account of the Venerable Richard Langley (*Ibid. M.* fol. 25 *e*). Latin.
5. Life, imprisonments, trial and death of the Venerable Nicholas Horner (Westminster Archives, vol. iv. p. 263; *Collectanea B.* n. 9).
6. (i.) Relation of Winchester Martyrs, *concluded* (Stonyhurst MSS. *Anglia*, vii. 25).
   (ii.) Letter from Father Garnet to Father Claud Acquaviva. Extract (Stonyhurst MSS. *Anglia*, i. 73). Latin.
   (iii.) Father Grene's *Collectanea E*. (St. Mary's Seminary, Oscott.)
7. Persecution and martyrdom of the Venerable James Duckett, written by his son, a Carthusian (Westminster Archives, vol. vii. p. 339).

1. Our previous chapters have consisted of a document, or a series of documents, concerning a single Martyr, or a group of Martyrs who suffered together; henceforth we propose to collect some shorter notices about different Martyrs, and we commence with some papers concerning ten out of

the eighty-three lay Martyrs who suffered under Elizabeth and her successors.

Of these the first is Blessed John Felton, and the account of him, which we now proceed to give, was written down by G. Farrar, a priest, who is elsewhere called a Notary Apostolic, in the year 1627 from the very words of Mistress Frances Salisbury, daughter of the Martyr, as appears from a Latin note appended to the paper.

BLESSED JOHN FELTON.

Executed at St. Paul's Churchyard in London, August 8, 1570.

John Felton, gentleman, of the family of the Feltons in Norfolk, dwelt at Barmesey [Bermondsey] Abbey, a place near to Southwark, London. When Pius V. his Bull concerning the excommunication of Queen Elizabeth was to be sent into England, Mr. Felton, being known to be a gentleman of approved resolution and virtue, was dealt withal to undertake the business of publishing it one way or other about the city of London. The danger of such an employment, which he took for an act of virtue, daunted him not a whit.

Whereupon promising his best endeavour in that behalf, he had the Bull delivered him at Calais, and after the receipt thereof came presently to London, where being assisted with one Laurence Webbe, Doctor of the Civil and Canon Laws, the five and twentieth day of May, 1570, betwixt two and three of the clock in the morning, he set it upon the gate of the Bishop of London his palace, but stayed not by it, as Sanders reporteth. He had given a copy of the Bull to a gentleman of Lincoln's Inn, a special friend of his. Now the houses and lodgings of all the Catholics about London being upon the publishing of the aforesaid Bull narrowly searched, the closet of this Inns-a-Court gentleman (for he was a known Catholic) was in his absence broken up, and the aforementioned copy found therein. The gentleman being hereupon apprehended and put to the rack, confessed of whom he had it.

Upon this were sent the next day to Mr. Felton's house the Mayor of London, the Lord Chief Justice, the two Sheriffs of London and other officers, accompanied with men and halberts to the number of five hundred, to apprehend him; whom as soon as Mr. Felton from a window saw knocking at the gate and ready to break it down, he desired them to have patience, saying he knew they came for him, and he would come down unto them. His wife, who then stood by him at the window, at those words of his, and the sight of the officers, fell down in a swoon. From his house he was carried by the Mayor and the Lord Chief Justice to the Tower, where he remained prisoner almost three months, having been in that space thrice put upon the rack, notwithstanding that at his apprehension he had confessed he was the man that had put up the Bull upon the Bishop's gate.

Being condemned, he was brought the eighth

day of August, 1570, from the Tower to Paul's Churchyard, near to the gate of the Bishop's palace, drawn upon a hurdle to the place of his execution. He hanged but a while, and was cut down and bowelled, being yet alive, insomuch that the hangman (whose name is said to have been Bull[1]) having his heart in his hand, he said once or twice, "Jesus." He was a man of stature little and of complexion black, about the age of   [2] years when he suffered.

His whole substance consisted in plate and jewels, which after his apprehension being forfeited to the Queen, were valued at three and thirty thousand pounds sterling. He used to wear a diamond on his finger worth 400*l.*, which the Lord Chief Justice having long before taken a special liking unto, would fain have bought of him, but Mr. Felton would no ways part with it. After his apprehension the Justice thought to have got it, which Mr. Felton prevented by wearing it still on his finger, and at his execution he gave it to an earl standing by (who is said to be the Earl of Sussex) to be delivered unto the Queen from him.

His wife had been maid of honour to Queen Mary, and wife to the said Queen's auditor, and by the same Queen at her death was recommended to Queen Elizabeth, whose playfellow she was in her childhood; for which cause Queen Elizabeth always bare a good affection unto her. After the execution of her second husband

---

[1] See p. 56, supra.   [2] Blank in MS.

Mr. Felton, Queen Elizabeth at her humble suit granted her liberty under her Letters Patent to keep a priest.

Hæc ex relatione Franciscæ Salisburie filiæ prædicti Joannis Feltoni.

---

2. James Layburne, the Martyr, was the head of an ancient family in Westmoreland, of Cunswick and Skelsmergh in that county. Anne, Countess of Arundel, the wife of the Venerable Philip Howard, was his first cousin, and this is a relationship of which any Catholic might well be proud. He married Bridget, daughter of Sir Ralph Bulmer, and we know that he had a child named Lucy, who was baptized in 1575,[3] and another named Susan, who became a nun at St. Monica's, for whom "the old Countess of Arundel gave eighty pounds" as a dowry for the sake of her father, "a holy Martyr."[4]

Challoner does not include James Layburne in his *Memoirs of Missionary Priests*, "because his case was different from that of all other Catholics who suffered at those times; for both at his arraignment and at his death he denied the Queen to be his lawful sovereign, as we learn from Cardinal Allen and other contemporary writers." And George Birket, a priest, writing from London at the time to Dr. Allen, expresses a doubt "whether his zeal was according to knowledge," because "he altogether denied the right and title of the Queen even in

---

[3] Paper read before the Cumberland and Westmoreland Antiquarian and Archæological Society in July, 1888, by Mr. W. Wiper, of Manchester.

[4] *Troubles*, i. p. 49.

temporals, and touched with some sharpness upon her illegitimacy." Dr. Allen was not likely to have shared in Birket's doubts, for in his *Justitia Britannica* he relates the "illustrious martyrdoms" of John Felton and John Storey, who neither of them regarded Elizabeth as the lawful Queen. These are now both of them honoured with the title of "Blessed," and so also are Thomas Plumtree and Thomas Woodhouse, who avowed the same. Sander names Felton, Storey, and Woodhouse in the paragraph in which he describes Layburne's death, and he calls them "four Martyrs." The honours of three of these have come to us from Rome, but the Cause of James Layburne has not yet been introduced. The passage from Sander is given by Bridgewater and Yepez, and the first of these two writers calls Layburne "a most glorious Martyr." And this is not to be wondered at, seeing that St. Pius V. distinctly says in his Brief to the Earls of Northumberland and Westmoreland that death in resistance to Queen Elizabeth was a death for the Church and for the Faith. Sander explains that if priests did not go so far, it was because it was not their business to interfere in matters of State.

James Layburne lost his father Nicholas and his mother Elizabeth before he came of age; and his mother in her will, dated Nov. 17, 1567, makes this curious mention [5] of her son, the future Martyr, "I have bought the wardship of my son James Layburne of my brother Thomas Warcoppe, and paid for him." From the same source we learn that "Mr. James Layburne of his liberality, for the use of the town [of Kendal] and those coming and

[5] Mr. Wiper's paper on the Layburnes.

resorting unto the same, did freely give and bestow all his clock, furnished with the sounding bell belonging to the same, from his manor-house of Cunswick, over and beside some oak trees for setting the clock upon." It is remarkable that in the *Book of Record* of Kendal, this gift is assigned to the year 1582, as at that time the donor was in prison.

Of that imprisonment a curious trace still survives. In the *Life of the Venerable Edmund Genings* by his brother, published at St. Omers in 1614, the following passage occurs: " Behold here Edmund's first entrance into the way towards Heaven, his first step towards his glorious martyrdom ... which I relate the rather because the gentleman [his Master] himself, being a priest in Brussels of Flanders, told it afterwards unto me; and this it was. The foresaid gentleman, having dealt in matters of great importance with many recusants of our country, it so fell out that one of them (whom for many respects I forbear to name) was taken and committed close prisoner in London; and because weighty matters had passed betwixt the prisoner and the foresaid gentleman touching lands and other affairs, and thereby was like to ensue some damage extraordinary to the gentleman, if some means were not wrought to advertise the prisoner how to answer to those accusations which would be laid against him; and having by himself sought all the means that he could to have access to the said prisoner, and perceiving no hope thereof without imminent danger, desisted, determining at last to send this his trusty servant [Edmund Genings], confiding more to his approved wit and lucky success in all his actions than to any probability of accomplishing the same. And (thus resolved) he sent Edmund, who was not yet seventeen years of age, to effect that enterprise which himself could not perform; and this only he imposed upon him, not directing him how it was possible to be achieved. The youth, having his charge, went with all readiness, committing his cause to God, for that 'nothing is impossible to God.' Determining therefore to do, as a trusty servant, what did lie in him, and thinking on no other means, he took up his lodging near to the prison, hoping in time to get acquaintance with the keeper or his man, and so to bring to pass his intended purpose. Neither was his hope frustrate, for within a few days he so ordered the matter, as he fell into great familiarity with the said keeper's man, who (as God would have it) had the charge of the foresaid close prisoner; and, to be brief, in a short time he dealt so judiciously in his business that he did not only procure to speak with the said prisoner, but also to have access unto him three or four times with paper and ink, to write his mind; and in the end concluded all things so effectually as if his master had been present, which was no small marvel to all those that were in danger or privy to the same."

In this passage Father John Genings neither gives the name of Edmund's master, nor of the "close prisoner" whom Edmund succeeded in visiting. Challoner tells us that Mr. Richard Sherwood, a Catholic gentleman, took him into his service in quality of his page. Where Challoner found the name does not appear, as he professes to quote only the Douay Diary and the Life by Genings, published in 1614. From the former we learn that Richard Sherwood reached the College at Rheims on the 14th of December, 1583, and he left it for England on the 2nd of August, 1584, having been ordained priest meanwhile. And further, John Genings has told us that his brother's *quondam* master was living as a priest at Brussels. Of this we have corroboration in the narrative of Thomas Sherwood, nephew and namesake of Blessed Thomas,[6] who says that his paternal uncle Richard was in Brussels when he passed through it on his way to the English College in Rome. From Father Christopher Grene[7] we also learn that Richard Sherwood was the Venerable Edmund Genings' master, and at the same time that the Martyr whom he visited was James Layburne. This information he has derived from a book which is entirely unknown to bibliographers. *A Brief Relation of the Life and Death of Mr. Edmund Jennings, Priest, martyred* 10 *Dec.* 1591, *in London: written by Mr. J. J., priest,* 1600, *and published of late by J. W. Printed with licence,* 1603. The edition of 1614 contains a letter from I. W. P., that is, John Wilson, priest, to his " Very Reverend, ever dear and worthy friend, Master I. G. P.," that is, John Genings, priest. The later edition has adopted the spelling "Geninges," and the date of the martyrdom is changed in error from December to November. From the title-page of this now extinct first edition, we learn that John Genings wrote his brother's life in 1600, and that John Wilson, priest at St. Omers, printed it in 1603. From this book Father Grene draws the substance of these two sentences. " A gentleman R. S. [Richard Sherwood] Catholic, by chance passing by Lichfield in the inn where then Edmund lived, about fourteen years old, took him for his page, and soon after converted him to the Catholic faith. Devout after his conversion, and fortunate in all

[6] Foley, *Records*, iv. p. 415.
[7] Stonyhurst MSS. *Collectanea M.* fol. 186.

business, and particularly when he was sent to speak with Mr. James Layburn, then most close prisoner in Lancaster, after a glorious Martyr."

It will be noticed that the later edition has changed Lancaster into London as the place of his imprisonment. It might be either, for Sander says that " he suffered sharp imprisonment in Carlisle, London, Lancaster, and Manchester." A similar variety of statement is to be found respecting the place of James Layburne's martyrdom. Sander's account is that " he shed his blood at last in Lancaster with the utmost cheerfulness and gentleness, all who were present at his death marvelling at his courage and patience." [8] The same is found in all the editions of Sander, but when this passage was reproduced in 1588 by Dr. Bridgewater, he substituted Manchester for Lancaster as the place of Layburne's martyrdom. Yepez translated the same passage in his *Historia Particular*, 1599, but, puzzled by the diversity, he has omitted the name of the place. In George Birket's letter to Dr. Allen, written in London about a month after the event, it is said to be at Manchester. The unknown Jesuit Father, who wrote the *Lives of the Earl and Countess of Arundel*,[9] names Lancaster, but with some hesitation. These are his words. " Mr. James Labourn was so resolute and constant therein [in the Catholic faith] that he lost his life for it, being put to a painful and ignominious death, hanged, drawn, and quartered at Lancaster, as I take it, in the year 1583, and 26th of Queen Elizabeth, for denying her supremacy in ecclesiastical affairs." In the archives [10] of the

[8] *Rise and Growth of the Anglican Schism*, translated by David Lewis, p. 317.
[9] Edited by the late Duke of Norfolk in 1857, p. 176.
[10] MSS. vol. iii. fol. 245.

Cardinal Archbishop of Westminster, there is a Latin document, the heading of which states that James Layburne was martyred at Lancaster a little before Easter, 1583. The paper is endorsed in Father Persons' hand, *De Domino Jacobo Laborno martyre anno* 1583, 22 *Martii*.

It is a mistake to suppose that this date is March, 1583-4. If it were the 26th of Elizabeth, as one of our authorities has told us, it would have been in that year; but this is entirely inconsistent with letters written at the time. George Birket dates his letter to Dr. Allen on the Friday after Low Sunday, 1583. Easter in that year was on the 31st of March Old Style, and the 10th of April New Style, and the letter was therefore written on April $\frac{12}{22}$.[11] This writer has given Dr. Allen an account of the martyrdom of Blessed William Hart, who suffered at York, March 15, 1582-3, and he adds that Layburne's death was "about the same time." And Father Persons wrote a letter[12] from Paris on the 24th of August, 1583, naming "the last six Martyrs, Kirkam [Kirkeman], Lacy, Hart, Jonson [Thompson], Thirkell, and Laborn." It is therefore clearly a mistake to say that James Layburne suffered with the Venerable James Bell and John Finch, who died at Lancaster on the 20th of April, 1584. The true date, and probably the true place, are those mentioned in the life of the Martyr's nephew George Layburne, D.D., where it is said that "the estate belonging to the family in Queen Elizabeth's days was still more reduced by the unfortunate circum-

---

[11] Its endorsement "April 24." is therefore wrong (*Douay Diaries*, p. 353).

[12] *Historia Missionis Anglicanæ, S.J.* a P. Henr. Moro. 1660, p. 124.

stances of James Layburn, who was executed at Lancaster, March 22, 1583," that is to say, 1582-3.

Father Grene came across another copy of the Latin document, which is to be seen in full in the Archives of Westminster, and he transcribed two or three sentences from it. He then broke off, and made this note: " Having copied thus far, I have found an English relation which seemeth more like to an original, and much better. It is as followeth."

Whiles he was prisoner in Carlisle, in Cumberland, and namely four months before his death, he was lodged for a season in the keeper's house, in a dampish and dark nether room, or parlour, having neither chimney nor glass windows, and although it was winter, viz., about Christmas, or a little before, yet could he have there no fire. His bedding was a thin mattress, and a poor coverlet, and very coarse sheets. His diet he had by himself, which I have seen, being coarse brown bread, small drink, and considering his calling, very homely meat; his clothing very poor and contemptible. After this he was removed unto the Castle, and there put into a very dark and loathsome cell, where he could not see to read but at one only very narrow window: in which room was also kept, besides another Catholic gentleman, two poor persons for felony, insomuch that for his own better quietness, he chose rather to lie without the chamber-door at the top of a stone stair, having nothing between him and the cold stones but a mattress, and upon

him an old coverlet and his clothes which he did
wear in the day, and so short and strait was the
place, that his bed's feet came over the top of
the stairs: and he had no other place to be
private alone but between the door and the stairs
(in the day time rolling up his bed to the wall),
where he was with the coming in and out of
others much troubled and hindered from his
devotion. In this time notwithstanding, such was
his patience, his cheerful countenance, his quietness of mind, his gladness to suffer, his comfortable persuasions to myself and to others which
came to him, his utter contempt of all worldly
things, as I have not perceived generally in any
the like. Touching the Queen, his opinion was
that she was an usurper, and unlawful, a lascivious
and very wicked person; in which opinion he was
very resolute, &c., and he declared divers reasons
which moved him thereunto. Such was his
charity and zeal, that if any came to him, he
would desire to know if they were Catholics. If
they were, he would greatly rejoice; if they were
not, he would, by all means he could, persuade
them, and that with so zealous affection as he
could not have used more to his very children,
although he were very often abused herein.
Shortly after Christmas, being about three months
before his death, he was removed from Carlisle to
Manchester, in Lancashire, and was brought hard
by his own gate, but not suffered to go in: and
passing by the doors of some of his old tenants
and neighbours, he spake to them very cheerfully

and comfortably, and so passing away, was lodged that night in Kendall, a mile or two distant from two of his manor-houses, whither his wife with one or two of his young daughters, and sundry of his former acquaintance and servants coming to him, he entertained them with very cheerful and loving communication, without any show of fear, grief, or astonishment [exhorting many to return to the Church, &c.]. The next morning, when he was to depart [a horse could hardly be found, and he prepared to make the rest of the journey on foot, which was near about fifty miles]. And so he departed from thence with no worse cheer than if he had gone to his own house at liberty. From which time till his death I cannot say ought but upon report, but what is here set down I can and do affirm of my certain knowledge, sight, and hearing. In all his opinions he would submit himself to the censures of Mr. Dr. Allen, and Father Persons, having in them a singular confidence, and he hath said to me that if he were able, he would give five hundred marks to see them and speak with them. Being demanded by a friend whether he could be contented to have his liberty procured, he answered, "Yea, so as the same might be with credit and furtherance of the Catholic cause, else not."

---

3. John Jetter is an excellent representative of the Martyrs who perished in prison. He was of a good family of Layscoffe in Suffolk, and his elder brother

George a student and priest at Rheims. Thither John followed him, but returned again in May, 1582, to England before he had received any Orders. On his return he was captured and had, for some unnamed cause, to sustain a singularly brutal persecution. Imprisoned at first in the Clink, he was moved to the Tower on the 7th of August, the prison certificate[13] which tells us so describing him as "servant unto one Mr. Higgins, scrivener, dwelling in St. Paul's Churchyard." On the 1st of September the prisoner in the Tower wrote: "John Jetter, after enduring the 'Scavenger's Daughter,' was thrown for eight days into the pit, then brought to the rack, and extremely tortured till he was nigh gone. Even when the pain was worst, and he seemed nearly dead, he called upon the name of Jesus with a wonderfully joyful countenance, and laughed at his torturers."[14] This is confirmed by other letters from the Tower,[15] but the following account[16] is more detailed.

You shall understand that one Jetter hath been monstrously racked, he showed great patience and courage. In the extremity of torment he never ceased to call upon the name of Jesus, so that Topcliffe in a great fury said, "What in the devil's name! Here is such a mumbling of Jesus Psalter as I never saw."

[13] P.R.O. *Dom. Eliz.* vol. 159, nn. 34, 35, 36. It is doubtful if he was the Jetter mentioned in *Troubles*, iii. 28.

[14] *Diarium Turris*, printed in Sander's *De Schismate*. The "Scavenger's Daughter" was an iron hoop, which, after the sufferer had clasped his knees in his arms, was fastened tight round his body, clamping it into a ball.

[15] Hart to Allen, November 15, 1582. Cf. *Troubles*, ii. p. 33.

[16] *Collectanea M*. fol. 82.

The tormented still calling upon Jesus, saying, "Sweet Jesu, have mercy upon me! With Thee is mercy, I see there is none with men."

His extremity was such, that being all in a burning heat, which proceeded of the stretching of his limbs to their highest power (unless they should have rent him in pieces), they poured upon his breast out of an ewer cold water, whether for a further torment, or *ad refocillandum*, I leave it for others to judge.

The poor man lieth in such misery that he is able to receive nothing into his body but with a quill at the hand of his keeper, who, God knoweth, looketh but slenderly to him. I think, notwithstanding this, he had been racked again, had they not feared he would die of this already done.

There is another now that far passeth the old rackmaster, Mr. Topcliffe.

This letter I had from the Tower, I thought to send you it, that you may see their countenance in such barbarous cruelty.

Yours to command,

Oct. 25.   G. B.

The bills sent in by the Lieutenant of the Tower for his expenses in keeping his prisoners, show that Jetter continued in the Tower till July 25, 1583, when he was removed to Newgate. Of his stay here Father Warford has something to tell us.

Mr. John Jetter (1585) died in prison. He has a brother, a priest, who is still living in England. Though but a youth, he showed more than a man's courage, for being bound with fetters in a most unusual manner in Newgate, his flesh nearly eaten away by the constant chafing of the irons, and his whole body swollen by the filth of the place, he was finally, after most acute sufferings, carried off by consumption, but could never be induced to abandon his faith in God, or to betray his neighbour.

I learnt these things from his brother George, the priest before mentioned, a faithful eye-witness who visited him in prison in order to encourage him, and who has himself suffered much during his many years of labour in the same cause. He has had two or three wonderfully providential escapes, and once suffered shipwreck, while flying into Ireland. Scrambling hurriedly along the cliffs, and not seeing his way in the dark, he so hurt one of his legs, that for a long time afterwards he lay sick and unknown, until I, happening to hear of it, found a remedy for his troubles. This shipwreck was caused by the bore of the Severn on the coast of South Wales.

In Newgate then he died, having been "long kept," says Mr. Penkevell, "cruelly in the Limbo of the same prison." [17] How long exactly we cannot say. Father Warford gives 1585, and Mr. Penkevell seems to imply the end of 1585 or the beginning of 1586,

[17] Infra, p. 286.

as the time of his death, but Challoner's date, 1582, is certainly wrong.

In common with the great majority of those who died in prison, Jetter's claims to the honour of true martyrdom have not yet been in any way recognized by the Holy See. The reason is evident. It is extremely difficult to prove that death in these cases was actually caused by their sufferings in prison, yet there must be evidence of death having been positively inflicted on the sufferer, before the Cause of his Beatification as a martyr can be admitted.

---

4. We have already printed many of the accounts of Martyrs, preserved to us by the diligence of Father Christopher Grene, who copied them out in full. He also sometimes wrote Latin summaries of longer stories, of which the originals were before him. The following is a translation of such a summary, the original of which was in an MS. volume entitled *Collectanea E.* p. 179. This volume is now at St. Mary's Seminary, Oscott.

VENERABLE RICHARD LANGLEY.
Suffered at York, December 1, 1586.

Richard Longley [Langley], Esq., was taken about the 21st of September in his own house by officers and a large band of soldiers, who had invested it. Among them was a certain Archdeacon (after the manner of the heretics) named Ramesdell, with some magistrates, Gayes, Vaughan, and Bethel,[18] and there were taken with

[18] See *Troubles*, iii. p. 93.

him two priests, who afterwards escaped out of prison. Mr. Longley was of such pleasant manners that he won the friendship of the gaoler, who in spite of his being a malicious heretic could scarcely refrain from tears when he was led out to execution. He was moreover of good family and fortune, yet he despised all these things, and declared before the Judges, that if he had greater riches and a hundred lives, he would willingly spend them all in that cause.

The accusation against him was that he had relieved the enemies of the Queen (for so they styled God's priests), whereupon he was urged to beg pardon for his crime of God and of the Queen. He answered with constancy that he had received them as messengers sent by God, and that therefore while he considered he had done an action pleasing to God, he could not admit that he had thereby done any injury to the Queen. This answer so irritated the Judges that they thought him unworthy of any grace, not even was the favour of an honourable burial allowed him, however much his friends begged for it. Permission was even refused for his corpse to be wrapped in the linen shroud he had prepared, and after his body had been thrown into the pit, the bodies of ten thieves were cast in over him. He died by hanging.

During the whole time of his imprisonment, he was so merry that many wondered at him, for he had always been shy at home, yet when brought out for execution he showed such alacrity of mind as to go to the scaffold even before the Sheriff, as if he were a bridegroom going to his nuptials. He suffered on December the 1st, 1586.

---

5. Our next paper is headed: "Of Nicholas Horner, that suffered martyrdom the year 1589: concerning in part the course of his life, his imprisonments, arraignment, and execution." In Old Style the date is in 1589, as it comes before Lady day, which was then the first day of the year.

VENERABLE NICHOLAS HORNER.

Executed at Smithfield March 3, 1590.

First concerning the place of his birth. It was either in the city of York or near by; his bringing up or education for the most part was in the said city, being by art or occupation a tailor.

The said good man was either his whole life, or for the most part, a good and perfect Catholic, a man of plain and just dealing, and one that always, according to such learning and skill that he had, endeavoured to draw and persuade others to embrace the said Catholic faith.

It happened in process of time for curing of a sore leg that he had, that he left York and came to London, where he had not remained long before he was apprehended and committed prisoner unto Newgate (where at that time myself in company of other Catholics was prisoner); but he was not brought into the same place where as we remained, but according to the accustomed usage of other Catholics, was kept close in the common gaol in a place alone, where through occasion of irons which were laid on his legs, and not being permitted to have his surgeon to come unto him, his said leg became incurable, so that afterwards when he had liberty of the house and was released of close imprisonment, he was enforced to have his leg cut off.

Before the time came of the cutting off of it, he always feared lest that he should give scandal by impatience when it should be done, and therefore prayed earnestly for patience against the said time. But afterwards when it was cut off it pleased God to give him such patience that he not only comforted the other Catholics that were there prisoners, but also drove the surgeons and other strangers that beheld the same into admiration. For whilst it was in cutting off, he being made to sit on a form neither bound nor holden by any violence, neither offered to stir nor used any impatient screech or cries, but wringing his hands together in very good order, often said, "Jesus, increase my pains and increase my patience."

As he afterwards reported, he did receive great comfort, not only by means that a certain good priest (to wit, Mr. Hewett, who was afterwards a

Martyr)[19] did hold his head betwixt his hands whilst it was adoing, but also by means of a certain meditation, which he purposely used at the beginning of his pain, which was of Christ bearing of His Cross to the Mount of Calvary. Which meditation at that time was so imprinted in his mind, and with such earnest apprehension, that it seemed unto him that he even saw our Saviour as He did bear His Cross on His shoulders towards the Mount of Calvary. Of all these things many other Catholics besides myself were eye and ear witnesses.

After that he had endured almost twelve months' great pains in the healing of his said leg, and after earnest suit made for him upon sureties, he was set at liberty and got him a lodging in Smithfield, where as he wrought for his living.

But he had not long enjoyed his said liberty, before Mr. Topcliffe took occasion to search his lodging, and after taking away all that he had, carried him prisoner unto Bridewell. There, to make him confess what priests were wont to come unto his said lodgings, besides many railing words and threatenings according to his accustomed tyranny, he hanged the old man up by the wrists of his arms in irons made for that purpose, leaving him in that torment until he was almost dead.

At the next Sessions he was brought forth and

---

[19] Venerable John Hewett, *alias* Weldon, *alias* Savell, was martyred at Mile End Green, October 5, 1588.

arraigned, and was condemned and adjudged to die, for no other cause nor on none other evidence, but that, as Mr. Topcliffe and Justice Young affirmed then at the bench, that he had made a jerkin for a priest. Of his own confession they had no more against him but that he had made a jerkin for a stranger, which he knew not nor was not acquainted withal.

From the Sessions House he was brought again unto Newgate, where he was kept close in the common gaol about the space of a week. The keeper, seeing his execution so long deferred, thought that he should not have been put to death at all, and therefore was contented that he should come amongst us into Justice hall; but within few days news came that he should be executed.

Whereupon he called us that were there prisoners unto him and told us, that seeing he was like to die (on condition that we would conceal it if he had lived), that he would reveal unto us a comfortable vision that he had had, to the end that when he was dead, to the comfort of others, we might declare it. Which was that after his condemnation one night, as he was walking in his foresaid close room alone, saying his prayers, happening to look aside, he did see about the head of his shadow against the wall, in proportion of a half circle, a far brighter light than that of the candle, even as bright as the light of the sun; and thinking that his sight failed him, did rub his eyes and looked again, and seeing the said light to continue, took off his kercher from his head to see whether it happened of any accident thereof; but notwithstanding the light continued all one a good space after. So that at last he began to think with himself, that it was a sign given him from God to signify a crown unto him. Therefore he immediately said, "O Lord, Thy will be my will," or to that effect, and so within a while it vanished away.

And so, within short time after, he constantly and patiently suffered martyrdom before the door of his foresaid lodging in Smithfield, having a title set on his head on the gibbet.

6. (i.) We have already [20] quoted twice from the Stonyhurst account of nine Winchester Martyrs, and the following descriptions of three martyrdoms complete the contents of the document, for the few lines which commemorate the rest add nothing to the fuller descriptions of the same scenes which we have already given above.[21] The account of John Thomas is the more valuable as he was unknown to Dr. Challoner, and has consequently been omitted altogether from the list of Martyrs whose cause of beatification has been already commenced, and who may therefore be called Venerable.

VENERABLE JAMES BIRD.

Suffered March 25, 1593.

James Bird was drawn to Bardich and there was hanged and quartered, for that he was

[20] Pp. 51, 95.   [21] Pp. 66, seq. and 83, seq.

reconciled by a Seminary priest contrary to a statute made treason in that case. Being asked of the Judge what he had to say for himself, why he should not have judgment to die, he answered that there was no just proof against him for that which he was condemned for. The like he answered at the gallows when the Sheriff bid him confess his treason. He said he had committed none, and desired the Sheriff that he might declare to the people for what cause he died, and said:

"Good people, I am here to suffer for my conscience and religion, and for that I was reconciled by a Catholic priest, which I did not confess, neither was there any proof against me concerning that matter."

Then the Sheriff bid him ask the Queen's forgiveness.

He said he never offended her.

Then he bid him pray for her.

"I beseech God," said he, "send her a long and prosperous reign to the salvation of her soul."

He was executed the 25th day of March, 1593, being on Lady Day and Easter Eve.

JOHN THOMAS.
Suffered August, 1593.

John Thomas was drawn to Bardich and there hanged and quartered, for the like offence as James Bird was. Being upon the ladder, he prayed in Latin in this sort, *Jesu, Jesu, Jesu, esto mihi Jesus.*

The Sheriff bid him pray in English, "and we will pray with thee."

Then he said, "I beseech all good Catholics to say one *Pater noster* with me."

Then the hangman brutally punched him two or three times in the breast with his feet, and bid him say, "Lord have mercy upon us," but he persevered still in his former prayers in Latin.

VENERABLE LAURENCE HUMPHREY.

Laurence Humphrey was drawn to Bardich and there hanged and quartered, for that in his sickness he said the Queen was a heretic, contrary to a statute made treason in that case. Being asked of the Judge as he stood at the bar at his arraignment, whether he did speak any such words or not, he answered, "Not as far as he could remember." His master, one Mr. Danstin, was called in as a witness hereof, unto whom the Judge said after his oath taking, "Answer to no more than I shall ask you. Whether did Laurence Humphrey speak these words or no that the Queen was a heretic?"

He answered, "I must needs say he did speak them."

The Judge caused a crucifix to be delivered unto him, which not long before had been taken from him, which he took and made obeisance thereunto and kissed it. The Judge asked him whether he did know it or not. He said he knew it very well. When the Judge had given sentence on him in the course of judgment, that is, "Thou shalt be carried to the place of execution and there thou shalt be hanged until thou be half dead, and thy bowels cut out and burned before thy face, and thy quarters set up on the four gates." Unto which in fear he answered, "And all this is but one death."

(ii.) In a letter from Father Garnet to the General of the Society, dated March 17, 1594, we have another account of the singularly interesting martyrdom of John Thomas, whose name he does not mention.[22] He first describes the trial of the Venerable James Bird, which is noteworthy. Judge Anderson's summing up to the jury was pithy, and pretty sure to bring a conviction.

"Here you have James Bird, a recusant. You know what a recusant is. A recusant refuses to go to church. No one refuses to go to church unless he has been reconciled to the Roman Church. To be reconciled to the Roman Church is treason, so you know what you have to do."

They martyred another layman there in the month of August. In the Lent Assizes he was sentenced at the same time as James for the same cause, but struck with horror at the sentence of death, he promised the Judge that he would go to church. The Judge could not recall the sentence he had given, but he ordered him not

[22] See Stonyhurst MSS. *M.* fol. 207.

to be executed, so that he might get for him the Queen's pardon. He going back to prison, and thinking of what he had done, helped probably by James Bird's exhortations, conquered the fear of death by the fear of Hell, and sent at once to the Judges, as they were leaving the town, to tell them that he repented of his cowardice, and firmly resolved to do nothing that a Catholic ought not to do. The Judges said: "Is he in such a hurry for the gallows? Let him not be afraid: if he persists, it will not be too late to hang him next Assizes." Yet when the thieves were led out to execution, he went too, carrying a winding-sheet, and presented himself to the Sheriff, who asked him what he wanted. He said he had been condemned and was come to die. "If you want to be hanged," said the Sheriff, "know that I would meet your wishes with the greatest pleasure if you were on my list, but as you are not written there, you must go." So he retired, lamenting his sin and accusing himself of his past life, for he had been a reader in the Calvinist ministry. But God did not fail him, for purged by long penance, with a large increase of merits, in the month of August he obtained what he desired.

(iii.) Another account of the Venerable Laurence Humphrey is given in Father Grene's manuscript at Oscott. It is there given under the year 1589, and Challoner assigns it to 1591. The manuscript account of the Winchester Martyrs evidently places this martyrdom in 1593.

In Hampshire a young man of eighteen years, having been a very earnest heretic, offering to dispute with Catholics, and yet being able but to read English, lighted upon Catholic books. By reading he desired conference with a priest: upon conference be became Catholic, and continued very constant and lived very virtuous. Soon after, falling into extreme sickness, in this extremity he used some words against the Queen, saying she was a heretic. This being overheard by some by chance in the house where he lay, he was forthwith taken out of his bed, committed to the gaol at Winchester for treason, fettered to one who was in prison for felonies, and there lodged among the felons on the ground. It pleased God to restore him his health. He then took upon him all the base offices of the prison, so far entreating his companion that he would stand still some two hours in a day whilst he said his prayers. The prisoners tried to persuade him to go to church; otherwise, they said, he would be hanged. He answered he would never alter his religion; and as for hanging, he prayed God to make him worthy of it.

At the next Assize, being called, the Judge showed him a pair of beads and a crucifix hanged to it, found with him. He desired to see it, which receiving, he reverently kissed it and blessed himself with fire. Said the Judge, "Thou takest that for thy God." "Not so, my lord, but for a remembrance of the death which my Saviour suffered for me."

He was indicted of high treason upon those words [that the Queen was a heretic], and being willed to confess them, he said that to his knowledge or remembrance he never spake them. But because the witnesses said he did, he would not stand in it; whereupon he had judgment to go to the place from whence he came, thence to be drawn to the place of execution, there to be half-hanged, so to be cut down, and then to be unbowelled, his head to be cut off, his body to be quartered, his head to be set on a pole, his quarters on the four gates of the city. "And all this," said he, "is but one thing." "What thing?" said the Judge. He answered, "One death."

Thereupon had away, be was beset by a rabblement of ministers, who asking him what he was, he answered, "A Catholic." They replying further, "What is a Catholic?" he said, "He that believeth that which the Catholic Church teacheth and preacheth, according to the consent of all ancient and holy Fathers." Hereupon the ministers forsook him. Being laid again in prison, he spent all that time that he had, in prayer, prostrate on the ground. When he was to be laid on the hurdle, he made the sign of the Cross, and laid him down. Going up to the gallows, the hangman reviled him, saying, "Thou holdest with the Pope, but he has brought thee to the rope, and the hangman shall have thy coat." At which words he smiled and said nothing. Thereupon the hangman gave him a blow under the ear, saying, "What! Dost thou laugh me to scorn?" And he mildly answered him, "Why strikest thou me? I have given thee no such occasion." His words scarce ended, the hangman turned the ladder, and so he happily obtained his wished for glorious martyrdom.

7. A note in the margin of the following undated Life of the Venerable James Duckett, tells us that it was written by his son, a Carthusian. This was John Duckett, Prior of the Convent of Sheen Anglorum at Nieuport from 1644 till 1647.[23]

THE PERSECUTION AND MARTYRDOM OF JAMES DUCKETT.

Executed at Tyburn, April 19, 1602.

James Duckett was son to N. Duckett of Gilfortrigg, in Shelsmore [Skelsmergh], in the county of Westmoreland. Mr. James Layborn, Lord of Shelsmore, and after[wards] a glorious Martyr, was his godfather in Baptism.[24] This James Duckett, after some years passed in studies, being a younger brother, was bound prentice in London, where he lived as he had been brought up, an heretic.

It happened he was visited by Peter Mauson,

[23] *The London Charterhouse.* By Dom Lawrence Hendriks, p. 317.

[24] James Layburne's aunt Catherine married Richard Duckett of Grayrigg, and his niece Elizabeth married Anthony Duckett of the same place.

a Catholic and countryman of his, who conversing familiarly one with the other, Peter Mauson (as God would have it), called him heretic.

"What is that," saith James Duckett.

"Marry," replieth Peter Mauson, "if thou wilt read such books as I shall give thee, thou shalt soon learn."

He accepts of his offer, and Peter brings him *The Foundation of the Catholic Religion*.[25] This book he having well perused, began to stagger in his religion, and he, who before being a Puritan was so zealous that he would have heard two or three sermons on a day, now having in some sort discovered their falsehood and bad doctrine, began to withdraw himself from their church and conventicles, till at last he left both their sermons and their service. This his change was soon perceived, by those chiefly with whom he lived; so that they began to observe his actions, and to discover the cause of this his change, which they soon found out.

---

[25] This book must be "*The Firme Foundation of Catholike Religion against the Bottomless pitt of heresies*. . . Compyled by John Caumont of Champanye, and translated out of Frenche into Englishe by John Pauncefoot the elder, Esquire, in the time of his banishment." No date, or place of publication. [Communicated by Mr. Joseph Gillow, who has kindly supplied much valuable information about the books hereafter to be mentioned.] The date of the Antwerp licence, viz., 1590, has been assumed to be the date of the publication of this book; but the exigencies of our story seem to point to some time before 1587 as the time when Duckett saw it. This seems therefore to show that there was an earlier edition privately printed in England. Pauncefoot and his son were in exile in 1585.

For he, whilst he kept his master's shop, was seen to read the foresaid book, which he endeavoured to conceal, hiding it under a cushion where he sat. This book while he was called away they got, and carried to one Goodacre,[26] Minister of St. Edmund's in Lombard Street. James Duckett was sent for and examined why he went no more to church. He said he neither did nor would go to church until he had better satisfaction in their religion than he could give them. Upon this answer he was committed to Bridewell, from whence after some time he was set free by his master's means.

Not long after, he was called again in question for not going to their church, and was sent to the Counter, another prison in London. From thence also his master delivered him; but durst not keep him any longer, lest that he himself should incur thereby some danger or obloquy. Whereupon James Duckett was forced to compound and buy out his apprenticeship.

Having thus cast off his temporal service and left his master, he found more convenient time and free access to those who could instruct him in the true service of his heavenly master. So that within two months (for as yet he was no Catholic) to his great comfort he was made a member of the Catholic Church by Mr. Weekes, a venerable priest and prisoner in the Gatehouse.

Two or three years he lived a single life with

[26] Thomas Gatacre was Rector from June 21, 1573, till June, 1593 (Newcourt, *Repertorium*, i. p. 344).

no little zeal and fervour of religion, and then he took to wife Anne Hart, widow to one Cooper. Their best means and remedies they had to begin and maintain their new family was what their own hands, labours and industry could bring in. The riches and only treasure they made account of was that they were both members of God's Church, and therefore he, to show himself in some sort grateful for so great a blessing and favour from Almighty God, offered up his best labours in exercising a poor tailor's trade, wherein his chief work was to accommodate priests and those who laboured for the conversion of souls, with garments fit for their necessities, to make and mend up vestments, to prepare church stuff and all necessaries for the altar.

This only is my relation as far as I remember, for I have seen him busied with such-like work.[27]

And that he yet further might be an instrument to help and set forward the common good, he resolved to deal and trade in books, wherewith he might furnish Catholics, as well for their own comfort and devotion as for the satisfaction and instruction of others, and thereby both benefit himself and them. So that the Divine Goodness (as it seems), out of His sweet Providence had ordained and pointed him out for this course and estate of life wherein He meant to make a full trial of this His servant.

For he had not long laboured in this kind, but that he was discovered and his house searched,

[27] This is added in the margin of the MS.

where they found a whole impression of *Our Lady's Psalter*[28] with pictures of the Rosary, together with the press. He was taken with the two printers and committed prisoner to the Clink on St. Thomas his day before Christmas, and before the Sessions he was removed to Newgate, where he continued prisoner two full years. And then some friends being bound for his appearance, he got his liberty, which he enjoyed but for a short time.

For some ten weeks after there comes a young gentleman to his house who called himself Flood, being, as he said, well acquainted with one Captain Bellice, a familiar friend of James Duckett's.[29] This gentleman seemed to pretend something that he durst not be seen at his own lodging, and therefore desired earnestly a chamber for one night. But the chambers being taken up he was content to sit by a fire in the kitchen; and all this was plotted to have taken a priest. For about midnight Sir William Sherrick, having a warrant from the Earl of Essex, comes with a constable and divers others and besets the house, where he found none he could suspect; only, for a show, he took the

[28] *The Rosary of our Ladie*, otherwise called *Our Ladie's Psalter*, &c., was printed at Antwerp in 1600, with cuts by John Collaert. The Preface is signed T. W. P. [Thomas Worthington, Priest]. Duckett's edition was evidently much earlier. There were many such works, one by I. M. [John Mitchell?], a Carthusian at Bruges, in 1576; others by John Fenn, and Father H. Garnet in [1580?] and 1598 (Gillow, *Bib. Dict.* vol. ii. p. 245, no. 7, p. 343, no. 5).

[29] "My father's," erased.

gentleman away with him, as though he had him in suspicion, and some *Jesus Psalters* and such little books of devotion.

Then he goes to my Lord of Essex to know what should be done, and from him he speedily returns with a warrant to commit James Duckett, who in the meantime was conveyed out of a back door without the least notice of those that stood to watch. Then presently those who before were bound for his appearance were called for, so that he was forced to render himself that night, to keep them harmless, and was committed to the Clink.

His wife being then great with child and near her time, in great perplexity went to solicit for his liberty first to Essex House, after to Whitehall, and so from place to place, the Earl of Essex being still gone before. At last she finds him returned home, presents her petition and expects so long for an answer till she began to faint and [fret]. Wherefore she was forced to return home, led between two women, as a wife comfortless for her husband's imprisonment, and there within two hours she fell in labour. These two women, heretics and strangers to her, seeing so pitiful a spectacle, made report to the Earl of Essex of her case, and in such a manner that they made him relent; whereupon he presently sent his warrant to discharge her husband, and caused her maid, who was detained from her in the constable's custody, [to return] [30] whilst she lay in her labour.

[30] Wanting in MS.

After this James Duckett having some Latin and English Primers[31] put out to binding, and they being discovered by the bookbinder's wife to be his, he was committed by Dr. Stannap,[32] the Bishop's Chancellor, to Newgate close prisoner on the top of the leads. In the meantime he had caused the *Manual* to be printed, and the *Second Birth* (or *Life*) *of St. John Evangelist. Mulier, ecce filius tuus*,[33] which being found and taken to be his, he was sent down into Limbos, a dark and dismal dungeon (through which the filth of the city ran with no small stench).[34]

There he had no light but when, at one time of the day, the sun shined in at two augur holes upon a white napkin, which he hung up for the same purpose. But the damp of the place made this napkin quite black, as it did the rest of his linen; which when his wife received from the keeper, and saw how foul the place had made them, she conceived (as she had reason) he needs must be ill. To increase her fears, it was told her that another, who was shut up in an adjoining

---

[31] This may have been, *The Primer or Office of the Blessed Virgin Marie, in Latin and English*. Antwerp, Arnold Conings, 1599. 12mo.

[32] Sir Edward Stanhope, LL.D., Chancellor to the Bishop of London in 1578, died in 1608 (Cooper, *Ath. Cantab*. i. p. 470).

[33] The second of these books is unknown even to such an authority as Mr. Gillow, who however aptly suggests that the *Manual* was *A Manuall of Praiers, gathered out of many famous and good Authors . . . Calice*, 1599, 16mo. This may have been the edition printed by Duckett, "Calice" being substituted for London as a blind, or he may have reprinted it.

[34] On the margin opposite this sentence: "I doubt of it, though I have heard it said."

dungeon after him, was already dead, through the filth and horror of the place. Wherefore to ease her mind she made means that she might at least have a sight of him, which was granted her. So that he, having a list[35] about his neck to bear up his fetters which well loaded him, came up to her smiling with a merry and full countenance, while she with a heavy heart stood weeping, thinking she should have seen in him the picture of a dead man, far from that cheerful countenance he brought with him.

From this place also after some time he was released by means of friends, two knights of the [shire] being bound for him. About half a year after they were both summoned to appear before the foresaid Dr. Stannap, concerning the christening of their youngest daughter Barbara.

The manuscript in the Archives of Westminster here ends abruptly, but Bishop Challoner, who had a copy of this story before him, quotes from it the following account of Venerable James Duckett's martyrdom.

Peter Bullock, a bookbinder, after he had been condemned a twelvemonth, in hope (as many imagined) of obtaining his pardon, informed Lord Chief Justice Popham, that James Duckett had twenty-five of [Father Southwell's] *Supplication to the Queen*,[36] and had published them.

[35] This seems to mean that he had a collar of folded or padded list to prevent the irons from wearing the flesh.
[36] This edition was printed early in 1602.

Upon this his house was searched at midnight, but no such book found nor sign thereof; yet they found the whole impression of *Mount Calvary*,[37] and some other Catholic books. However, he was apprehended and carried to Newgate, it being the 4th of March.

At the next Sessions he was called to the bar, and Mr. Watkinson (a virtuous and worthy priest, who newly was come into England and taken) was also brought in. James Duckett perceiving him to look pale, and thinking it might be through fear (which indeed was only his sickness), began in his best manner to encourage him. Which Popham understanding (Mr. Watkinson being first arraigned), he calls out, "Duckett, now speak for thyself."

Then evidence being called in, the same Peter Bullock accused him that he had some of Father Southwell's *Supplication to the Queen*, which he denied, having had none of them. Bullock also avouched that he had bound for him divers Catholic books, and amongst the rest Bristow's *Motives*,[38] which he acknowledged. The jury being called and hearing what was alleged against him by one only witness, went out, and

---

[37] *Mount of Calvarie*, by Anthony de Guevara, translated out of Spanish into English. A quarto edition of this was published in London in two parts, the first in 1595, the second in 1597. But neither of these can be Duckett's edition, printed, seized, and entirely destroyed in 1602.

[38] Gillow, *Bib. Dict.* The second edition was printed in 1599, with Antwerp on the title-page, but as Duckett had the book in sheets, he may have printed another edition.

having consulted returned again and found him not guilty. Judge Popham, who was bloodily bent against him, stood up and bid them consider well of what they did, for that Duckett had Bristow's *Motives* bound for him, upon whose words they went out again, and soon returning, declared him guilty of felony. The jury's verdict being given, sentence of death was pronounced against him, as also against the three priests, Mr. Page, Mr. Tichburn, and Mr. Watkinson.

On Monday morning, the day designed for his death, his wife came to speak with him, which she could not without tears. He bid her be of good comfort, and said his death was no more to him than to drink off the caudle which stood there ready for him. "If I were made," said he, "the Queen's secretary or treasurer, you would not weep; do but keep yourself God's servant, and in the unity of God's Church, and I shall be able to do you more good, being now to go to the King of kings. As you love me do not grudge, that the good men [the three priests] are reprieved and not I.[39] For I take it for a great favour from Almighty God, that I am placed amongst the thieves, as He Himself my Lord and Master was."

As he was carried towards the place of execution, in the way his wife called for a pint of wine to drink to him. He drank and desired her to

[39] The Venerable Martyrs, Thomas Tichburn, Robert Watkinson, and Francis Page, S.J., were executed April 20, 1602, the day after the Venerable James Duckett's martyrdom.

drink to Peter Bullock and freely to forgive him, for he, after all his hopes, was in the self-same cart carried also to execution. Being come to the place, and both Peter and he standing up in the cart,

"Peter," said he, "thou art the cause of my coming hither, as God and thyself knowest, for which I from my heart forgive thee. And that the world and all here may witness that I die in charity with thee"—he kissed him, both having the ropes about their necks.

Then he said to him, "Thy life and mine are not long, wilt thou promise me one thing? If thou wilt, speak. Wilt thou die, as I die, a Catholic?"

Bullock replied he would die as a Christian should do, and so the cart was drawn from under them.

CHAPTER XII.

FATHER WARFORD'S RECOLLECTIONS.

DOCUMENT.

Father W. Warford's Relation of Martyrs (Stonyhurst MSS. *Collectanea M*. fol. 131—143). Latin.

Father William Warford was a native of Bristol, and, though only thirteen when sent to Oxford in 1574, he shows throughout his narrative that he possessed much knowledge of Somersetshire and its inhabitants. On June 13, 1576, he became Scholar of Trinity, and Fellow two years later, and was made Master of Arts in 1582. That same year he resolved to become a Catholic, and accordingly left the University and went to Rheims; then making up his mind to become a priest, he was sent to study theology at Rome.

The confidential account of him sent from Rheims to the Rector of the Seminary at Rome is a very favourable one: "The second is named Warford, a man most excellently instructed in Greek and Latin literature, and endowed with capacity for any branch of study. We have not his like. I recommend him most earnestly to your Paternity on account of the very special hope I entertain in his regard, that he may turn out not only a learned scholar, but also a good and holy man. Indeed, I have no doubt at all but that he will prove a man after your own heart."[1]

His career in the Seminaries of Rome and Valladolid justified the high opinion early formed about him; and his ministry in England, whither he returned in 1591, is described as fruitful in good work.[2] On May 23, 1594, he entered the Novitiate of the Society of Jesus at Sant' Andrea in Rome, and was afterwards appointed English Penitentiary at St. Peter's, during which period he wrote the following reminiscences. In 1599 he was sent to Spain, was professed of the four vows in 1607, and died the year following at Valladolid at the comparatively early age of forty-eight.

A note at the end of the document informs us that Father Persons has given it the following heading:—

FATHER WILLIAM WARFORD'S RELATION ABOUT MARTYRS.

Mr. John Nelson, priest (1578),[3] was the next after Mr. Cuthbert Maine who suffered for the faith. His friends relate that he was accustomed to say, that no effectual help would be given to the cause of the faith in England, unless it could be restored by the same methods as those by which it was planted, that is, by the blood of the Martyrs. Though many bright hopes sprang up in different quarters, he declared that he remained always strongly inclined to that opinion.

---

[1] Dr. Barret to Father Agazzari. August 11, 1583 (*Douay Diaries*, p. 330).

[2] Foley, *Records*, vol. ii. p. 574.

[3] Blessed John Nelson suffered at Tyburn, February 3, 1577-8.

Mr. Thomas Ford (1582),[4] priest and Bachelor in Divinity, was educated at Oxford. He was a Fellow of Trinity, and the colleague of Dr. Blackwell, the archpriest. A man of the most straightforward character, of singular modesty, and most fervent zeal. I have heard the following among other stories of him.

In one of the usual theological disputations of his College, a fellow-master of Ford's tried to please the company by abusing the Pope as is their fashion. When the defendant had finished, Ford said resolutely, "I cannot submit to such insulting language towards so good and holy a Father," and accordingly commenced to argue.

For this and other similar reasons, being unable to repress the warmth of his feelings, he at length abandoned the advantages of the University, and had to leave the country, or shall I not rather say, was freely drawn abroad to seek the priesthood. On his return from the Seminaries he lived mostly in Oxfordshire, where, although his residence was known to many in his College, yet on account of his unassuming conduct he was never informed against until he was apprehended with Father Campion. On that occasion he wanted to give himself up to save Campion, but the latter altogether refused. He was above the average height, as I have heard, and wore a reddish beard.

[4] Blessed Thomas Ford suffered at Tyburn, May 28, 1582. He took his degree in Divinity in 1574 at Douay (*Diaries*, p. 273). He incepted as Master of Arts at Oxford, July 14, 1567 (*Oxford Register*, Boase, I. 251).

William Hart,[5] priest (1583), died quite young. He was born at Wells in Somersetshire, and had as godfather Father William Good, who was for many years Confessor of the English College in Rome, and who afterwards died at an advanced age in the Neapolitan Province. Father Good had much to tell of his godson's noble qualities, and kept many of his spiritual letters[6] written in prison just before his martyrdom, worthy of so bright and apostolic a spirit. For he was called by his friends and spiritual children the Apostle of York, on account of his successful labours, his remarkable spirit of prayer, and the charm of his sermons and letters.[7]

Mr. James Fenn,[8] of Somersetshire (1584), was a man of much virtue and learning, with a great disesteem of himself. It was remarked of him that he had so great a dislike for fine clothes, that even when required for a disguise, he could not be persuaded to wear them. He was apprehended on the highway near the house of Giles Bernard, a Catholic, and a man of civic rank, who also suffered much because he was found near his

---

[5] Blessed William Hart suffered at York, March 15, 1583.

[6] These are probably the nine letters of which Latin translations are printed in Father Bridgewater's *Concertatio*, fol. 105. Another translation of them, including one to his mother, is in the Westminster Archives, vol. iii. p. 229.

[7] Father Warford next gives the account of the Venerable John Bodey and John Slade, quoted above, p. 56.

[8] Venerable James Fenn suffered at Tyburn, February 12, 1584.

house, which was not far from that of the Sydenhams.

Thomas Hemerford[9] took the degree of Bachelor in Civil Law at Hart Hall in Oxford; and held a disputation with Isaac Glisson, of Bristol, a student of the same Hall as his opponent. After he was hanged at Tyburn, being mutilated in the usual manner while still alive, he was seized with such an agony of pain that the vehemence of his cries was much noted.

His friends (as Mr. Thomas Jones, now in Spain) have many stories of him. Thus Mr. Thornell has often told me that he was so careful in regard to chastity, that as often as any troublesome carnal thought occurred to him, he at once retired to some secret place, and gave himself a discipline, until, warned by his confessor, he was obliged to treat himself less rigorously. He was a short man with a dark beard, severe of look, but of a sweet disposition, and very pleasant and exemplary in conversation.

[*Note by Father Grene.*—Mr. Edmund Thornell died at Rome in 1617. He was admitted into the College at Rome, May 16, 1581, at the same time as the Martyr, Thomas Hemerford, and lived with him for two years.]

---

[9] The Venerable Thomas Hemerford suffered at Tyburn, February 12, 1584. The *Oxford Register* (II. iii. 53) says that he was admitted B.C.L. 30 June, 1575, but gives Christ Church as his College.

Mr. James Lomax[10] died in prison. His health was delicate, on which account he was sent from Rome before he had completed the full time of studies. Educated at Cambridge, he was reputed to know Greek better than most. He preached well and with unction. I heard him in the year 1583 at Rheims. Rather short, with a long face, inclining to paleness. He had no beard.

Mr. Edward Stransam[11] (1586) was born at Oxford of good, honest Catholic parents, in the parish of St. Mary Magdalen, near the north gate, which is called Bocardo, and educated in the College of St. John the Baptist, where he was made Bachelor (or Master) of Arts. Thence he passed over to Rheims, where, being gifted by nature with a good wit and the faculties requisite for preaching, he made much progress in that art, and was greatly famed for his sermons when he returned to England.

He there attached himself to Father Gaspar Heywood, with whom he lived on very intimate terms, and after awhile returned to Rheims with quite a crowd of Oxford students, twelve or

[10] The exact date and place of his death are uncertain. Dr. Barret wrote to Father Agazzari, February 21, 1584: "Pater Lumaxius in carcere est mortuus præclarus confessor" (Stonyhurst MSS. *Anglia*, vi. n. 3). As sufficient proof is not yet forthcoming that his death was *caused* by the privations of prison life, the title of Venerable has not yet been awarded him.

[11] Venerable Edward Strancham suffered at Tyburn, January 21, 1586. Father Warford's account of John Jetter has been already given in chapter xi. p. 224. It would otherwise have come before the account of Strancham, who, by the way, was B.A. only (1576), not M.A.

fourteen of whom he conducted into Catholic countries, of whom five or six were from Trinity College. He remained some time at Rheims with Allen, who in 1583 was still living there, and had much affection for him. Afterwards he returned to England, and laboured strenuously, chiefly in London and among the upper class.[12] At length, through the frequency and openness of his visits to the prisons, in order to console and assist the Catholics, he was apprehended in London and brought to trial. He defended himself with such applause, so ingeniously and eloquently, against the insidious questions of the pleader and the Judges, that even the heretics admired him.

He generally wore a hair-shirt, and though he frequently suffered from ill-health, he was ever unwilling to be without this provocative of piety and chastity, but kept it with him and resumed it as soon as he was well again.

He often escaped in a wonderful manner, having great presence of mind. I heard once from himself that returning to the house of a Catholic, where he mostly lodged, he found it surrounded by the Queen's officers, who had come to take him, and when he found that he could not fly without being seen, he feigned to be going in

[12] The Douay Diaries (p. 197) give July 22, 1583, as the date of his return, and mention the names of ten of his companions. The Trinity men were John Atkins, William Morgan, John and Walter Oven, and Richard Blount. From his very interesting examination (P.R.O. *Dom. Eliz.* vol. 180, n. 22) it further appears that he had stayed in Paris and thereabouts about a year and a half, and returned in July, 1585. His arrest followed much sooner than Father Warford seems to have thought, viz., after a fortnight.

another direction, but being confused and not noticing the way, he fell into a deep swamp, and having extricated himself with difficulty, he was compelled by that band of persecutors to return and give an account of himself. Having his breviary with him, he wrapped it in a small handkerchief, in order that it might not betray him, and gave it to one of the simplest standing at the door, to hold. God so disposing, the man returned it to him without any suspicion, and by his cautious answers and presence of mind he safely evaded the examination of the Justice at the head of the searching party. He had more than one such escape afterwards.

He was very zealous in gaining souls, discreet in daily life, most exact in speech, and more than commonly learned. He was tall and dark, slightly but becomingly bearded, his head small, and very emaciated in person.

Some good Catholics relate that once when Father John Cornelius was exorcising a possessed person, the devil, seeming to rejoice in the death of such a man, said (and his word turned out to be true): "You, too, shall shortly follow Stransam. Oh, how sweet his bowels smelt when they were burning at Tyburn. Ah, what a scent it was!"

The Martyr was wont to say that he would like to go to Italy (though in fact he never went) for many reasons; ranking, next after his desire to visit the tombs of the Apostles, a wish to see the place and examine with his own eyes the rails, whence Theodosius was turned away by Blessed

Ambrose. In the writings of that holy Doctor, he took great delight, and loved especially his greatness of mind, a greatness which was seen renewed in Stransam, while withstanding with his life the Queen of England.

Writing to him afterwards, I gave him a description of Milan and its Cathedral, with which he was so charmed, that, writing to me about it, he confessed that nothing had ever given him so much pleasure, and that he esteemed it a great favour. These, his last letters, are still in my possession in England.

He was at that time sick unto death in Paris with a slow fever and consumption, insomuch that he took nothing but asses' milk, yet he was preserved to give God greater glory, and to receive the crown of martyrdom. He used to say his Office with great attention and reverence. Thus, once in England, where frequently there was no convenience for saying it otherwise, a certain priest, a friend of his, said it lying in bed, whereupon he was severely scolded by Stransam, who said that such a fault was not to be tolerated in a priest. Strict, however, as he was in finding fault, he was also full of tact. He has still an elder brother alive,[13] who is a priest now labouring in the vineyard, a worthy and unassuming man.[14]

[13] The Douay Diaries make mention of three Stranchams, Thomas, ordained in 1578, Edward, our Martyr, ordained in 1580, and George, ordained in 1585.
[14] Father Warford next describes the martyrdom of the Venerable William Marsden and Robert Anderton, which we have given above, p. 66.

Mr. Francis Ingleby [15] (1586). He was born of a good family, I think, in the county of York, and studied law in London. I saw him in 1583, when he had made a good start in his profession, and heard him commenting with great discretion, but very fluently, on the frauds practised by the Earl of Leicester in perverting the laws of the country. He studied at Rheims scholastic theology and at the same time cases of conscience.

He was arrested, as I have repeatedly heard, in this manner. On a certain day he left York on foot and in the dress of a poor man without a cloak, and was courteously accompanied beyond the gates by a certain Catholic of that city.[16] The gentleman, though intending to return at once, stayed for a few moments' conversation with the priest on an open spot, which, unknown to the priest, was overlooked by the windows of the Bishop's Palace. It happened that two chaplains of the pseudo-bishop idly talking there espied them, and noticed that the Catholic as he was taking leave, frequently uncovered to Ingleby, and showed him, while saying good-bye, greater marks of respect than were fitting towards a common person meanly dressed. They ran therefore and made inquiries, and finding he was a priest, they apprehended him, and after casting him into prison delivered him to death.

Great was the loss to York, for he was most

---

[15] Venerable Francis Ingleby was martyred at York, June 3, 1586.

[16] This story is also told by Father Grene, *infra*, p. 305.

highly esteemed by all Catholics [17] on account of his great zeal for souls, and especially for his remarkable prudence. He bore himself most constantly and bravely, and left all good Catholics sore afflicted at his loss. They have preserved the memory of many of his sayings and doings, which are indeed worthy of note, though I cannot now recall them in detail.

He was a short man but well made, and seemed a man of thirty-five years of age or thereabouts. He was of a light complexion, wore a chestnut beard, and had a slight cast in his eyes. In mind he was quick and piercing, ready and facile in speech, of aspect grave and austere, and earnest and assiduous in action.

Mr. John Adams,[18] priest, at first a Calvinist minister, afterwards a Catholic Martyr. I saw him at Rheims, when he had returned from England with Mr. Jessop, who was afterwards a distinguished confessor, and brought with him some boys of the greatest promise, including Father Henry Tichborne, S.J., and Father Mayo, who now labour in England. From Rheims he returned after a few months back to England, where he was apprehended and put to death. He is said to have laboured very strenuously, especially at Winchester and in Hampshire, where

---

[17] He was one of the priests received by the "Pearl of York," the Venerable Margaret Clithero (*Troubles*, iii. p. 411).

[18] The Venerable John Adams suffered at Tyburn, October 8, 1586. The visit to Rheims was in July, 1583 (*Douay Diaries* p. 196).

he helped many, especially of the poorer classes. He appeared to me to be about forty years of age, of average height, with a dark beard, a sprightly look and black eyes. He was a good conversationalist, very straightforward, very pious and pre-eminently a man of hard work.

Mr. Stephen Rowsam. I knew him at Oxford about the year 1578, where he was minister of the parish of St. Mary's, the University Church. Soon afterwards he went to Rheims, and being, as it seemed, naturally somewhat fearful, no sooner did he find himself in safety on the French coast after his flight, than he cast himself, it is said, on his knees, gave thanks and offered himself to God with great earnestness. Then he told his companions, that now, provided he might live as a good Catholic, he cared not if henceforth he had to earn his daily bread at the plough tail.

Being a person easy to recognize on account of a certain twist in the neck (though not a very ugly one), and an inequality of his shoulders, he was apprehended on his return to England and confined in the Tower of London, whence he was led out to execution.[19]

The following story, which would seem to be miraculous, is related of him by many of his friends. Once as he was saying Mass in the

---

[19] This is not correct. The Venerable Stephen Rousham was banished in 1585, and returning to continue his apostolic labours, he suffered martyrdom at Gloucester in March, 1587. The day is uncertain. In 1572 he was a commoner at Oriel.

Church of St. Stephen at Rheims, not long after his ordination, a large spider, crawling on the dirty roof, fell into the chalice as he uncovered it to adore the Precious Blood. He was sorely disturbed and quite at a loss what to do. At last his simplicity, swayed by his great piety and devotion to the Blessed Sacrament, won the day. Having silently invoked the Divine assistance and commended himself in spirit to the mercy of Christ, he bravely swallowed the spider together with the Precious Blood, and suffered no hurt thereby. Nay, he told his friends, chief among whom was Mr. Lewkner, a grave man who told me all this, that he never received anything with more zest, and that he was from that time forward wonderfully confirmed in his faith in the most Holy Sacrament. Although he was not sure that the poisonous drink would have caused his death, he had made up his mind to die rather than allow the Precious Blood to be exposed to disrespect.

He was a man of a pleasant and manly countenance, with a brown beard, and a full and sweet voice. He was low in stature, and (as I have said) a little crooked. He was much devoted to prayer and piety.

Mr. Thomas Pilchard[20] (1587). I knew him at Oxford as Fellow of Balliol and Master of Arts

---

[20] Venerable Thomas Pilchard suffered at Dorchester, March 21, 1587. He matriculated at Balliol, 1574 or 1575, æt. 18.

[1579]. He went from Oxford to Rheims and was made priest, and here again I was intimate with him in the year 1583. He gave great edification by the remarkable sobriety of his demeanour, his candour and sparing talk, and above all, his piety and devotion in saying Mass.

He returned to the English Mission, where he bore himself in so praiseworthy a manner, that there was not a priest in the whole West of England who, to my knowledge, was his equal in virtue. Certainly to this day his memory is in benediction throughout all that country, where he was universally held for something more than a Seminarist, having the reputation of being a true apostle. Many were the souls he gained to God. Whether at home, on a journey, or in prison, he was always at work and never excused himself from preaching and administering the sacraments. An unwearied chastiser of his own body, he was accustomed to sleep on the ground even in prison and in fetters, and when he had a bed to sleep on if he chose. Accordingly, he was glad to give it up to his fellow-prisoners, and by such acts he brought more to God when in prison than when free.

He was imprisoned at Dorchester, whither there ran to him from every side those who were solicitous about their souls. All were helped, all consoled, no one left him without receiving a lesson in some virtue or other. The very thieves were attracted and converted by his meekness, and though in close imprisonment, he was accounted the oracle of the whole county. His prudence and constancy frustrated all the stratagems of the gaolers.

When he had lived a good while in prison, his fervour remaining unchecked by any of the dangers that beset him, the magistrates decided to bring him to trial, and he was condemned to death. But as sentences of this sort were rare in that place, an executioner could hardly be found to carry it out, until at length a cook, or rather a butcher, was hired at a great cost, to take it in hand.

But after the rope was cut, and the priest being still alive stood on his feet under the scaffold, the fellow held back, either struck with fear or stupefied by some supernatural agency. At length compelled by the cries of the officials to finish his work, he drove his knife, hardly knowing what he did, into the belly of the priest, and leaving it there he again hung back horror-stricken, whereat all the spectators groaned and murmured. This lasted so long that Mr. Pilchard coming completely to himself and finding himself naked and horribly wounded, inclining his head to the Sheriff who was present, said to him, "Is this then your justice, Mr. Sheriff?"

On his saying this, the executioner taking fresh courage, rushed on him, and throwing him to the ground laid open his belly and brutally tore out his entrails to the horror of the spectators, and so finally completed his cruel task.

On the scaffold before being hanged, Mr.

Pilchard said several things which showed his great piety, and it was remarked by all the Catholics of that county, that of those who had part in his death, there were none but came to a bad end, such as for instance befell the cook and the greater part of the jury almost immediately afterwards. Others were overtaken by great misfortunes, the Sheriff, for example, from being a rich and powerful man died miserably within two years, having fallen into great adversity.

Among those who were put to death with our Martyr, there were some whom he converted to the faith. One of them was a young man of great bodily strength, who had been a notorious robber. Mr. Pilchard, the night before, reconciled him to the Church, and brought him to an excellent confession of his sins, and he fearlessly professed himself a Catholic on the scaffold.

Mr. Jessop in the prison and elsewhere was Mr. Pilchard's most faithful companion, and his chief instrument in helping souls. Though he was a man well skilled in secular business, he devoted himself so energetically to gain souls that he astonished every one. Mr. Pilchard was taken in London, being recognized in Fleet Street by an acquaintance who had known him very well some years before at Oxford; for he was a person easily recognized owing to a decided squint, though his eyes were nevertheless not without a charm. At this sight Jessop was unable to conceal his grief, and, being known to have kept Mr. Pilchard's company elsewhere, was also cast into prison.

There is a noteworthy story told in this connection. Whilst he was led along on horseback with his hands tied behind him, the officers on entering a town wished for his sake to put a cloak over his shoulders, but he shook it off and said, "I am not ashamed of these fetters, nor is it right to drag me secretly like a thief; I wish all men to know that I am held in bonds on account of the Catholic religion."

Jessop, then, was used to minister in all things to Mr. Pilchard, whom he loved most devotedly and venerated because of his eminent virtues, and therefore when his friend was taken from him by death he thought his life a burden, and often grieved that it had not been his lot to meet death in company with so great a servant of God; indeed I know not why he was never tried for his life.

At length he died in prison from grief or the filth of the place, though he was a man in the flower of his age, being less than forty years old. In his will he gave special directions that his body should not be buried in a graveyard, but as closely as possible to the body of Pilchard in the fields by the place of his execution. When his friends and his wife asked him to consult in this matter the honour of his family, and not to make light of consecrated ground, he replied that all graveyards were now profaned by the bodies of heretics, and that it could not but be, that the blood and members of so great a Martyr would abundantly sanctify the place he had chosen. He therefore begged that nothing more might be said on that subject, for that he would die the more willingly if he knew for certain that he should be buried with his Father, Mr. Pilchard. It was, therefore, so done, but at night so as not to be publicly known.

I learnt all these things from his sister and other relations of his, whom I know to be persons most worthy of credit. They also informed me as an indisputable fact that Dorchester and the whole surrounding country was stricken with such terrible storms and terrified with such horrible and unusual lightnings, until the limbs of the Martyr were taken down from the walls, where they had been hung as usual, that the like had never been heard of. Thus, too, when Father John Cornelius, who had been admitted into the Society of Jesus not long before his apprehension, was condemned to death for the same cause, the leading men of the town came to the Judges, and begged that the quarters of this priest might not be fixed on the walls according to custom, because it was known for certain that tempests had of late years occurred on account of the exposure of Mr. Pilchard's body, causing great loss to many, and especially destructive to the harvest.

Whilst I was living in England less than six years ago, it happened that a joiner in that same town named Pike[21] was put on his trial for having spoken in prison too freely in favour of the Catholic religion. The bloody question about the Pope's supremacy was put to him, and he frankly confessed that he maintained the authority of the Roman See, for which he was condemned to die a traitor's death.

When they asked him, as is their wont, whether to save his life and his family he would recant, he boldly replied that it did not become a son of Mr. Pilchard to do so.

"Did that traitor, then, pervert you?" asked the Judge.

"That holy priest of God and true Martyr of Christ," he replied, "taught me the truth of the Catholic faith."

Asked where he first met him, "It was on a journey," said he, "returning from this city."

Until he died, Mr. Pilchard's name was constantly on his lips, and he recalled with heart-felt words the Martyr's memory, and so the son followed the father. Thus did that holy and glorious Martyr beget other Martyrs.

He was of a most gentle disposition, more than moderately learned, a remarkable pattern of priestly life. He was above the middle height, and had, as I have said, a cast in his eyes; his countenance was modest and sedate; he wore a small beard round the mouth and chin; was

---

[21] The Venerable William Pikes suffered at Dorchester in 1591. The day is not known.

sparing in food, with most sweet and holy manners; and what I used most of all to admire in him, he was always like himself. He was between thirty and forty years old.

Mr. John Hambley or Hambeling [22] (1587), of Somersetshire, taken, as I have heard from trustworthy persons, at an inn, where he met a gentleman's servant that had once been his fellow-lodger, who recognized and denounced him. He was taken to prison at Westchester, where he lived for two years among the thieves and robbers in great hardship, for which certain Catholics living in the neighbourhood were partly responsible, for they could have assisted him in his necessities. But when he was taken, there were found on him some letters he had written to a lapsed Catholic, on account of which Popham took occasion to harass the latter. This, it is believed, was the reason why he received so little assistance.

Men of various sorts, many of them very trustworthy persons, relate of him a thing very fit to be recorded. At the Assizes, when he had been condemned to death, being mildly urged by the Judge, whose name was Gent, he showed such pusillanimity as to promise to yield in those things which the Judges required, which prac-

---

[22] Venerable John Hambley suffered at Salisbury about Easter, 1587.

tically amounts to denying the faith.[23] Great hereat was the jubilation of the heretics, and not least the joy of the Judge. But whilst other business was proceeded with, and the priest was standing between the constables like the rest of the condemned, there came up to him (for the Assizes were held in booths in the open) a certain unknown man, who, after placing some letters in his hand, at once withdrew. No one preventing him (which in itself was a kind of miracle), Mr. Hambley read and re-read them until at length he broke into tears, and gave signs of being strongly moved. Then he was asked by the officials of the Court what had happened, what those letters were, who had brought them, and the like; he, however, excused himself, and gave no answer.

Next morning, when asked by the Judge as usual for the second and last time whether he would adhere to his promised conformity (this is their word for recanting), he answered very promptly and resolutely that he was ashamed and sorry that he had promised conformity of that kind. The Judge getting angry, and demanding the cause of this sudden change, he answered that there was no new cause beyond that which had so long held him in fetters; that

---

[23] Hambley's confession is still extant at the Public Record Office; it confirms what is here said of his pusillanimity, and corrects some details of Father Warford's story. He was born at St. Mabyn, Cornwall, was only one year in prison, and he named several Catholics in his examinations (*Rambler*, Nov. 1858, p. 325). P.R.O., *Domestic Elizabeth*, vol. 192, n. 46.

he grieved from the bottom of his heart for having so basely yielded to the Judge's threats and blandishments; henceforward let them not expect any more such weakness. Then the Judge threatened him with a most cruel death, to which he answered that he would accept it most gratefully. To that determination he adhered with great constancy. Sentence was pronounced, and the next day he was crowned with martyrdom.

Although it is certain that these letters restored him to a right mind, yet to this day it is not known who wrote or brought them, although diligent search has been made in the matter. Hence many not without reason believe that they were brought by his Guardian Angel.

Alexander Crow, a priest of Rheims (1587),[24] where I knew him; a man humble in birth and still more in heart. In England he had been a bootmaker, and was for a time a servant at Rheims, willingly performing all, even the lowest offices. At length by his virtue and exemplary patience, by his modesty and humility, he deserved to be admitted to the study of letters, and in fine to be promoted to the priesthood.

But what exceeds all this is that he won the crown of martyrdom at York, where he had lived, and where, I think, he was born. A simple man,

[24] The Venerable Alexander Crow was executed at York, November 30, 1587. The Douay Diary (p. 178) says that "on the last day of April, 1581, there came from England Alex. Crawe, cobbler." The editor has not identified him with the Martyr.

but with a wonderful zeal for souls, so that he could not be held back or deterred by any dangers. He was of more than medium height, with a serious countenance and black beard; well grown and strongly made. His age about thirty-six.

Inquire about his parents.

Martin Sherson,[25] though ordained priest at Rheims, he studied at Rome for about three years or more. I knew him first at Oxford, in St. John's College, a poor scholar of George Mannering, who taught Rhetoric there, and again in the year 1583, at Rome. There through an over-zealous application to study and prayer, he began to spit blood, and was therefore sent to Rheims for the recovery of his health, and afterwards to England. He was a young man of good abilities and well trained in piety and obedience. He was of moderate height, had a slight beard, a pale, oval face, and a rather large head.

Inquire as to his birth-place and parents. I think they came from Staffordshire or thereabouts.

William Hartley (1588),[26] a priest of Rheims. I knew him at Oxford, at St. John's College, where he acted as chaplain, from which post he was removed by Toby Matthew, then president, because he was suspected of Catholicism.

[25] Died in the Marshalsea, February, 1587. His claim to the honour of martyrdom rests on the same grounds as that of James Lomax and John Jetter, *supra*, p. 225.

[26] The Venerable William Hartley was executed near the Theatre, London, October 5, 1588.

Without demur he straightway betook himself to Rheims, was ordained priest, and returning to England, was apprehended and thrown into prison — I do not know which, but I think the Tower. Afterwards with eighteen others he was condemned to perpetual exile; on which occasion he came to Rome, where I saw him in 1585 or 1586.

In the pontificate of Sixtus V. he returned a second time to England, was apprehended, and, being beset by the deceits of the heretics, incurred the suspicion of having apostatized. But the event showed how unjust that suspicion was, for when he suffered at Tyburn, he won the greatest credit for constancy, and every one testified to his loyalty towards all Catholics.

One of Hartley's achievements was to rescue from the galleys, to convert and thoroughly instruct Captain Cripps, who is now in the naval service of the King of Spain. Hartley had been the spiritual Father of that man's mother. He was a man of the meekest disposition and naturally virtuous, modest and grave, with a sober and peaceful look, a blackish beard, moderate height, over thirty-five years of age.

Robert Morton,[27] who was nephew to Dr. Morton, to whom he erected a monument in this College [the English College in Rome], on the wall in the middle of the church. Called from

[27] The Venerable Robert Morton was executed in Lincolns Inn Fields, August 28, 1588.

a secular life to the priesthood shortly before his uncle's death, he studied here cases of conscience about the year 1586, and after his ordination was sent into England, and was apprehended almost on his arrival. He was remarkable for piety, and a hater of heretics like his uncle; a man who deserved well of the Catholic cause. He was prudent in action; about thirty years of age; a good height, his hair and beard inclining to red; his face somewhat inflamed owing to the heat of his liver. For his birth-place, see his uncle's epitaph.

William Spenser,[28] a priest of Rheims; born of respectable parents at Glisburn, or Ghisborne, in the district called Craven, in the bishoprick of Durham, or certainly of York. Educated from his earliest years in Oxfordshire by his maternal uncle, whose name was Horn, a priest of Queen Mary's time, and who until the return of his nephew from Rheims, about 1586 or 1587, held a benefice at a place called Cornwell, near Chippingworth.[29] He brought up his nephew the aforesaid William with great care at Trinity College, Oxford, of which he afterwards became a scholar and Fellow, and Master of Arts [in 1580], about two years before he quitted Oxford.

There I knew him for about eight years, always leading a most upright life, but suffering much

---

[28] The Venerable William Spenser was executed at York, September 29, 1589. See *F.* fol. 71 in Foley's *Records*, iii. p. 740.
[29] Chipping Norton, Oxfordshire.

at the hands of the heretics even before he left the University, because he was looked on as leaning somewhat towards the Catholic faith. They brought many charges against him, and he would argue against them, but never recklessly. From the time he was a boy his zeal for souls was marvellous, and he never neglected the first rudiments of the faith taught him by his uncle, but acted up to them with zeal and constancy to the time of his death. He read nearly all the books of controversy he could obtain at that time, setting down in a special book some or rather all the remarkable passages to be found in each.

He made great use of these extracts in instructing in the true faith the young men and boys who came fresh to his College, many of whom he was happy enough to convert from heresy. He then taught them a method of prayer, and put into their hands pious prayer-books, especially the *Jesus Psalter* and the *Verepæum* [sic]. In fine, he laboured so hard that I have often doubted whether he gained more souls after he became a priest, than he did before.

Hence, as I have said, many storms were raised against him, which, owing to the iniquity of the times, he was unable to withstand, and at length, becoming weary of the life he led at Oxford, he left with me and three or four others. Of these one was John Fixer, another Anthony Shirt, both now priests, a third was that worthy gentleman Mr. Edward Stanford, who is still alive and married, distinguished for his constancy and his sufferings for the faith. Last, though in dignity first, let me name Mr. John Appletree, one of the oldest of those who have laboured in England, and a man who has rendered the greatest service to the whole Catholic cause. He accompanied us, to see us safe, and also on private business of his own.

We landed at St. Germain, near Cherbourg in Normandy. We had started from the Isle of Wight, not far from the Needles at night time, but we were driven back, and re-embarked next day in a small boat manned by only two sailors. There were many things new to us in our journey, but hardly, perhaps, worth mentioning. The constant rain, however, was very troublesome to us in our journey, and Spenser's wonderful force of character and patience were pre-eminently conspicuous. We escaped the snares of English merchants, &c.

At Rheims he studied cases of conscience, Holy Scripture, and controversy, and worked hard to get back the sooner to the harvest in England, and also because he was very anxious about his uncle's health. So, after about two years, he was ordained priest, and returned.

At first he acted cautiously, as it were feeling his way; and at last he arranged to meet his father and mother in the fields, having dressed himself for the occasion as a peasant. There he spoke to them about the state of their souls, and reconciled them to the Church by means of another priest. Finally his uncle, now past sixty, gave up his rich and comfortable benefice, and went to live under the roof of a Catholic gentleman of rank.

Now that he had recalled these dear ones to a state of salvation and communion with the Church, he began more freely and boldly to expose his life to danger, and to work more earnestly in order to help souls. He carried his zeal to the pitch of voluntarily making himself a prisoner in York Castle, in order to help those confined there, but this he did so covertly that the gaoler himself, owing to the size of the place, and the number of Catholics always imprisoned there, was not, it seems, aware of his presence. Thus he secured a hiding-place in which he could shut himself as often as he liked. There he acted very cautiously, and consequently was able to be very serviceable to a good many.

At last his hour came, for as he happened to be on a journey, a certain gentleman out hunting, who was also a Justice, met him in the open country, and asked him, perhaps from mere curiosity, who he was. He answered readily enough; but, on being asked where he came from, he said, "York;" and, further questioned where he was going to, he again repeated, "York." Now doubtless God ordained this so, that he might win his crown. For the Justice, who was a notable and bloodthirsty heretic, at once laughed and said: "People don't travel towards the place they start from."

Supposing, as was in fact the case, that Spenser had returned so silly an answer because he was ill at ease, and that the question had taken him by surprise, he said to him: "You are, if I mistake not, some Papist or Seminary priest, are you not?"

"And if I were a priest, what then?" was Spenser's answer, for he saw there was no escape. Thereupon they laid hands on him and held him.

He was a man faithful to his friends, and exceedingly charitable in doing good to all; a bitter hater of heretics, and a champion of the faith; he feared God, and spoke of nothing more frequently than death and the last things. When asked, especially by friends at Oxford, why, since he was so devoted to Catholics and the Catholic faith, he continued living so long with heretics, and conforming to the times, I have often heard him answer: "True, if I die in this state, I know right well that I shall suffer eternal punishment."

He always longed for the peaceful state of the priest and the true believer, but was hindered by a variety of circumstances. When, however, he had once embraced this life, he bore himself in all things with courage and faithfulness. He answered at the bar with intrepidity, and met his death with joy. No one at Oxford was a more general favourite, or had more scholars, or a nobler following; no one lived more chastely, or more in conformity with Christian philosophy. At Rheims no one was more beloved; he recited his Office piously, was most devout at Mass, a bitter enemy of sleep and sloth, most diligent in attending lectures, from which he acquired a more than ordinary share of learning, for from his youth he had always been extremely studious.

He had a keen and clear understanding, especially in practical matters; his countenance like his mind was cheerful; his eyes vivacious; his face was long and freckled; his hands also were covered with freckles; he had a yellowish beard, and his cheeks were sparsely covered with hair. In other respects he was robust, squarely built, and of moderate height. I remember while he was still at Oxford, the news was brought us of Father Campion's apprehension, and while all Catholics grieved, he was so affected that his grief was remarked by the whole College; so much so that his friends had to warn him of the danger he incurred from the heretics. He always carried about with him Father Persons' book *Of Resolution*, and was very devoted to the Society of Jesus.

Once when in the hearing of some friends, he said that many falsehoods were spread abroad from the pulpit about the Roman Pontiff, he had to undergo a regular persecution. If anything favourable happened to Catholics, he was delighted, and used to call his friends into his room and rejoice with them as though for some personal happiness. All this he used to do, as I have said, before he left England.

CHAPTER XIII.

SELECTIONS FROM THE WEST-MINSTER ARCHIVES.

DOCUMENTS.

1. Execution of Blessed Thomas Cottam, by Arthur Pitts, priest (vol. ii. p. 5).
2. Relation of the sufferings in England from 1584—1591, by Peter Penkevel (vol. iv. p. 255; *Collectanea B*. fol. 1).
3. Trial and execution of Venerable George Gervase, O.S.B., by his confessor (vol. ix. p. 287).

That the Archives of the Cardinal Archbishop of Westminster contain documents of the highest importance as materials for the history of the English Martyrs, the reader has already had the opportunity of judging. But we would remind him that here, as throughout this volume, the selections do not pretend to represent the most valuable or most interesting pieces in the various collections, whence materials have been sought, for our object has only been to bring to light what others have left unused.

Before we come to the papers themselves, we would fain renew our earnest thanks not only to his Eminence the Cardinal Archbishop for his kindness in allowing us to see his Archives, but also to their custodians, the Fathers of the London Oratory, of whose care in keeping them, and courtesy in showing them, it would be difficult to speak too highly.

1. The account we are about to give of Blessed Thomas Cottam is prefaced by the following sentence in Latin: "The Acts of his martyrdom are printed in the *Concertatio Ecclesiæ Anglicanæ*, part 2, fol. 93. What follows is taken from the account of Mr. Arthur Pitts, priest, who was a prisoner in the Tower at the very time Cottam suffered." This Arthur Pitts sent through Dr. Allen[1] to Father Agazzari in Rome the corporal on which five of the Martyrs had said Mass in the Tower of London. Blessed Thomas Cottam was one of these five, and the corporal is now at Stonyhurst. Dr. Challoner has mistakenly said, in his list of the priests banished in January, 1585, that Arthur Pitts, who was one of them, was "afterwards Dean of Liverdun." It was John Pitts,[2] the author of the well known book *De illustribus Angliæ Scriptoribus*, who became Dean of Liverdun, and died there in 1616. Arthur Pitts was one of the first Canons of the English Chapter, and died in 1635, æt. 80.

OF MR. THOMAS COTTAM, PRIEST.

Executed at Tyburn, May 30th, 1582.

Mr. Cottam having been condemned long before with Campion, Sherwin, Briant, and others, received a bill from the Lieutenant of the Tower the 20th[3] of May, in the year 1582, that the next day he

---

[1] Cardinal Allen's *Letters*, p. 202.
[2] Dodd, ii. p. 374 ; iii. p. 80.
[3] This should surely be the 29th of May. Curiously enough, his diet in the Tower was only charged for till May 27th. He suffered on the 30th.

should suffer. Whereupon he came to his window out against my door, saying with joy of heart and voice, "Give God thanks with me, for to-morrow is my day. And now I hope I shall not escape the happy hour which I have earnestly so long desired, because I find my name first in the roll of the four assigned to die to-morrow!"

The next day he departed joyfully, but arriving to the place of his martyrdom, he was quailed again; for albeit he was first taken up, yet the officers fearing that his example might draw many to be of his religion, because he was well known and beloved in the city, having been before a schoolmaster there, they desirous to save his life, solicited him earnestly to recant his religion, in which he persisting, they take him down to see if the death and torments of the other his brethren could move him. But when they perceived that his courage by their blood increased, he had his desired crown of martyrdom.

The reason that he had so much this crown printed in his head, and the fear of losing it, was this. Being a scholar in the English College at Rome (whither he had been sent from the Seminary of Rheims), he had a desire to be a Jesuit, and to this end entered the Novitiate at St. Andrew's in Rome, but for his infirmity was dismissed. Where at his departure the porter bidding him adieu, said, "Beware, lest some other receive your crown!"

[From Rome he came again to Rheims in April, 1580, and the month following was made priest at Soissons, and soon after sent into England, not being able to prosecute his studies through want of health. *Added from the Douay Diary*].

He came into England in the company of Dr. Ely, and arriving at Dover was apprehended. The searcher having great acquaintance with Dr. Ely, gave him in charge to Dr. Ely to convey him to the Council, which he willingly undertook, but being a Catholic, at his arrival at London, dismissed him. The searcher having had news that the prisoner was not delivered, came post to London, and meeting with Dr. Ely, apprehended him; who making excuse that for cause and upon assurance of his forthcoming, he had given him a few days' liberty, and promising the searcher to bring him unto him or to answer it in his own person, he was content. Dr. Ely therefore coming to Mr. Cottam, told him the case what had happened, who presently said, " Now God be thanked, for I was never quiet in my mind since you let me go. Still it came in my head that which the porter of St. Andrew's said unto me." And so he yielded himself.

2. The writer of the next document was Peter Penkevell, a Cornish name, which not being very familiar was variously spelt Penkwell, Pencavell, and Penckevel, and then by mistake of the " v " for an " n," Penkenel, and so Penkennel, which is the form it takes in the heading of the paper. The family which bore it was, as far as we know it, entirely made up of Catholic confessors. Its history indeed is beside our present purpose, so we only add a word about

those who will appear in the course of the story. The last we hear of the mother, who was imprisoned in 1586, is that she was still in prison in 1600, at which time Mark, one of her younger sons, entered the Society of Jesus. Thomas and John are traceable for years through the State Papers, owing to the persecution they underwent, while another brother, presumably our author, Peter, became a Capuchin friar, in Spain.

THE RELATION OF THE PENKENNELS [PENKEVELS] OF THE SUFFERINGS IN ENGLAND, 1584—1591.

First I came into London about the year 1584, my brother [Thomas] then being prisoner in Newgate in the company of Mr. [Leonard] Hyde, Mr. [William] Wiggs, Mr. [Isaac] Higgins, priests, and Mr. Robert Bellamy, layman, with others. I then for a time was placed in service with a gentlewoman, in part of which time I prepared myself, and was reconciled at Newgate by the foresaid Mr. Hyde.

Shortly after this I did serve one Mr. Richard Shelley,[4] who was then prisoner in the Marshalsea, committed thither for giving up a supplication unto the Queen; the effect whereof, whether it was for craving a public dispute for trial of religion, or in favour of them that were troubled for their

---

[4] Challoner records that "Mr. Shelley, of Sussex, presented a humble address to the Queen one day as she was walking in her park at Greenwich. But this address had no other effect than the causing the gentleman who presented it, to be cast into the Marshalsea, where he died a close prisoner."

conscience, I do not perfectly remember, but I think it was for the first, for it greatly chafed both the Queen and her Council. The said gentleman being very sick at my coming to him, shortly after died, a constant confessor in the said prison.

About this time was executed Mr. Transon, priest out of the Clink, arraigned at Westminster, who behaved himself in such sort that he blacked the Judges. Two other priests suffered in his company, whose names I know not.[5]

After this I did dwell with a certain doctor of physic, and coming, according as I had accustomed, on a time to see my mother, who was then lately come up unto London, it happened (by means that her chamber was searched the same day) she with my brother and sister being carried to prison and the house watched, that I was also apprehended, brought before Justice Young, by him examined, threatened, and sent to the Counter in the Poultry (the year '86), where I found Mr. Emerson[6] prisoner.

It happened in the time of my being there, that one Richard Robinson, who had been long beyond the seas, arrived about Rye, and being there presently taken, was after by Justice Young sent to the same prison, where in our company

[5] This paragraph is added in the margin. Venerable Edward Strancham and Venerable Nicholas Woodfen suffered at Tyburn Jan. 21, 1586. There was no third priest.

[6] Ralph Emerson, the well-known lay-brother companion of the Blessed Father Campion, was committed September 24, 1584. See *Life of Father John Gerard*, p. 146; *Troubles*, ii. p. 43.

he died. About the same time one Glynn, servant unto Sir John Arundel, was thither committed, who also within short time died in the common gaol, being a sely poor old man that had not the proper use of the senses.

About this time suffered the fourteen gentlemen, to wit, Mr. Ballard, priest, Mr. Babington, &c., being accused of conspiring the Queen's death, who were butchered in most cruel manner.

Near unto this time also suffered Mr. Dibdale, Mr. Adams, and Lowe, priests.[7] Mr. Dibdale, had dispossessed one of wicked spirits, and caused the said spirit to bring out of the party possessed, a knife and other things which they had carried in by the means of witchcraft. He was at his death charged by Topcliffe of conjuration, and that he did those things by delusion of the devil. Mr. Dibdale answering hereunto, protested on his death then openly before the people, that he did it by virtue of the name of Jesus, and by the authority which He had given unto His Church. Being demanded by the said Topcliffe whether he did it by his own merits, answered, "No, but by the merits of Christ and by His power."

Near this time there died in Newgate a Queen Mary priest, and one Mr. Reynolds, a layman, being both prisoners for their conscience. Also somewhat before this time Mr. Jetter, who had

---

[7] Venerable Robert Dibdale, John Adams, and John Lowe, were executed at Tyburn, October 8, 1586. For the exorcisms, see Challoner, and *Troubles*, ii. p. 96.

been long kept cruelly in the Limbo of the same prison.

After I had remained two years at the Counter, Mr. Felton[8] and I were removed unto Newgate and put into the common gaol. After wearing of irons one day for fynes of iron, we were removed where my brother and the rest were in the crown side, where I remained about three years, in which time there were very many priests and other Catholics put to death for their faith in divers places of England.

The year that the Armada compassed England about, at St. Bartholomew tide, there were fourteen priests and laymen at one Sessions at Newgate arraigned, who all very constantly suffered martyrdom, except Mr. Foxwell, who was reprieved. Margaret Ward at that time was arraigned, condemned, and suffered martyrdom. [She was] condemned for bringing a rope to a priest being prisoner in Bridewell, who by that means escaped, but was put to death for refusing to go to church, on which condition life was offered unto her openly at the bar. The laymen, that then suffered, for the most part were condemned, because they said they had confessed their sins unto a priest. The names of the priests that I remember were first Mr. Deane, who had been some time a minister, Mr. Holford [Acton], or

---

[8] Venerable Thomas Felton, son of Blessed John Felton, was afterwards by favour set at liberty, but was soon re-arrested, and suffered near Hounslow, August 29, 1588. He was a postulant of the Friars Minims.

Bude, Mr. James or Clarkson [Claxton], Mr. Earth or Ley [Leigh], and Mr. Mourton.[9]

At that time there was executed divers other priests out of the Clink and Marshalsea, of whose names I remember no more but Mr. Flower [or Way], and Mr. James.[10]

Also in company with these was Mistress Lowe[11] arraigned and condemned for harbouring of priests, who was brought unto the place of execution willing to die, [but] by her husband's means was reprieved.

Also at York and other places there were divers priests and laymen executed at that time, whose names I know not. It was determined that within short time after, there should be all the priests in Wisbech and very many other Catholics arraigned, but the Earl of Leicester dying the same while in extraordinary manner, caused a sudden stop in those proceedings.

But within two months after the magistrates returned unto their accustomed practice, there

---

[9] The others were, William Gunter, priest, Henry Webley, Hugh Moor, Thomas Felton, Edward Shelley, Richard Martin, Richard Flower, John Roche, laymen. They have all been declared Venerable. The six priests and eight laymen were not bowelled and quartered (*Collectanea N.* i. n. 6, p. 65).

[10] The others were, Robert Wilcox, Edward Campion, Christopher Buxton, Ralph Crockett, John Robinson, William Hartley, John Weldon, priests, Robert Widmerpool and Robert Sutton, laymen. They too have all been declared Venerable. The next paragraph is in the margin of the MS.

[11] Mistress Philip Lowe died in the White Lion prison in 1588 (*Troubles*, iii. p. 36).

were arraigned Mr. Hewett[12] and Mr. Hartley, priests. Mr. Hewett refused to be tried by the jury, for that he was loth, as he told the Judges, that those ignorant men that understood not the case, should be burdened with his blood, and referred the matter unto the Judges' consciences. And notwithstanding that he proved there openly that they had no just matter against him, and that he, being banished, was from the Low Countries sent into England prisoner by the Earl of Leicester, yet nevertheless they proceeded against him, and without a jury condemned and judged him to be hanged and quartered.

The next morning he was carried into Mile End Green, where he in the cart disputed openly with two preachers, whiles one went into the Court to know the Queen's pleasure concerning his quartering, who was found so favourable that she would have him but hanged. In this space he reproved and proved the said ministers of many shameful lies, and behaving himself in all respects both discreetly and constantly, was there martyred.

The foresaid Mr. Hartley, priest, being brought forth in the same cart, was, after the dispatch of Mr. Hewett, carried near the Curtain and there hanged.

[12] Challoner wrongly says that John Hewett was martyred at York. He did not know that he was the same as John Weldon, whom he has rightly given as martyred at Mile End Green. The Martyr appears in the list of Venerables under the names of "Hewett, *alias* Weldon."

Also at that Sessions there were two laymen arraigned and condemned, to wit, Mr. Sutton, a schoolmaster, and one Symonds,[13] who presently before was greatly suspected and slandered to be a spy. Mr. Sutton suffered at Clerkenwell and Symons at Tyburn, who blessed himself, and kissing the halter said it was the happiest collar that ever went about his neck.

Also at that time Mistress White was arraigned and condemned for harbouring of priests, who was reprieved, and after the space of one year and a half, for money had both pardon and liberty.

Not long after this, Mr. Nichols and another priest, Mr. Yeats [Yaxley] was taken at Oxford, and two laymen, one Mr. Belson, and a chamberlain.[14] The priests, and I think the other two, were brought to London, and after cruel torture in Bridewell, were all sent again to Oxford, and there arraigned and put to death. Both the priests were hanged and quartered [July 5, 1589].

After this, Mr. Bayles, priest, was apprehended, and cruelly tortured in Bridewell by Top-

---

[13] There can be no doubt that we have here the notice of a Martyr hitherto unrecognized, and that this omission was due to the false report of his being one of those iniquitous spies, whom the Catholics dreaded more than any of their other enemies. He is probably the same as the John Harrison, *alias* Symons, a carrier of letters, whose apprehension is mentioned in a list of recent arrests, which belongs to the commencement of 1587 (Lansdowne MSS. vol. 51, n. 67). These Martyrs suffered October 5, 1588.

[14] Challoner calls him Humphrey ap Richard, servant of the St. Catherine's Wheel Inn.

T

cliffe. . . .¹⁵ Afterwards he was arraigned at Newgate bar, where amongst other things he proved that he was such a priest, as was sent into the land by Pope Eleutherius to convert the Britons, and such a priest that St. Augustine was that after converted the Saxons. Judge Anderson seemed to cavil with him about the histories, but the other Judges being weary of the dispute, stayed it: condemned and judged him to be hanged and quartered in Fleet Street [March 3, 1590].

At that time, as I remember, Nicholas Horner, a layman and a tailor, was arraigned and condemned to be hanged, for that he had made a jerkin for a priest. The evidence against him was only given by Topcliffe and Young. He was executed at Smithfield before his lodgings, with a title set over his head. He had been before that time prisoner in Newgate, where he, not being suffered to have a surgeon to come to him to dress his leg that was sore, was afterwards enforced to have it cut off in the same prison.

Not long after, Mr. Jones, priest, was taken, extreme tortured and arraigned, and in a discourse which he made concerning the execution of Protestants in Queen Mary's time, and the persecution of Catholics now, concluded in such sort that it was to the education of many of the hearers and a great mager to the Judges and other persecutors. For they suffered him to make a large discourse, uttering it in such manner

---

¹⁵ The outrages here recounted cannot in decency be specified.

as they hoped the conclusion would make for their purpose, and not so much against them. So being condemned, was hanged and quartered in Fleet Street [May 6, 1590].

At the same time was Mr. Middleton, priest, arraigned, hanged, and quartered at Clerkenwell, with a title over his head.

The same time [16] a poor man that was an hostler in Gray's Inn Lane, was arraigned, and after hanged in the same lane, with a title over his head, because he had lodged a priest in his house.

After this was Mr. Beesley, priest, taken, and committed to the Tower by Topcliffe. There he was very hardly kept and cruelly racked, and was afterwards arraigned in the company of Mr. Scott, priest, who by the means and help of one Baker was to be banished by order from the Council, which he obtained for money. When the time of his banishment was come, he was committed again to prison by Topcliffe, and afterwards brought to the Sessions, where for want of other matter Topcliffe signified that it was good policy to put him to death, and said that his austere life was a mean to draw the people unto him; for he said that Mr. Scott was accounted for a saint. So he was condemned, and after was hanged and quartered in Fleet Street [July 2, 1591]. His mild behaviour pierced the hearts of people so much, that many of them said it was pity he

[16] Venerable Alexander Blake was really the companion Venerable Christopher Bales and Venerable Nicholas Horner.

should be done to death. "For," they said, "he is likely to be such an one as meant no evil." Both Mr. Beesley and he had titles over their heads.

Endorsed by Father Persons.—The Relation of the Penkevels of the sufferings in England.

3. MR. GEORGE GERVASE, BENEDICTINE PRIEST, HIS ARRAIGNMENT AND MARTYRDOM, 1608, IN LONDON.

Written by one who was present at both arraignment and death.

Mr. George Gervase, gent., was banished in the year of our Lord, 1608, and the [6th of] King James, and [had also been] one of the number of those which were of the first banishment after the coming of the aforesaid King James. That same year he arrived at Rome with another banished priest named Mr. Nuport, to visit the Holy City, where in poverty and great devotion he remained some three months, and with extreme difficulty obtained ten crowns of alms, with which he departed again into England.[17]

Two months after his arrival he was apprehended in Smithfield, going into the house of one Mr. Bluntstone, gent.—where he intended to

[17] The Pilgrim Book of the English College, Rome (Foley, *Records,* v. p. 581), shows that our Martyr was at the Hospice from November 20 to December 6, 1606. But his companion, Venerable Richard Smith, *alias* Newport, who had been a student of that College, made three visits between October 10, 1606, and April 29, 1607.

celebrate—by the same Justice, who had charge to banish him in Northumberland. Who meeting there with him, demanded of him how he durst presume again to enter into the land, to which he answered little. The Justice carried him into a tavern, where after some speech, Mr. Gervase desired him not to seek his blood.

"No," saith he, "but seeing you are come, you shall see my wife." Which done, he desired him to walk abroad, Mr. Gervase hoping that the proceeding would be favourable.

But drawing unto St. Paul's, he led him unto the Bishop, where, after notices given by the Justice, he was examined, and the Justice presently demitted without any thanks. He answered the Bishop gravely, resolutely, and religiously, but was committed unto the Gatehouse. Being sent for by the Judges, he was demanded whether he was a priest? To which he answered, "Yea;" and whether he was of any Order, to which he answered also, "Yea, and of the Order of St. Benet."

The Recorder demanded whether he would take the oath, which he denying, the Recorder and Justices demanded whether the Pope could excommunicate or depose princes. To which, with a vehement voice, to the great admiration of standers-by, he answered, "Yea, and also all princes in the world;" at which the heretics fell into a great laughter.

The jury was panelled, and the charge given by the Bench unto the Jury according unto his confession [of his] banishment, Order, denial of the oath, and confessing of the Pope's authority. Which done, he was condemned, and kept secret until the next day.

The next day being called unto the bar, the Recorder standing up, spake: "George Gervase, thou hast been condemned for that in the year of our God, and King James, . . . according to the common proceeding," &c.[18]

Which ended, the Recorder began again—

"George Gervase, priest, &c. . . . This last day before this honourable Bench and assembly, thou hast not only approved and defended thy traitorous opinions, but also extolled the Pope before God, making him able to command and dispose of princes, more than God doth, and this blasphemy thou hast avouched—besides much more to this effect. Hast thou, therefore, anything to say for thyself?"

Unto which Mr. George Gervase, in most mild and sweet manner answered: "What I have said my blood is ready to answer" (and such like).

Judgment was given upon him according to their order; and so, committed unto the gaol, he remained close prisoner until execution.

The Bishop sent seven ministers on the Sunday morning to deal with him, the one was Dr. Morton, whom I saw. They all tormented him according to their diversities of spirits, and as the keeper said, he remained a most obstinate

---

[18] "The words of Sir Edward Montague, Recorder, as myself heard, being near unto him."—*Margin*.

Papist. Only this much I will adjoin from the mouth of Mr. Richard Cary in Holborn, and also of my own knowledge (he being dearest unto me), that since the first persecution in England, never any priest for the space of two or three days ever had more affliction amongst ministers, and that by the means of the Bishop,[19] for then the oath was in its first entrance. The Sunday night after his judgment he was accompanied with five ministers the whole night, the day afore with seven, being all this time in close prison.

The next morning being Monday,[20] a great concourse of people expected at the prison, at seven of the clock he was put on the hurdle, attended by the Sheriff and many officers. By them I still accompanied him on horseback, and after often turning unto him, he ever lifted up both his hands (which were bound) unto me, making signs that I should pray for him.

Being come unto the place of execution, his first words were, viz., " I am hither brought to suffer death for being a priest, and for refusing to take an unlawful oath." To which the Sheriff once demanded whether he would yet take it; to which he answered no, but willingly would take any oath not prejudicing his conscience or the Catholic faith. Which the Sheriff understanding, commanded the executioner to do his office.

[19] The Bishop of London was Thomas Ravis, who was translated from Gloucester in 1607, and died in 1609.
[20] The date given by Challoner is April 11, which in 1608 was a Friday.

The minister who accompanied him told him that now it was time to remember himself for denying that out of the Church there could be no salvation. Mr. Gervase with these words put him aside, "Tut, tut, look to thyself, poor man." Something more he spoke, but I heard it not by reason of the sway of the people.

After which he prepared himself, holding open his hands, which were not bound, with eyes fixed up towards heaven, never moving joint, not even at the drawing away of the cart, which was very little before a serjeant cut the halter, and the executioner received him in his arms alive, but somewhat amazed. Being laid on the block, by chance he catched hold of the executioner's knife, as he intended to have ripped up his belly, which act caused the executioner to cut his own hand; but with help of the master executioner he was quartered and bowelled, and his members disposed upon the walls of the city. His soul now enjoyeth all felicity, being most devout unto our Blessed Lady, having made three or four special vows, the which with great devotion he observed, as I myself best know upon secret reasons, having been his ghostly Father.

Rob. Cha^l.
Pr[iest].

Father Gervase [21] both at the bar, at his arraignment, and at his death did declare himself

---

[21] The postscript is in a different hand, with the marginal note, "Extract out of a letter received from London in April, 1608."

to be a monk of St. Benet's Order. Being asked at the bar if the Pope can depose princes upon a just cause, he wished them not to urge him in this point, it being a bloody question; at last he answered that the Pope can depose. At his martyrdom he was cut up cruelly, while he was in his senses.

CHAPTER XIV.

SELECTIONS FROM STONYHURST MANUSCRIPTS.

DOCUMENTS.

1. Remnants of *Collectanea A.* preserved in Father Grene's transcripts (Stonyhurst MSS. *Collectanea M.* fol. 49, 50, 187, 197, 201).

>   (i.) Martyrdom of Venerable Monford Scott and George Beesley (*Coll. A.* fol. 88).
>   (ii.) Another account of the same Martyrs (*Ibid.* fol. 283).
>   (iii.) News from London, April, 1591 (*Ibid.* fol. 103).
>   (iv.) Martyrdom of Venerable Francis Ingleby (*Ibid.* fol. 116).
>   (v.) Account of Venerable Richard Langley (*Ibid.* fol. 120, 123). Latin.
>   (vi.) Account of various Martyrs by Venerable Father Henry Walpole (*Ibid.* fol. 144).
>   (vii.) Relation of Mr. George Stoker and Mr. Heath, concerning Martyrs (*Ibid.* fol. 204).
>   (viii.) Father John Curry to Father Persons, May 12, 1590 (*Ibid.* fol. 177). Latin.
>   (ix.) Martyrdom of Venerable Roger Dicconson and Ralph Milner (*Ibid.* fol. 183).
>   (x.) Relation by a Priest in England (*Ibid.* fol. 273).
>   (xi.) Father Christopher Walpole to Father Persons (extract) September 19, 1604 (*Ibid.* fol. 287).
>   (xii.) Varia (*Ibid.* fol. 183, 255).

2. The preservation of the relics of Venerable Robert Sutton By Father John Gerard (*Collectanea M.* fol. 47, 48). Latin.

3. Summaries by Father Grene of accounts of Martyrdoms (*Collectanea E.* pp. 179, 302 ; *Collectanea M.* fol. 55 *f.* 25 *e*).

4. A Relation of divers persecutions, *anno* 1588 et seq. (*Collectanea M.* fol. 143 *e*—146).

The Archives of Stonyhurst College contain a large number of important papers concerning the English Martyrs, and many of them have been already printed. We have already for our present purpose drawn largely on these documents, and especially on the valuable transcripts made by Father Christopher Grene. In this chapter we propose to lay before the reader such remains of the volume *Collectanea A.* as concern the Martyrs. This volume was the first of the series of *Collectanea* which was put together, and, though now broken up, it has not been entirely destroyed, for some of the original documents, which it once contained, survive in the collection called *Anglia A.* at Stonyhurst. But of the greater number the memory has entirely perished, except where Father Grene's care has provided us with whole or partial copies of them. These we now proceed to give.

(I.) THE MARTYRDOM OF MR. SCOTT AND MR. BEESLEY.

Set down by one that was present.

At Mr. Scott's arraignment his own confessions made to Justice Young and Topcliffe were read, wherein he had confessed himself to be a priest, made after the Roman order. Mr. Topcliffe objected many other things very absurdly, which the Martyr denied.

Topcliffe said he thought no ten priests in England did so much hurt as he.

Mr. Scott answered: "I thank God I never did hurt in all my life, neither do I care, though you and all the Bench be privy to my doings."

[He and Beesley were then condemned to death. Both confessed that they were priests, and refused to conform to the Church of England, which the Judge urged them to do, holding out hopes of life. Both were executed together. Mr. Beesley first began to speak to the people][1] on the ladder. *Absit mihi gloriari nisi in Cruce Domini Nostri Jesu Christi:* but being interrupted added little more. Mr. Scott said also little on the ladder, prayed for the Queen, and ended with saying the *Pater noster* in Latin and *In manus tuas Domine commendo spiritum meum,* and *In te Domine speravi.*

[*Note by Father Grene.*—The present Relation, if it be true, seemeth little to the praise of these two Martyrs, they seeming to have showed very little courage; and Mr. Scott prayed for the people and desired them to pray for him.]

Father Grene's last note shows us how important the question of praying or *communicatio in sacris* with heretics was held to be among English Catholics. It is notorious that England lost the faith through this weakness, and the reader has already had many examples of the persistence with which the English Martyrs refused to countenance it. Happily Father

[1] The passages in square brackets in this chapter represent Father Grene's Latin summaries of part of the document copied. Some names and dates have also been added.

Grene has himself given the best defence possible of the Venerable Monford Scott and George Beesley, by writing out a fuller account of their deaths, which satisfactorily explains how far they went in praying with heretics.

(II.) MARTYRDOM OF MR. MONFORD SCOTT AND MR. GEORGE BEESLEY.

Mr. Monford Scott, priest, being by Judge Anderson, at his arraignment in the Sessions House at Newgate, demanded "whether if the Pope should send in forces into England, he would pray for the good success of the Church of England—yea or no?" answered that "he would pray for the Catholic Church."

Being asked what Church that was, he said, "The Universal Church."

"Aye," saith the Judge, "you mean the Church of Rome," to which Mr. Scott answered nothing.

He confessed himself to be a priest, made after the order of the Church of Rome, coming into England to no other end than to do good. . . .

[I omit Topcliffe's most impertinent questions and objections.]

The jury finding them guilty, they had their judgment; and first Mr. Beesley said that for anything he could perceive, he was condemned for being a priest, which he did acknowledge.

"Nay," saith the Queen's Attorney, "you confessed you came into England."

"I did so," saith he, "and with all my heart

I am glad of it." Mr. Scott then answered . . .

[Here some lines are missing.]

The words which Mr. Beesley used at his death in Fleet Street, 1 June, 1591, between six and seven in the morning.

Being by the Sheriff offered that if he would recant, he should have favour, answered that he minded by the grace of God to die a good Catholic, and being wished to desire the people to pray for him, answered that he desired all good Catholics to pray for him, using also these words, *Absit mihi gloriari nisi in Cruce Domini Nostri Jesu Christi,* and pausing awhile said, "Good people, I beseech God to send all felicity;" and not suffered to speak any more, was turned off and cut down, and laid upon the block; he stretching forth his legs when the hangman began to unbowel him, and so he ended.

Words used by Mr. Scott at his death, 1 June, 1591, in Fleet Street.

Being in his shirt, and coming to the gibbet, he kneeled down at the foot of the ladder, saying some few prayers unto himself. Then he went up the ladder, and the rope being about his neck made this speech, that he prayed for his country, that he prayed for his prince: and being demanded who that prince was, answered, the Queen of England, which the people liked well. He likewise prayed twice or thrice that God would send some good Abraham into this land to pray to God that He would avert His wrath from this realm, thanking God that he came to die for his conscience and religion.

Being demanded of Sheriff Mosly whether the people and he would pray together, his answer was that he thanked his worship, and said unto him, "Mr. Sheriff, pray you for me and I will pray for you," whereupon the Sheriff said: "Then let us say the Lord's Prayer together."

Mr. Scott answered that he had said it, and by the grace of God did mind to say it again, and so began *Pater noster;* and they bade him say it in English, but he would not.

Then he thanked them for having given him leave to speak, and being bid to make an end, he said, *In te Domine speravi, non confundar in æternum,* and *In manus tuas Domine commendo spiritum meum:* and so was turned off and hung till he was dead, by commandment of the Sheriff. Some took notice, when the hangman held up his quarters, that his knees were hardened as horn by much prayer.

One saying, "Is this the treason? I came to see traitors and have seen saints," was thereupon cast into prison.

(III.) NEWS FROM LONDON, APRIL, 1591.

Mr. Beesley was kept in Topcliffe's house, tied by the neck with a chain and in a cellar, to make him confess where he had been harboured.

Father Scott has his liberty to depart gotten by one Baker, and was in the country among his good friends where he had gotten £20, of the which he made the same Baker acquainted, by whose means he was presently apprehended and is close prisoner, and it is thought that he shall be hardly dealt with for to know of whom he had the money.

[Mr. John Nutter is said to have been naturally a very timid man, but in undergoing death for the glory of the name of Christ he bore himself most bravely. The same is related of Mr. Anderton.]

(IV.) MARTYRDOM OF THE VENERABLE FRANCIS INGLEBY.

Mr. Francis Ingleby, son to Sir William Ingleby, knight, having occasion to go to York, a Catholic gentleman, by name Mr. Lassie,[2] met him in a place called Bishopfields, and kneeling down craved his blessing, which being espied by one of the President's men, he was taken and brought to the Council. They said unto him they marvelled, that he being a gentleman of so great calling would abase himself to be a priest. He answered that he made more account of his priesthood than of all other titles whatsoever.

Brought unto the Castle, he had a pair of fetters laid upon his legs at the prison door. The

---

[2] This "Mr. Lassie" cannot be the Blessed William Lacy, who was martyred at York, August 22, 1582, but it may well be one of the same family.

Catholic prisoners craved his blessing. With a smiling countenance he said, "I fear me I shall be overproud of my new boots," meaning his fetters. In the time of his imprisonment a minister came into him for to dispute, &c.

Being arraigned, and refusing to take the oaths, &c., said, "I will give unto the Queen subjection so far forth as she hath protection." Being adjudged to die, he spake these words, *Credo videre bona Domini in terra viventium.*

Coming from the place of judgment again to the Castle, the Catholics looking forth of their windows craved his blessing. Privily he gave them it, saying, "O sweet judgment." After his condemnation he showed such tokens of inward joy that the keeper, named Mr. Meverell, said that he took no small pleasure to behold his sweet and joyful conversation; for his joy was such that the keeper, a very earnest Puritan, could not abstain from tears.

At his martyrdom one Humphrey Mountain, who would have taken some of his flesh or blood, was carried to the Castle, and there remaineth.

(V.) VENERABLE RICHARD LANGLEY.

Richard Langley, Esq., a man of great soul and remarkable piety, spent all his estate in succouring priests. He built a very well hidden house underground, which was a great place of refuge for priests during the persecution. When this was divulged by a certain Catholic, the

President ordered him to be arrested and committed to prison with Mr. Mush and Mr. Johnson, two very learned priests. After a short confinement they were brought to trial and condemned to death.

That very night the two priests Mush and Johnson, together with a third named Patinson,[3] escaped from prison, but Mr. Langley was separated from them, and received the crown of martyrdom a few days later with great alacrity and constancy.

(VI.) A RELATION BY THE VENERABLE FATHER HENRY WALPOLE.

[August 30, 1588], Mr. Richard Lee [Leigh], priest, brought forth of Newgate to be executed with four other Catholics, who demanded his benediction, which he gave unto them and likewise unto others that stood about the cart, desiring God to make them all partakers. . . . Then being drawn to Tyburn (they all sang their service by the way), after long speech Mr. Lee desired to have respite to make his petitions unto God. Being in his meditations his colour changed and his legs began to bend, insomuch that it was thought that his soul had been already in Heaven; whereupon Topcliffe cried out very loud, saying, " Lee, Lee ! " divers times, " it is the devil that doth deceive thee." The hangman pulling him

---

[3] This must have been Bernard, ordained 1585, not William (the Martyr), ordained 1587.

by the sleeve, he came to himself, and looking about demanded what the matter was.

Then being asked whether that the Queen were Supreme Head of the Church, he answered, "No!" and the people crying, "Away with him!" the carts were drawn away; and so he died, and the four others also, not quartered. One of their names was Shelley, a man of 50 or 60 years of age, condemned for keeping of the book called my *Lord of Leicester's Commonwealth*. There was of those four a woman that was servant of Mrs. Whittle, condemned for giving of two shillings unto a priest in Bridewell.

Mr. Way or Flower was brought to Newgate Sessions, and there his indictment read. He denied to be tried by a temporal Judge, wherefore the Bishop of London was sent for; and the Recorder said that because of his refusal there was a spiritual Judge.

Mr. Way asked, "Who made him a Bishop?"

The Recorder said, "The Queen, who is Supreme Head of the Church."

He answered that she was not Head of the Church, neither would he acknowledge him for Bishop.

Then upon the Statute he was condemned, and at Kingston very cruelly martyred, unbowelled alive, and his bowels burnt before his face [September 23, 1588].

Mr. Rivers (*vere* Christopher Bales), executed about Easter, 1590, in Fleet Street. Being stripped and on the ladder, making the sign of the Cross, he turned round and beheld the people, and said,

"Good people, you are come hither to see a man die, but why or wherefore you know not. A traitor! But now wherein a traitor? In that I am a priest, and seek to reconcile souls unto Almighty God according to my office and calling; but this word *traitor* is such that you cannot see into the cause. But I would that you might but see the soul and the change it makes, and then I doubt not but that this word *traitor* would take no effect."

Then Topcliffe interrupted him, and would let him say no more, but demanded him of the Supremacy, which he denied, and then was hanged, drawn and quartered. Before his death he desired all good Catholics to pray with him in that his last agony. . . .

The same day that Mr. Rivers [Bales] was executed, there was father Horner, a layman, executed in Smithfield, being condemned for giving of Mr. Rivers the making of a jerkin. The said Horner had long lain in Limbo, whereby his leg was fain to be cut off, and not long before released out of Newgate.

Mr. Jones, or Parker, and Mr. Middleton not long after were martyred [May 6, 1590], Mr. Jones in Fleet Street, where after long speech had with Topcliffe, he desired the people to bear witness that he died a priest of the true Catholic, Apostolic, and Roman Church, and praying for the conversion of his country, was turned off the ladder. He made the sign of the Cross upon his breast, and after closed his own eyes, and then was cut down and quartered.

Mr. Middleton the same day being brought to Clerkenwell, desiring that he might have liberty to speak, it was denied, and was hasted to despatch, and presently was to be turned off. He said that he did not doubt but that the shedding of his blood would confirm a great many of Catholics in England, and so was hanged, drawn, and quartered.

About Michaelmas, 1589,[4] was Mr. Savell, or Weldon, executed at Mile End Green, who always, by the way, desired our Saviour to aid him with grace to persevere. Being brought to the place of execution, Topcliffe said how that the Queen was merciful, "and whereas by his deserts he was condemned to be hanged, drawn, and quartered, her pleasure was that he should be but hanged." He said "the less was his merit," and so he died.

He hanged very near a quarter of an hour before he died. They would suffer no man to strike him on the breast or pull him down. There was then in the cart Mr. Hartley, priest, and a layman, who desired him by the name of Martyr to pray for him, whereat the people cried out.

Mr. Hartley, priest, was then drawn from thence to Finsbury Fields, and there was demanded

---

[4] See pp. 229, 289. The year should be 1588.

if he would ask the Queen forgiveness. He said he had never offended her, and then, being in his prayers, he said he did confess that he had offended the Queen and Almighty God, and therefore was sorry, for that he had worn his apparel otherwise than by his calling he ought to have done, and therein he had offended the Queen in breaking of her laws.

The people cried out that he spake in derision, and was straight turned off without further speech, and was not quartered. [Robert Sutton], the layman, was executed at Clerkenwell, and died very constantly. He was a schoolmaster, some time in Paternoster Row.

Father Grene adds: All this is copied out verbatim of a relation original of B. F. Henry Walpole.

(VII.) RELATIONS OF MR. GEORGE STOKER AND MR. HEATH CONCERNING MARTYRS.[5]

When I was in the Tower after my extreme racking, my keeper Gaskin told me that there were two things that did very much move him touching Papists; the first was the death of Father Campion, who died so patiently after all his racking and torments; the second [Sherwin's kissing the hand of the executioner, which was stained with Campion's blood].

This reporter also being in the prison at Newgate called Limbus, it was told him that there

---

[5] For some other extracts of this document, which do not concern Martyrs, see *Troubles,* ii. pp. 115, 189.

was a Papist made the devil run away, whose name was Mr. Horner, an old layman. Coming afterward unto the Justice hall, they examined Horner of the former thing.

He said also that being in bed with one of my Lord of Leicester's men, about midnight the devil appeared in the likeness of a bush of thorns, and after in likeness of a blackamoor; but after father Horner had blessed himself and began to speak to him, he vanished away.

The same father Horner was so long kept in Limbus and in the common gaol as one of his legs rotted, and in the Justice hall was cut off. Afterwards for money he had his liberty, but shortly after they apprehended him again, at which time Mrs. White came unto him, to whom he told that in the night there was a great light in his chamber, and that an angel did come and comfort him. He desired her that until he were executed she would not utter it to any, neither did she: but being he was shortly after executed, she made relation; who afterwards was also executed [6] herself. Mrs. White was condemned upon a Statute for receiving and harbouring of priests. There was none to allege anything against her, but other's accusation in writing. She desired to have him brought to her face, but it was not granted.

There was also one Mrs. Ward, who came to

---

[6] Mrs. White was condemned to death for receiving Mr. Green or Gray (*Troubles*, ii. p. 385), but she was not executed.

Bridewell to visit Mr. Watson, a priest.[7] She provided him also a rope to come out of prison withal, a man to accompany him, and a boat to convey him, assigning the hour when he should come down; the time was between 10 and 11 o'clock. When she came afterwards to the boatman he altogether refused, at which she was much grieved, thinking she had utterly cast away the good priest.

By chance she met with a young man[8] whom she had not seen in half a year before, who seeing her in that mournful plight demanded the cause. She denied to tell him; he more enforcing her, said he would willingly adventure his life to do her any pleasure; and she said that so he must if he would help her in that respect. To this he accorded with faithful promise, whereupon she told him the whole matter. Then he went and provided another boat, and she came to the place appointed, and so received the priest and went his way.

At his coming down there fell a stone which awaked all the house, so that they followed him with hue and cry; and his keeper making haste overtook them at Lambeth Marsh. The priest

---

[7] Father Grene notes, "Watson was afterwards in 1603 executed in a less happy cause." This is William Watson (Challoner calls him Richard), who was executed with Clarke, another priest, for a plot against King James, which was reprobated by all good Catholics. He was the author of the notorious *Quodlibets*, for which he expressed his sorrow on the scaffold (See also *Collectanea P.* fol. 527, and *N.* i. n. 6, p. 21).

[8] Venerable John Roche, an Irishman (See *P.* fol. 527).

seeing him come after them said unto the man, "Sure we be undone, for yonder comes my keeper." Whereupon he returned towards him and bade him good-morrow; but the keeper ran away, not knowing him. When he was gone they [changed] clothes, but the man upon his return was taken by the priest's apparel, and so both he and the gentlewoman were executed at Tyburn, and made a most constant and blessed end.

(VIII.) FATHER JOHN CURRY, S.J.,[9] TO FATHER PERSONS.

May 12, 1590.

First of all I journeyed to York, where there are Catholic laymen in prison to the number of sixty, more or less. We greeted them through a messenger, and they seemed greatly comforted at our arrival. In this city, as they gave me to understand, a certain priest [Mr. Burden is noted in the margin] remarkable for learning and piety, had a month or two before given a noble testimony to the Catholic faith by the shedding of his blood. He had sent little presents of a pious character to those of whom he had charge, and his memory was in benediction.

Then I visited as many Catholics as possible in their homes, and at last I fell in with our

---

[9] Father Grene notes: "Father Curry was companion to Father Holtby on his return to England at the beginning of this year. He died a holy death in England, as Father Gerard bears witness in his notes" (See *Life of Father John Gerard*, p. 209).

Father Superior, who received me in our customary manner, and after a short time sent me to London, where I found the whole city black with gibbets, on which many Catholics had been hanged in the storm which the Earl of Leicester had raised not long before. . . .[10]

At the beginning of the following year there were sent from the Seminary at Rheims two priests [Miles Gerard and Francis Dickinson], who were betrayed before they embarked at Calais, so the report runs, and given up to the pursuivants ere they left the ship. They were first most cruelly tortured to force them to give information as to what was going on beyond the seas. Nowadays to give colour of clemency the heretics use this form of torture instead of the rack. They hang up priests, and sometimes other Catholics, fastened only by the hands or forearms, and that for several hours together, adding weights if the victims were light, so it is said.

But having gleaned no information thereby, they approached these Christian Martyrs in another fashion. They sent them to a prison where they were treated somewhat more liberally. The gaoler feigned himself their friend, and persuaded them to write to their friends for necessary supplies. One of them (Gerard) sent letters to one of good family, named Drieland, which the

---

[10] Father Grene notes: Here he narrates the martyrdom of Mr. Nichols and Mr. Yaxley and their companions, which is found more at length, *Collectanea M*. folio 222.

gaoler handed to Topcliffe, the rack-master. He substituted for them forged letters, and sent them to Drieland as if they came from the priest. Drieland received them, and wrote back as though to an unknown correspondent. The priest, not suspecting fraud, wrote again.

At last finding that this trick did not succeed in compromising any one, they charged the priests with a fresh crime—viz. that they had been commissioned to draw off sailors from England for the service of the Catholic King. This they most emphatically denied. But the Judge deeming it sufficient that some asserted the fact, condemned them to be hanged. Meantime they held discussions on points of doctrine, stoutly and bravely professing the Roman and Catholic faith. One of them also undertook the defence of the primacy of the Roman Pontiff against certain of the heretics.

After some days they were taken to Rochester in Kent, disputing with their adversaries on the way, and making the foolishness of their reasoning clear to all. They were hanged and quartered, giving in their death a splendid testimony to the Catholic faith.

About that time there was another priest captured in London. [He describes the martyrdom of Christopher Bales and Horner, which we have elsewhere written out more at length.] These priests were shortly followed by two others (Jones and Middleton), one of whom was in great repute with the Catholics for his sermons, by which he moved many to a better life, and filled them with courage to profess the faith. He was betrayed, it is said, by a woman who had pretended that she was about to become a Catholic. As soon as he was captured they hurried him to the usual place of torture. His tormentors pressed him with questions as to those with whom he had lived, where he had said Mass, &c. But he would not utter a word to compromise any one.

He was, therefore, sent to prison, but being allowed some liberty wrote to a certain young man. As usual the letters were intercepted by the satellites of Topcliffe, and they discovered that the priest had certain moneys deposited with this young man, and [these they got from him].... But to return to the priest. Being brought to trial, the only charge against him was that he had acted as a priest. His defence was long and bold, showing plainly to all men the cruelty of the heretics and his own innocence.

After a day or two [May 6] they are led to the place of execution [in Fleet Street near the Conduit], where the populace had gathered in great numbers. Mr. Jones, seeing this charge written on top of the gallows, FOR TREASON AND FAVOURING OF FOREIGN INVASION, cried out that it was utterly false. Then having mounted the ladder he was allowed to speak a few words, and said that he was being put to death because he had tried to help his hapless country, and other such things as showed his true faith. Hearing this the heretics ordered him to be thrown from the ladder, and so, while yet alive, his belly was ripped open and his bowels pulled out and flung into a fire, he bearing all with marvellous constancy.

Meanwhile, to terrify his companion by the sight, for he had been captured but two days before, they placed him so near that he is thought to have been besprinkled with his fellow's blood; but the sight seemed to inspire him with greater courage. So they drew him on the hurdle, according to their wont, to [Clerkenwell] another part of the city, where a gallows had been made ready for him.

Mr. Middleton was a man of slight figure and short of stature, but of an indomitable soul. Arrived at the appointed place of execution, he briskly climbed the ladder, saying to a certain minister who had annoyed him by his garrulity, "Farewell, heretic, I am now out of thy power." There was hardly any one who did not wonder at this freedom of language, and at the face of the Martyr, which shone with a marvellous beauty.

Topcliffe was standing by, pale with rage to see himself beaten by so small a man, when the Martyr asked his permission to speak.

"Yes," said he, "if you have anything to say to the glory of God "—the formula of the heretics —" otherwise be silent."

Understanding by this that he might utter nothing but what was agreeable to them, he said,

"Be it so; if I may not confirm the Catholic and Roman faith by my words, I will confirm it with my death;" and saying this he resigned himself into the hands of the executioner.

In these martyrdoms there is a fact we must not omit to mention. While they were being tried, they had cast friendly glances at their companions and acquaintances. These were forthwith seized and imprisoned in the closest confinement.

About the time this was going on, there landed in the north four other priests who had been sent from the Seminary, who are said to have been apprehended, and to have stoutly endured the extremity of suffering.[11] They are said to have been betrayed by a pretended Catholic, who shortly after came to a miserable and shocking end.

(IX.) VENERABLE ROGER DICCONSON AND RALPH MILNER.

Mr. Welby [Dicconson] having done much good by his labours in God's vineyard, was apprehended in Hampshire, brought up to the Clink in London, arraigned at Winchester, where

---

[11] The date of their death, of which Dr. Challoner was uncertain, is fixed by the following extract from the Parish Registers of St. Oswald's, Durham, 1590:

Duke, Hylle, Hogge, Holiday, iiii. Seminaries Papists Tretors and Rebels to hyr Mages- tye were hanged and quartered at Dryburne for there horrible offences the 27 day of May.

(R. E. Chester Waters, *Parish Registers in England*, 1883, p. 56).

many that were taken with him being at the bar, they cried that they might have the same sentence that he had, and that they were as guilty of death as he was, both being only for their conscience. The Judge, angry at their speeches, caused them to be indicted, but when they came to be arraigned, and again craved to receive the same sentence as their priest, the Judge turned to Mr. Welby and angrily told him that their blood should be exacted at his hands.

"Yea, my lord," said he, "so said Pilate, turning the fault upon the Jews. I pray God that both theirs and mine be not exacted upon you."

One named Miller [Milner] was condemned with him, a poor honest farmer, having a wife and ten children. This man being very zealous, had been an earnest and most diligent furtherer of God's service and helper of priests. When he was arraigned, the Judge said that he was worse than any Seminary priest, meaning that he did more good to the Catholics.

"Yea," answered Miller, "you say most true, my lord; I am far worse than any of those good men, and am not worthy to be compared to them."

They both with great joy accepted the sentence of death, and with no less constancy suffered the execution thereof. When Miller, who suffered after Mr. Welby, was going up the ladder, the Justice said, "Come down, fool, and look to thy children." He thinking he had meant he should live, came down, and then the Sheriff told him that if he would go to church the Queen would spare him. He presently goeth up the ladder again, saying that she might keep that mercy for others, but he said he had not lived so long a Catholic to go now to heretical service.

When he was on the ladder, his children asked him blessing. He desired God to bless them and to send them no worse death than their father, at which all the people laughed; but he thought it a high blessing to wish them to die Martyrs.

(X.) RELATION WRITTEN BY A PRIEST IN ENGLAND.[12]

Mr. Pilchard, priest, being taken and imprisoned in Dorchester gaol, betwixt that and his death, which was but a fortnight, he made thirty Catholics that sought unto him being in prison. He used himself so well that his keeper began to show him what friendship he could, and therefore he had a new keeper. Condemned to die, he was so cruelly drawn upon the hurdle that he was almost dead when he came to the place; but afterwards recovering himself something, he was hanged, and as I think quartered, being so soon cut down that he was half alive.

One being at his execution told a person that had fallen, that there was no other way to be saved but in that faith in which Mr. Pilchard died, whose soul he saw carried by angels into Heaven,

[12] This relation commences with an account of the Venerable Roger Dicconson and Ralph Milner, which has already been given, pp. 88, 96.

and that he should shortly follow him, as he did, for that he presently fell sick and so died. The keeper of the gaol fell presently sick, and said openly unto many standing by, that the devils did strive for him, and that they would presently carry him away; but that he saw Mr. Pilchard stand with a cross betwixt him and them.

Mr. Pilchard had no sooner his judgment, but was presently commanded to execution, so that he had not an hour's space between judgment and execution. As he was laid on the hurdle the minister and preacher of the town said, *Oportet te gloriari in Christo Jesu.* His quarters were buried in the field: the manner of his execution was, as before, with such cruelty, that the people murmured much at it.

[All this relation is written by a priest then in England, as appeareth, but no year is expressed.]

(XI.) FATHER CHRISTOPHER WALPOLE TO FATHER PERSONS.

"From Spain, September 19, 1604.

"From Father Michael [Walpole] I received one from Bruges in Flanders of the 17th of August. He writeth no particulars but only of the death and martyrdom of one Swete, *alias* Cope, and a layman in Warwickshire,[13] at whose condemnation the Judge protested the rigorous execution of the law hereafter, it being both commanded

---

[13] Venerable John Sugar, *alias* Sweet, *alias* Cope, priest, with Venerable Robert Grissold, layman, suffered at Warwick, July 16, 1604.

by Parliament, and again in particular by the King [James I.] so straitly, as that he would not have his own letters to have credit to the contrary and much less any other Councillor's."

[*Note by Father Grene.*—The Catalogue of Douay puts this martyrdom of Mr. Sugar, August, 1604. If this be true, the author of that Catalogue meaneth August, *stylo novo*, for Father Blunt in a letter dated London, 1st August, 1604, relateth this martyrdom as done at Warwick the last Assizes.]

VARIA.

Cheek, one of the Council of York, having derided Mr. Francis Ingleby for making a cross at the bar, within few hours broke his neck down a pair of stairs.

Hurlston of the same Council going to the Bishop of York to have leave to torment some Catholics, expecting in *anticamera*, fell down dead and stunk horribly.

Topcliffe having cruelly tormented Mr. Francis Dickinson, priest and martyr, after his death defamed him for being naughty with women. He objected the same vice unto Mr. Bales, Martyr, openly in the Sessions House, but Mr. Bales so answered him that the whole shame returned upon Topcliffe [whose great wickedness in regard of this vice, see *Collectanea M.* p. 105.[14]— *Note by Father Grene*].

[14] See above, p. 119.

Mr. Hugh Moor, who was martyred at London 1588, was persecuted to death by his own father.

I knew one Mary, a young woman, dispossessed of many devils by Mr. Dibdale the Martyr.

Robert Sutton, priest, martyred at Stafford, being taken as he visited the gentlemen prisoners John Wolsey Esquire, William Maxfield Esquire, Edward Sprat, Francis Thornbery and his elder brother, gentlemen, condemned for that they received Mr. Sutton into the prison.

2. Of the Venerable Robert Sutton, Stonyhurst College possesses a very noble relic, the history of which is given in the following document.

THE RELICS OF MR. ROBERT SUTTON, PRIEST.

Taken from some note-books existing at the English College in Rome in the handwriting of Father John Gerard, S.J., this 22nd Jan. 1689.—*Note by Father Grene.*

Mr. Robert Sutton, who suffered martyrdom for the Catholic faith at Stafford in the year 1587, had previously been minister, and usurper of the office of parish priest in the parish of Lutterworth in the county of Leicester, where formerly the impious heretic Wyckliff had held that office. Here Mr. Robert was converted to the true faith, and at the same time to a sound and holy mind by his younger brother, Mr. William Sutton,[15] a learned and pious man [who afterwards joined the Society of Jesus].

By whose advice, in order the better to satisfy

[15] William Sutton was sent to England from Douay in the year 1577.—*Note by Father Grene.*

God and his parishioners, before quitting a place he had held so many years unjustly, he brought them all together to speak to them. He began by showing great sorrow, and begging their pardons for having been so long not only a blind guide, but one who had led them into pitfalls and noxious errors. Then he declared that there was no hope of salvation outside the Roman Church, &c.

Having uttered these words he came down from the pulpit, threw off his gown (being otherwise ready booted and girt for the journey), and with another younger brother, whom he had brought up in his house, mounted their horses, which a trusty servant had ready outside the churchyard, and rode to London, whence they immediately crossed to Belgium, to study at the English College. On the completion of his studies Mr. Robert Sutton, having been ordained priest, came back to England, where I knew him for some years, labouring strenuously and holily in the Lord's vineyard.

Apprehended at length in the house of a Catholic relative of mine, with whom he had spent no short time in the chief town of that county (Stafford), he was cast into prison, and when, in the course of the year, the Judges came there according to custom, he was arraigned, convicted, and condemned as guilty of high treason, for having, as a priest of the Roman Church, presumed to come to England contrary to the laws, &c.

In the night preceding his passion he was heard by some Catholic prisoners in conversation with others; but they, knowing that he was in strict solitary confinement, and fearing lest some attempt might be made against him secretly, descended to the door of his cell and found it securely shut, but looking through a window, they saw him enveloped in light and praying. Next morning the Catholics waited at the door of the prison to see the Martyr go forth and to commend themselves to his prayers; on seeing them the good Father commended himself to theirs, that God would be pleased to grant him constancy and perseverance to the end, "from Whom," he said, "I have this night received greater consolation than I deserved."

He was drawn, as usual, to the place of execution, and hanged. When he was half dead, the rope was cut, and he fell to the ground. His head was cut off, his body divided into four parts to be hung up in various places.

After the lapse of a whole year, the Catholics, wishing to have some relics from the holy body of the Martyr, carried off one night by a pious theft a shoulder and arm. All the flesh was consumed, torn, and eaten by the birds, except the thumb and forefinger, which were found whole and uninjured and clothed with flesh; so that on these, which had been anointed with holy oil and sanctified by contact with the most holy Body of Christ, a special honour above the other fingers was conferred, even in this world, before the day of the Resurrection, when the whole body will shine like the sun in the sight of the Father.

His brother, Mr. Abraham Sutton (whom Robert had left at Douay), and who is now also a priest, showed me both these fingers thus wonderfully preserved, and gave me the forefinger.[16] I have kept it deposited in a silver and glass reliquary with great reverence, with a paper on which the above account is briefly set down. Our Fathers in England have the reliquary with its sacred treasure, unless perchance, by the iniquity of the times, it have been made the spoil of the heretics.

[Father John Gerard, *alias* Tomson, wrote the above A.D. 1630, the 27 April.

The above is from the autograph.]

3. We now give some summaries made by Father Grene of fuller accounts of martyrdoms in his *Collectanea E*.

At York, Mr. Taylor, having received sentence of death with a layman on a Thursday, and on the following day, Friday, having said Mass and his Office; "How happy," said he, "should I be, if on this day, on which Christ died for me, I might encounter death for Him."

---

[16] Father Gerard should have said that the thumb, not the forefinger, was in the possession of the Society. See *Life of Father John Gerard*, Third Edit. p. 120, for an account of this and other relics that have happily been preserved to our time.

Scarcely had he said this when the officer unexpectedly came to lead him off to execution, and leaving the layman for Saturday (the usual day for executions), put him immediately to death.[17]

Edward Campion [suffered at Canterbury, October 1, 1588], a man both in name and in deed like Edmund Campion. Being in prison with some who meditated flight, they tried to induce him to join them, but he replied: "I would readily consent, if I did not hope to suffer martyrdom with the rest."

When any one was condemned to death, his Catholic fellow-prisoners met on the day on which he was to suffer, and recited first the litanies and the *Stabat Mater*, and with other prayers besought Almighty God to grant constancy and courage to those about to die.

George Douglas, a Scotch priest. He was taken at Ripon and brought up for examination, for alleging that the children of priests were illegitimate, and denying the false bishops to be really bishops, and was thereupon cast into a dark prison. Being afterwards removed from thence, he gave lessons to the sons of a certain Justice, who was also a warden of that prison, and who detained him in free custody. He still, however, communicated with heretics, and did

---

[17] Challoner gives November 26, 1585, as the date of his death. This was a Friday.

not himself altogether shun their churches. Being afterwards removed to York Castle, he was thrust into a low dungeon, where he suffered much, and contracted a fever, and after a time was reconciled to the Catholic Church.

He was a learned man, and handled Catholic controversy with such force against the ministers, and so manifestly got the better of them that they retired in confusion and could answer nothing. He was sharp in speech, and inveighed without stint, against the wives of ecclesiastics, and the ministers themselves. Being afterwards examined by the heretics, whether he acknowledged the Queen to be Supreme Head of the Anglican Church, he most freely denied it, and proved his point with such authorities and arguments that for that cause alone he was convicted of high treason. He suffered on the 9th of September, 1587.

Edmund Sikes, priest, was put to death on the 23rd of March, 1588. He was accused and betrayed by his brother. He was first exiled, then slain.

Edward Burden, priest, was martyred 29th November, 1588. He was a very weak man, and one who kept his learning in the background. When Father Dalby was led off to his trial he complained, saying: "Shall I always lie here like a beast, while my brother hastens to his reward? Truly I am unworthy of such glory as to suffer for Christ."

He was then ill with consumption, but next day as he lay sick on his bed, the gaoler came to him and called him to the court. The summons so invigorated him that, dressing himself at once, he hastened thither with as much alacrity as if he were not ill, so that the Judges found fault with the gaoler for having said he was sick.

He was a very mild man and endowed with a wonderful sagacity in dealing with spiritual diseases, especially in confession, and gifted with an admirable prudence in consoling wounded souls. He used to journey on foot, for though slight and infirm of body, the vigour of his mind overcame this weakness. When he went on an errand of mercy to souls, he seemed rather to fly than to walk.

Robert Dalby was martyred 16th of March, 1589. He was apprehended at Scarborough, at the very time of his landing. He seemed to contend with Father Burden as to which of them should first be called to receive the crown; for as soon as he was brought before the court, he answered with such boldness, that the Judges openly declared that they found him guilty, because he professed himself to be a priest. Among other things objected against him was this, that a sixpence was found in his purse, on which the Queen's likeness was nearly rubbed off, and they said he would do the same to the Queen herself if he could.

When he was led to execution with John Amias they both went as joyfully as if they were going to a feast, and having kissed and blessed the hurdle, they of their own accord lay, nay, threw themselves upon it, so that the bystanders wondered at the joyousness of their countenances and the alacrity of their movements. They would not suffer themselves to be tied down to the hurdle as was usual.

Though Dalby was very downcast before his sentence, at being put off to another Session, because he could not attain his crown in Father Burden's company, yet after judgment such joy welled up in his heart that he could not conceal it, and therefore on the road he kissed Father Amias and encouraged him in the conflict.

In former days, when Father Dalby was still a minister, being admonished by some Catholic of his state, he fell into such despair (considering his past life) that he attempted to kill himself with a knife. The stroke not being mortal, a boy called for help as he fell, and the neighbours came to his assistance. Then a certain priest having reasoned him into a sounder frame of mind, he left his country and betook himself to Rheims, where he was made priest, and returning to England he finally washed out with his own blood the stains of his former life.

John Amias was martyred with Father Dalby. When these two stood at the bar, a man imprisoned for theft, named Bramley, who had been brought up in heresy, thought he saw a globe of light over the heads of these priests hanging from the roof of the court. When they were answering the charges and questions of the Judges, the light moved over their heads, but when the Judges were speaking, it moved over the place where they sat and then returned again towards the priests. At the sight of which the aforesaid Bramley experienced great delight, but when the speeches were over the light vanished.

The thief was so much moved by this, that repenting of the sins of his past life, he desired to be admitted into the bosom of the Catholic Church, and having been made a living member of the Body of Christ, he behaved with such constancy, that he refused to pray with the heretical ministers, declared that he no longer belonged to their synagogue, but believed in all things according to the teaching of the Catholic Church. Many were the tears he shed over his past sins, and commending himself to the prayers of Catholics, he bore with patience the punishment due to his crimes, at the same time and place as the aforesaid priests.

4. The following document is thus introduced by Father Grene: "No author is noted. It wants one or two pages of the beginning. Yet here I will copy

some things, changing as little as possible the words, but omitting what seemeth of less moment. It was written in 1595, or in end of 1594."

A RELATION OF DIVERS PERSECUTIONS.
1588—1594.

Stephen Rowsam.—After the Judge had condemned this servant and priest of God, he was returned to his prison. But by the way a graceless company of apprentices and youths of Gloucester were gotten to one of the dunghills, from which they pelted this holy confessor most spitefully and all berayed his face and clothes.

The morning he was martyred, he offered the Divine Sacrifice of Mass, and there were with him at it Mr. Thomson aforesaid (there called Groves) and many more Catholics. They all confessed and did receive at his hands. When Mass was almost ended, the Sheriff's officers called at the prison door to have the holy man to his martyrdom. They were told he was not as yet ready, and entreated to have patience a little, unto which they yielded. After Mass, he said his Evensong, blessed, kissed, and embraced every one present, he went down cheerfully to the hurdle, all his company much lamenting his departure from them.

Before he came to the hurdle, one of the under-keepers said thus to him:

"O, Mr. Rowsam, if I were in the like danger as you are, and might avoid it as easily as you may by going to church, surely I would soon yield to that."

. The good Father answered, "I pray thee be contented, good friend; within this hour I shall conquer the world, the flesh, and the devil."

He was then so laid on the hurdle that one of his legs draggled on the ground as he was drawn, and being admonished by a schismatic woman to draw up his leg to him, he said, "No, all is too little for Christ's sake."

He was hanged until he was dead, but so was not Mr. Sandys[18] that died there before him, but most bloodily and beastly used, so that the very common sort of people cried out upon the officers, and some preachers sued that Mr. Rowsam should not be so handled.

This Mr. Rowsam had divers strange visions, even being a schismatic, and many more after he was a Catholic and priest. The said Mr. Thompson, his fellow-prisoner (as before is said), got them of him, and let the writer have a copy, which he dispersed into many counties of England, but yet at the writing of this present had none with him, else he would have set them down all. This only he doth perfectly remember, Mr. Rowsam being in [Oriel][19] College in Oxford, and running forth with many others one day to see strange meteors that then

---

[18] Venerable John Sandys executed at Gloucester, August 11, 1586.

[19] Blank in MS. In a list of Oriel College in 1572, S. Rowsam appears among the commoners (Oxf. Hist. Soc. *Registrum Un. Oxon.* vol. ii. pt. ii. p. 40).

appeared in the sky, he beheld over his own head and very near to him a crown very bright and splendent, which he showed to his fellows that stayed by him. God the Father and God the Son appeared sundry times to him when a priest; so did our Lady with words as he would not utter. For the space of one night and day, or thereabout, being a prisoner, he lived in unspeakable joy, which he deemed a taste of Heaven. As he prayed once in the Tower of London, many singing birds came over his book and pictures which stood before him.

The 28th of March [May], 1582, were martyred at London Mr. Thomas Ford, and Mr. John Shirt, and Mr. Robert Johnson, priests. The same day they appeared to Mr. Rowsam in the Tower, and let him feel what pains their martyrdom had been to them, and with what joy they were rewarded. Before he was banished, being prisoner in the same Tower, and most desirous to celebrate Mass, he had all things necessary thereto conveyed unto him, he not knowing how or by whom. This Dr. Stafferton told and bade us report on his knowledge and credit.

It followeth in the said relation, anno 1593.

These fellows [he has been speaking of the pursuivants, enumerating their many and most unjust vexations of Catholics] could get no Justice in Shropshire to aid them, but they met with a monstrous apostate, one Lewis, that had been a schoolmaster and Catholic. He hath six fingers on every hand, and as many toes on either foot, a monster five times over in making and manners. This monster directed them to all places he knew.

In July of the same year, 1593, with an outcry they apprehended Mr. John Pybush, priest, at Morton Henmarshe in Gloucestershire, had him before the Lord Giles Shandis (now dead) who offered him often the oath of the Queen's Supremacy, then sent him up to the Privy Council, where the Lord Treasurer, understanding he was a Seminary priest, bade him show his crown. The holy confessor bowed down his head and told him he had none, and that his Lordship could easily guess at the reason.[20] "O," said my lord, "you think yourselves wiser than all the world. Will you stand to the law?"

"I must, whether I will or no," said the priest.

"Then have him to Topcliffe," quoth my Lord Treasurer, showing all this while great anger.

Topcliffe put him close prisoner in the Gatehouse at Westminster and never returned to him till the year's end, and then he examined him what preparation of wars he knew, when he came into England, and so sent him to Gloucester gaol, there to be tried, where he was taken.

The last Summer Assize (which was 1594) the holy priest was arraigned of high treason, who, before he could answer guilty or not guilty, asked of the Judge, who was Mr. Clench, whether the treason they laid to his charge was anything else

---

[20] His crown means, of course, his tonsure, which would not be worn by a priest in disguise.

but his priesthood and the exercise of his priestly office.

The Judge answered, they had nought else to lay against him.

Then the holy man replied, "If to be a priest be to be a traitor, then am I one. I thank God for it."

But the Judge never gave sentence of death on him, but returned him to prison, where he yet remaineth joyfully and resolutely expecting martyrdom the next Assize, which shall be ere Easter, 1595, and daily he provideth for that high honour.[21]

I told you before that Mr. Sandys, who was martyred at this Gloucester, was bloodily butchered. I will here set down some particulars. When they had condemned him, they could find none for any money to murder him; they could hire no knife or other instrument in all the town to mangle him. At last they found a most base companion, who yet was ashamed to be seen in that bloody action, for he blacked and disfigured his face, and got an old rusty knife full of teeth like a sickle, with which he killed him.

[21] The Venerable John Pybush was not destined to die so soon as the writer of this paper imagined. For, some of his fellow-captives breaking prison, our Martyr escaped with them, but taking little care to hide himself, he was rearrested, tried once more, and this time sentenced to death at Westminster, June 25, 1595 (P.R.O. *Coram Rege*, 37 Eliz. Trin. n. 146, 2°). Execution was however deferred until February 18, 1601, when after a day's notice he was hanged, drawn, and quartered at St. Thomas Watering.

The holy Martyr had requested the High Sheriff (who was Paul Tracy of Stanwaye) to suffer him to hang until he died. He then granted the request, yet caused him to be cut down as soon as he was cast off the ladder. The holy man was nothing past himself, but said, "O, Mr. Sheriff, you have not kept your promise." Unto which Mr. Tracy replied not, but commanded his men to pull down the traitor, the hangman to bowel him, and himself laid first hands on him. The hangman did his bloody office, the holy Martyr ever catching his ragged knife in his bare hands, thereby to save himself, but it was even pulled out most forcibly, wherewith they cut and mangled his sacred hands most pitifully. When he had pulled from him his bowels, the blessed saint cried ever with St. Stephen, "Lord, forgive my persecutors," and so fell asleep in the Lord.

That monstrous Lewis I talked of caused Nicholas Smallman, his wife, brother, and sister, all of Shropshire, to be apprehended and committed to the Castle of Shrewsbury in 1582 or 83, where they have been in prison ever since, because they will not go to church; but Nicholas was removed to London to the Gatehouse, 1584, where he yet remaineth, because he was too resolute and stout in God's cause and therefore thought to do much harm in the said country and city. He was a good freeholder, &c.

Finis hujus relationis.

w

CHAPTER XV.
PAPERS FROM NYMPHENBURG.

DOCUMENTS.

1. Relation of the martyrdom of the Venerable Thomas Reynolds and the Venerable Bartholomew Roe, O.S.B. Latin.
2. Martyrdom of the Venerable Edward Morgan.
3. Martyrdom of the Venerable Thomas Bullaker, O.S.F. Latin.
4. Martyrdom of the Venerable Thomas Holland, S.J. French.

1. Nymphenburg is the central house in Bavaria of the famous teaching order of the Institute of Mary, commonly called the Englischen Fraülein or English Ladies. It represents the Paradeiser Haus in Munich, which was founded in 1626 by Mary Ward and her English companions. A search through a considerable collection of documents relating to the foundation and history of the Institute brought to light four contemporary papers relating to the deaths of English Martyrs in the year 1642. By the kind permission of the Reverend Mother General, we produce them here, and they shall be the closing chapter of this volume. Fortunately they refer to Martyrs of whom nothing has as yet

been said in this record of Acts, and they will serve as specimens of the later class of our English Martyrs.

The names of all the Martyrs with whom we are here concerned figure near the top of the list presented to Parliament in 1651 by four pursuivants, Wadsworth, Newton, Mayo, and Luke. This list [1] contains the names of thirty-six priests, all tried and condemned through the agency of these four priest-catchers, who apply to Parliament for a reward for their services. Of these thirty-six priests, thirteen were martyred at Tyburn, and now bear the title of Venerable, ten are recorded in the pursuivants' list to have died in Newgate, four are said to be "now in Newgate," six were banished, two seem to have been pardoned, and one escaped.

The first of our Nymphenburg papers is dated London, February 1, 1642, the year being given in New Style. It tells us of two Martyrs, a secular priest and a Benedictine, who suffered together at Tyburn on Friday, the 21st of January, O.S., in that year. The one Martyr was the Venerable Thomas Green, otherwise called Reynolds, to whom our manuscript erroneously gives the Christian name of Richard; and the other the Venerable Bartholomew Roe, a Benedictine, called in religion Dom Alban.

VENERABLE THOMAS REYNOLDS, SECULAR PRIEST, AND VENERABLE BARTHOLOMEW ROE, O.S.B.

Suffered at Tyburn, January 21, 1641—42.

On the 31st day of January two priests suffered a glorious martyrdom at Tyburn in London. One of these was Mr. Richard Reynolds, a

[1] Lingard, Edit. 1849, vol. viii. p. 45; *Troubles*, i. p. 336.

secular priest, who fourteen years ago had been condemned to death on account of his priesthood, but who had been reprieved by a royal warrant and discharged from prison.[2] He was a man of singular meekness and most gentle manners, whereby he so far won the affections of the Protestants that many of them publicly declared with tears before his martyrdom that such a man ought not to be put to death.

On the scaffold he openly proclaimed that his death was ennobled by the cause for which he died. That cause was Religion, which, he said, needed no glory from his death; and, although he had by a royal warrant been exempted from ordinary judicial authority, he nevertheless declared that he forgave all who had been in any way whatsoever instrumental in bringing about his execution. Here he was interrupted by the Sheriff, who presides at public executions of this kind, and who out of reverence for the man of God had remained with head uncovered the whole time he was speaking to the people, which was for about half an hour. "And do you, sir, forgive me?" he said, "for in this matter I must do my duty." "Most freely I forgive you," answered the Martyr. Then he raised his heart awhile in prayer to God, sweetly embraced his companion, and, after having tenderly kissed the halter, at once placed it round his neck; the

---

[2] He remained in prison from 1628, when he was condemned to death, to 1635. He was again arrested in June, 1641, and executed on his former condemnation.

cart was then drawn away, and he gave up his blessed soul to God.

Many had feared that he would waver when brought face to face with death, because he had seemed to show some timidity, and to be struck with terror of the difficulties of the time, more particularly as, instead of execution on the scaffold, his life was offered him if he would give up the Catholic faith. But the love of God prevailed, and despising this corruptible life, he was led by that love to the possession of eternal life.

Immediately after him followed Dom Alban Roe, of the Order of St. Benedict, a man of dauntless soul, and brave in all things. When he also, according to custom, began to speak on the scaffold, he declared that enough had already been said by his brother, pointing to Mr. Reynolds with his finger, so that it would be unnecessary to repeat it; but that if he had as many lives as he had committed sins during his whole life, he would willingly lay them all down in so good a cause. When he began to speak a little more sharply of the laws against priests made under Queen Elizabeth, and called them tyrannical and heretical, he was commanded by the Sheriff to desist from this manner of speech. He then asked the Sheriff whether his life would be granted him if he embraced the Protestant religion, and was answered that his life would without doubt be spared, and that there was nothing they wished more. The man of God then called upon God and men to bear witness that he died for his God and his religion only. The cart was then drawn from under him, and he gave up his soul to God.

The two Martyrs had for companions in death several criminals convicted of various offences. Of these it is said that two were converted by the Martyrs under the very scaffold itself. For while Mr. Reynolds was speaking to the people, Mr. Roe was seen to be in serious conversation with them, and they in turn were observed to make signs of sorrow and repentance; and when they were asked by the Calvinist minister to sing a Psalm after the Puritan manner, they turned away their faces, would not join in the Psalm, and, as others say, asked the prayers of the Catholic bystanders.

While all these things were passing, the wonderful fervour and piety of the Catholics were openly manifested. Some of them ran in the streets to the servants of God as they were led to execution, and threw themselves down to kiss their hands and garments; others implored their blessing; while others, again, exhorted them to constancy, exclaiming, "Courage, Soldiers of Christ; we would willingly give ourselves and our children to a similar death for the Catholic faith." The men of God answered with a smiling countenance, giving thanks and blessing the people, and saying they were going as it were to a wedding, adding that the hurdle upon which they were being dragged to execution for the

Catholic faith was far more pleasing to them than could be any royal chariot upon which they might be drawn in triumph. Upon that hurdle they heard each other's confessions.

The Catholics piously vied with each other in taking away relics of the Martyrs. Many dipped handkerchiefs in the dismembered bodies: others carefully collected the blood-stained straw from off the ground; while some snatched from the flames the intestines, which, as usual, had been thrown into the cauldron, and carried them home.

At the death of these two Martyrs were present some Protestant noblemen, who could scarcely refrain from tears, and openly proclaimed that by the example of these two holy Martyrs many persons would without doubt be converted to the Catholic faith.

2. The Venerable Edward Morgan, *alias* Singleton, may be claimed by most of the English Seminaries as one of their Martyrs. He seems first to have been at Douay. Thence in the year 1606, when he was over twenty, he went to the English College at Rome, where he received the minor orders. He entered the Society of Jesus in October, 1609, but he left from ill-health. For the same reason he left St. Alban's College, Valladolid, to which he went in 1615. He remained some time at Madrid, and was ordained priest at Salamanca, as he tells us in his speech on the scaffold. In 1621 he came on the English Mission, where he laboured for twenty years before he received his crown.

He is called Edward in the Roman register, John in that of Valladolid, and Edmund on his picture still existing in that College.

The following narrative is headed, "A brief relation of the cheerful, devout, and constant death of Mr. Edward Morgan, a Seminary priest." It appears to be the original English of the Latin account used by Challoner. The final phrase, which says that the officers asked the bystanders for their handkerchiefs and gloves to dip in the Martyr's blood, is very remarkable. The later martyrdoms vary in some respects from those of Elizabeth's time. The Sheriff standing uncovered all the while that the Venerable Thomas Reynolds was speaking is a great contrast to Topcliffe, who browbeat his victims to the very end of their lives.

VENERABLE EDWARD MORGAN.

Suffered at Tyburn, April 26, 1642.

He was condemned at the Sessions House in the Old Bailey in London on St. George's day, and received the sentence of death with great joy.

In the prison after condemnation, being visited by many, both Protestants and Catholics, he took much pains in answering the objections which the Protestants made concerning religion; which he performed with so much zeal, charity, and moderation in the manner of his speech that, although he confounded them exceedingly by the force of his arguments, and made clear their absurdity and the truth of the Catholic religion, yet he left them not offended, but satisfied, showing much respect and compassion towards him.

To the Catholics he spoke of his happiness for being condemned for so glorious a cause, and desired their prayers, that (to use his own words) he might die a true Roman Catholic priest—that is, that he might not be daunted with death, nor presume too much in himself, that he might die with courageous humility and with humble courage; that he pardoned all that had concurred to his poverty, or were the causes of his being called madman, of the misery of his imprisonment for fourteen years, and of his being condemned to die.

He told one who was with him upon Sunday night, that he had said Mass that day (not having had opportunity in a whole twelvemonth before to say it till then), and never in his life had more difficulty than to make an end of Mass, by reason of the extreme abundance of joy and comfort by which he said he was transported; and having used the words of St. Francis Xaverius, *Satis est Domine*, was enforced to divert his mind from thinking on the name of Jesus, that so his joy and tears being somewhat moderated he might make an end.

A good man[3] coming again to him the next day after, with such alms as many Catholics willingly offered for the satisfying of such debts as, for his mere necessary sustenance, he had contracted in

---

[3] This term was commonly used by Catholics to avoid mentioning the word "Priest." See, p. 247 *ante*.

two years, he found him in the same or rather more alacrity, having been tired all that day with satisfying all sorts of people that flocked to him, begging his prayers, of which some procured to take off all they could that was about him, as buttons, handkerchiefs, and at length tore off pieces of his coat, so much that he was brought to yield that his whole coat was taken from him and another sent him, and the whole night he did not go to bed.

Tuesday morning, which was the execution day, being drawn (as the custom is) after eight o'clock in the morning upon a hurdle, the people seemed to incline more to compassion than to offer any affront or uncivil words. And being somewhat straitly tied, by the neck especially, on the hurdle, and his head very low, whilst they stayed to settle and compose him, one desired him to drink a cup of wine. The while the whole multitude staying, he took occasion (upon some question made) to say he went to die for being a priest, and showed so much alacrity as all the people wondered. And one saying that the Popish priests could drink wine and be drunkards, another Protestant told him that because their ministers were such, therefore the seeing this man drink a cup of wine made him think their priests were drunkards too, but he was much deceived.

Another Protestant hearing how great care he had taken for the satisfying some small debts said, "This man will rise in judgment against Protestants, for (said he) he and those of his profession are just, and do no wrong." Yet some there were who upon occasion of some monies brought and paid in the prison to his creditors, said there were divers come to buy pardons of him, and that one lady gave him 25*l*. for a pardon of all the sins she should commit.

After the aforesaid halt, as they proceeded by the way, a Welsh footboy spake to him in Welsh, and he answered him in the same tongue very cheerfully, advising him and counselling him very cheerfully to be careful in serving God, and not to offend His Divine Majesty, with other holy admonitions, till upon notice taken by the officers the footboy was taken off.

When he came to Tyburn, the place of execution, the throng of coaches, horses, and people were so great and pressing that the hurdle could by no means pass (as usual) to the gallows; till at last, after some stay, and the much difficulty of the officers, a cart, with a basket in it to receive his blessed quarters after his death, made way till it was under the gallows, into which he very cheerfully ascended, and bending very devoutly upon his knees, recommended himself upon his knees to Almighty God. He rose up (no other noise being made after his arrival but of such as cried, " Peace, peace, peace, that we may hear him;" others demanding what he had said, and most standing with their hats off). Then, having cast away his hat to some one of his acquaintances, he looked so cheerfully and courageously as if he had mounted a triumphant chariot; and so walking to and fro in the cart till the multitude was somewhat appeased.

His first words were to desire Mr. Sheriff to hear him. His demand was whether he might be admitted to speaking, saying he so much respected authority that he would not speak one word without licence first had. The Sheriff with much ado laboured to get through the multitude, but not being able, sent word to him that he had leave to speak so much as he would. Then blessing himself he spake as followeth.

"Now having leave by authority to speak (without which," said he, "I would not), I must tell you that standing the other day at the Sessions, I have taken cold, and thereby fear I shall not be able to express myself so well as I wish, yet I will adventure to do so well as I am able, and will take for the subject of my discourse a short and brief sentence out of the words of God, and read this week in the holy Mass according to the custom of our religion: *Bonus Pastor animam suam dat pro ovibus suis*—'A good pastor giveth his life for his flock.' Mistake me not. I bring not these words to apply them to myself, who am most unworthy of this title and dignity, and a poor sheep of that grand Pastor of souls, Christ Jesus, Who suffered and died for us all. But before I expound this sentence, I will clear some doubts or questions, which some here present may have, or ask to be satisfied, in prevention of all idle and false billets and pamphlets after my death upon such occasions, and therefore do assure you I am neither Jesuit, monk, or friar, but a true Seminary priest. And further, to satisfy such as shall inquire after my name and country and education, I am by nation a Welshman, and by name Edward Morgan, my father's name was William; one of my mother's kindred had rule and government in the Low Countries, and afterwards made Lieutenant of the Tower of London. I speak not this out of ostentation, but that people may not be misinformed. I was born in the year 1584, and am now fifty-seven years of age. I went over in my young days into the Low Countries, where I studied some years, then in Rome, afterwards in Spain,[4] and was made a priest in Salamanca, from whence returning into England, I was taken and committed to the Fleet, where I have remained these fourteen years in much need, and hardly have had the wherewithal to satisfy and sustain nature, and have been held by some as a madman, which God forgive them for, as I do wish from the bottom of my heart."

After which he turned himself to the people, and began to expound the text before mentioned, but the noise of the tumult was so great that little could be heard. He showed that the death of Christ was an example and sufficient to all His to give willingly their lives for Him, and that to die for being a Roman Catholic priest is to die for His Church, and so consequently for Him. And as there was one God, one Baptism, one

[4] Challoner wrongly says, "From Spain he went to Rome."

faith, so there must be one Church, and if ever he had had any true reason or disproof of the Roman Catholic Church, he would never have continued a member thereof, but that he was sure there neither was, nor is any. He brought proofs of the antiquity and universality of the true Church, both in time and place, and the constant and uninterrupted succession thereof. And further, he showed the novelty of sects. And for the aforesaid true Church of Christ, he was ready and most willing to die, and offer up his blood, and pray for the good of his country and the greater union betwixt the King and Parliament (or to this effect).

And hereupon the doctor or minister-assistant interrupted him, and said, " Mr. Morgan, I would wish you to dispose yourself for death, and not to go about to seduce the King's people." He turning about to the minister told him it was not a time to dispute, which said, he turned again to the people, and went on with his former discourse, expressing how that he died only for being a true Seminary priest.

Here the minister again stopped him, saying, "No, Morgan, you mistake; you die for no such matter."

"For what then?" said Mr. Morgan.

The minister replied, "For going out of the kingdom against the laws of the land."

"Good sir," said Mr. Morgan, "trouble me no more," and returned to his discourse with great zeal, alacrity, and to the content of all the people;

until at last the minister spake to him the third time, and wished him to put his trust in the merits of the Lord, and not in angels and saints. Whereunto Mr. Morgan replied, "Mistake not yourself, sir, for I put my whole trust and confidence in the infinite merits of my Lord and Saviour Jesus Christ, Who died for me."

"That is well said," said the minister, and let him alone.

Then having ended his speech, and recommended himself most fervently to Almighty God, he with a merry countenance wished Gregory to do his office, and gave him a piece of money. Gregory going to dispose him in some posture, he said, "I pray thee, teach me, for I never was at this sport before."

Whereupon the minister said, "Mr. Morgan, this is not a time to sport, nor is it a jesting matter."

"Sir," said Mr. Morgan, "I know it is not jest, but good sober earnest; but you cannot deny but that God requireth a cheerful sacrifice, and I hope it is no offence to you and these good people that I go cheerfully and merrily to Heaven."

By this time Gregory, having made the rope ready, was putting it over his head, but Mr. Morgan desired to see it first, and then took it, and kissing the same, put it on, and so, recommending himself again to Almighty God, he pulled down the handkerchief over his face, and so was turned over, never once stirring, and hanged so, while Gregory was putting on his apron, sleeves, &c., and preparing his block and knives, &c., so that he hanged above a quarter of an hour, and was quite dead. And then Gregory fell to his butchery. So ended this glorious Martyr, to the admiration and astonishment of all the people, all crying, " Lord, receive his soul." And the officers calling for the people's handkerchiefs and gloves to wet in the blood, which they did, and delivered them again to their owners, and one got almost his whole heart out of the fire.

3. Our next document gives the "Death for the Catholic Faith of the Reverend Father Thomas Bulaker, of the Order of St. Francis, in London, October 22, 1642." The Venerable Thomas Bullaker, as his name is more commonly spelt, was in religion called Father John Baptist. He was born in 1604, he went to St. Omers at the age of seventeen, according to the *Certamen Seraphicum*, and in three weeks he was sent thence to the College at Valladolid. He arrived there in 1621, and while there he went by the name of Thomas Tailer. Making known to Father Alexander Baker, S.J., the vocation that he felt to the Order of St. Francis, after a retreat he was advised to ask admission to the Recollect Convent of Abrojo, and there he entered as a novice on the feast of Corpus Christi, 1622. After his profession and ordination Father John Baptist left Spain for England. On landing at Plymouth he was arrested, and was sent first to Exeter County Gaol. There he was not tried, as there was no evidence against him, but he was sent

to London in custody and there discharged. He had been twelve years in England, when by Wadsworth's means he was twice arrested, and thus at last obtained the crown of martyrdom. The following narrative is independent of that in the *Certamen Seraphicum*, which is Challoner's sole source of information.

VENERABLE THOMAS BULLAKER, O.S.F.
Suffered at Tyburn, October 12, 1642.

The English Catholics continue to fill up in Christ's Body, that is the Church, those things that are wanting to His Passion. Within less than two years' time from the beginning of the present Parliament, nine Martyrs have entered Heaven in the ranks of His purple-clad warriors. London, ever fruitful in holy Christian athletes, has been the scene of five of these martyrdoms, God so disposing matters, that in the capital of the whole kingdom and its most populous city, the constancy of Catholics should be conspicuously manifested to the greater praise of His Church.

The last to suffer was the Rev. Father Thomas Bullaker, of the Order of St. Francis, who died on the 22nd of October [N.S.], a priest of singular holiness, and a pattern of fortitude, modesty, and cheerfulness of demeanour, a cheerfulness which he manifested even in his execution. He was the son of a doctor at Chichester in the county of Sussex, and while a priest in England he devoted himself diligently to the care of souls. When scarcely more than forty years of age he gained the palm, for which, as one athirst, he had long yearned with burning desire.

The previous year, when he was in the country and heard of the death of Mr. William Ward, of happy memory, the first Martyr under the present Parliament,[5] he said to some friends who were with him: "How can I remain here when so great a crown is to be won in London? Did I not come back to England for this very end?" Forthwith he went to London, where he was apprehended when he was coming from the house of the Portuguese Ambassador. He boldly declared that he was a Catholic, and that he had often been present at Mass, although he had not this day had this consolation. He could not be induced to take the unlawful oath of allegiance, or to acknowledge the royal supremacy in matters spiritual; and he openly stated that he would swear to nothing that was contrary to the laws of God or against his conscience. But the fatal, and to him happy, hour had not yet come; for, bail being offered for him by his friends, he was released.

A few months afterwards, when other Martyrs had been put to death, Father Bullaker impelled by an increased hope of sharing their blessed lot, and moved in great measure by the death of Mr. Edward Morgan, again returned to London, and there fulfilled the holy offices of the priesthood with great fervour, zeal, and benefit to the souls of others. At last—I know not through

[5] Venerable William Ward suffered at Tyburn, July 26, 1641.

whose treachery—he was again apprehended while he was saying Mass in the house of Lady Powell, a noble matron of the family of the house of Montague. When taken before some members of the House of Commons, he bore himself with undaunted courage, and gave excellent proof of the truth of the old religion. His sentence was delayed until the sitting of the Judges on capital cases, which takes place at given periods in London.

When he was again called up for trial, he avowed frankly and bravely that he was a priest, but he absolutely denied that he was on that account guilty of any crime; and this he confirmed with such convincing reasons that the jury would not deliver their verdict without first consulting the Parliament. Two days afterwards, Father Bullaker was condemned to be hanged and quartered, which is the punishment adjudged in England to those found guilty of high treason. When he received the news of his death-sentence he had but one cause for sorrow, viz., that on account of the poverty he had vowed, he had nothing wherewith to make a present to the bearer of the good tidings; otherwise he would by no means have allowed him to go away without a gift, seeing that he had brought him the happiest news he had ever in his life received.

A pious fellow-prisoner lamented bitterly with feminine tears, but with manly courage, that she was not permitted to share his martyrdom. Two of his other penitents walked by the side of the osier hurdle on which he was dragged to the scaffold, and this through roads everywhere deep in mud. These holy women frequently kissed the outstretched hands of the priest, and eagerly drank in his pious counsels.

When he arrived at the place of execution, few could hear him speak, partly because his words were drowned by the noise of the assembled crowd of people, partly because his voice was weak, owing to his general exhaustion resulting from previous labours, night watches, prayers, and fasting. He had not been suffered to say much, before he was frequently interrupted by an importunate preacher, who, when the Martyr began to speak of the Real Presence of our Lord in the Blessed Eucharist, made himself most troublesome. But the Sheriff, a more humane man, willingly allowed the herald of truth to proceed, and he himself often and humbly petitioned the minister that he might do so, but the chattering impostor pretended that it was not fair that the faithful, that is the people, should be seduced by false doctrine.

When the servant of God was about to be hanged, the Sheriff in mercy promised that he should not be cut down until he was quite dead; for the executioners out of hatred usually cut down the priests while still half alive, and disembowel them while still breathing, and capable of feeling. The Martyr thanked him, but bravely answered that, though he acknowledged the kindness, he did not in the least fear any torture, and was even ready to be quartered before he was hanged. As he was found worthy of the contempt of the Cross, he was hanged amongst thieves and others guilty of crimes deserving death; but there was this difference, that the Master was placed between the crucified criminals, while His Martyr was the first of the condemned company to suffer.

The rope being ready, and all things else prepared, the servant of God remained awhile with his hands raised to his head. He had previously agreed with a priest of his Order who was present that when he gave this sign he should receive the last absolution. Thus gloriously died Father Bullaker, laden with merits rather than with years, ready for Heaven in the prime of life, a splendid example of Christian fortitude not to Catholics only, but also to heretics. Many of these last strongly condemned the exercise of such cruelty towards innocent men, and predicted many evils for the city of London on account of the unjust sentences there carried into execution against priests.

---

4. The Venerable Thomas Holland, S.J., who went by the names of Saunderson and Hammond, is said by tradition to be of Upholland in Lancashire. He was born in 1600. For about six years he was a student at St. Omers, where he was more than once elected Prefect of the Sodality. In 1621 he went to the Seminary at Valladolid, and while there he was sent to Madrid to deliver a Latin speech on occasion of the visit of the Prince of Wales, afterwards Charles I. In 1624 he entered the Society at

Watten, and he was ordained priest at Liège. He was Minister at the Tertianship at Ghent and then Prefect and Confessor at St. Omers. He took his last vows as Spiritual Coadjutor at Ghent, May 28, 1634, and in the following year he came on the English Mission, which he served for seven years. These were spent in London in the midst of the greatest dangers. He is reported to have been very ingenious in disguising himself, speaking French, Flemish, and Spanish, and perfectly able to imitate a foreigner's pronunciation of English. An interesting episode in Father Holland's ministry, which must have occurred soon after his arrival in London, was the part he had in the conversion of Lady Falkland's daughters by the refutation of William Chillingworth, an apostate, whom Archbishop Laud was employing to prevent their becoming Catholics.[6] The following paper needs no further introduction. It is written in French, and it is headed, "The happy and saintly death of Father Thomas Holland, priest of the Society of Jesus, which he suffered in London on suspicion of being a priest."

VENERABLE THOMAS HOLLAND, S.J.

Suffered at Tyburn, December 12, 1642.

On Wednesday, the 7th of December, 1642, Father Thomas Holland, of happy memory, after having endured two months' imprisonment, was summoned before the Judge and the twelve jurors, according to the form of justice in England. Where, being accused by three pursui-

---

[6] *The Life of Elizabeth, Lady Falkland*, 1585—1639. By Lady Georgiana Fullerton. London, 1883, p. 185.

vants, and an unfrocked Jacobin,[7] he answered courageously, and showed clearly to all the world that according to the laws of this country he was guilty of no crime. He was, notwithstanding, found guilty by the twelve jurymen, which caused so much astonishment to the members of Parliament that one of them, named Garoué [Garroway],[8] said loudly and clearly before them all, that if he had been one of the jurors he would not have agreed to the verdict for all the gold in the world.

The Saturday afterwards, when the time came to pronounce sentence of death against him, the Judge, named Sergeant Luisant,[9] said, "Sir, I have no fault to find with your life or with your actions. You have always acted honourably, but as the jury have convicted you, it is my duty to give sentence;" which was done, and Father Holland was taken back to prison until the Monday following.

During this short time hundreds of Catholics came to ask his blessing, and to recommend their needs to him. The Portuguese Ambassador sent a painter to him, being desirous to have his portrait;

[7] Thomas Gage, an apostate friar, had a share in the deaths of several Martyrs. See Foley, *Records*, ii. p. 520. His brothers were all excellent Catholics, Sir Henry Gage, Governor of Oxford, George, a secular priest, and William, a Jesuit.

[8] Father Tanner gives this name, and adds that the Lord Mayor, Sir Isaac Pennington, said the same. The latter name figures as "Ponnigagnoni."

[9] Peter Phesant was made Sergeant in 1640, Recorder for a month in 1643, Judge of the Common Pleas in 1645, and he died in 1649 (Hadyn's *Book of Dignities*).

and the Duc de Vendôme sent one of his gentlemen to say that if he wished, he would petition Parliament to grant him a respite. The Father humbly thanked them both, and said he did not merit it.

The Spanish Ambassador had him recommended in the Masses and prayers in his chapel, and sent him a message begging him to remember His Catholic Majesty and the affairs of his kingdom. The Father thanked him for the favours he had shown him, and promised to say on the morrow his last Mass for this intention.

On Sunday, the Capuchin Fathers brought the necessary furniture for the altar, and were present at the Mass in the prison, where several went to confession to the Father, and received Holy Communion at his hands.

In the afternoon, at five o'clock, he made his general confession to one of the Fathers of his own Society, and remained all the night in prayer.

On Monday, at about four in the morning, he celebrated Mass, confessed and communicated several persons, and about eleven o'clock he was taken on a sledge to the gibbet at Tyburn, one league from the city of London, where he was met by a Father of the same Society, who saluted him, and taking his hand, said, "Courage, Mr. Holland, good courage." To which he said, "Yes, with God's grace." Then standing up on the sledge and looking round, he said, "The silence and attention of this large company seem to show that I am to be allowed to speak. I declare to all that I do not intend to offend any one, and if in speaking a word should escape me, I beg to be excused, as it would be against my will. But I forget, I ought to begin with the sign of the Cross, the sign with which we overcome our enemies."

He then said in Latin, *In nomine Patris*, &c. "I hope," he said, "that no one will be offended at this, as it is the sign of the Christian. I have been brought here to die as a traitor, a priest, and a Jesuit; but I may say in truth that none of these things have been proved. My accusers are Newton, a pursuivant, John Cook, his servant, and Wadsworth, another pursuivant, and one that it pains me very much to name—a man on whom I pray God to have mercy and to bring back to the Church from which he has apostatized miserably,—Thomas Gage, an unfrocked Jacobin priest. All that Newton and Cook could testify against me is, that they saw me in the company of Mr. Smyth,[10] who they say is a Jesuit priest; and to render me more detestable Newton says, though most falsely, that Mr. Smyth was principally concerned in the Gunpowder Plot. John Cook was asked by the Judge if Mr. Smyth had ever said that I was a priest. He answered, 'No, he had not said so.' The other two reported they had seen me studying at the Seminaries on the Continent, and nothing more. This is important. If they are now present they know I am speaking the truth.

[10] Father Henry Floyd, *alias* Smith (Foley, *Records*, i. p. 549).

"These proofs, if they are examined into, are as much against my accusers as against me, as they have themselves kept the same company, and lived and studied in the same Seminary as I have, and many others, too, who are not priests.

"Having been maliciously accused, as you see, I put myself (according to the forms of justice of this kingdom) into the hands of God and my country, thinking to find people of judgment and good sense to conduct my trial; but I was, contrary to the laws of the country, convicted as a criminal without any proof, but solely by suspicion, jealousy, fear, and presumption. For according to law, to condemn a man who is accused of what is attributed to me, the witnesses ought to swear to the time and place where the order of priesthood was first received, or that I have been seen to exercise the functions of the priesthood, such as preaching, catechizing, saying Mass, hearing confessions, and the like. But nothing of all this was proved against me—nor can they name any one whom I have seduced or persuaded to change his religion—so that the Judge, Sergeant Luisant [Phesant], for his part, discharged me from all crime, saying on the bench, that he had nothing to say against my actions or behaviour. So that I am here only as a suspected person, and I am not obliged to say anything except that I am a Catholic and have lived with Catholics, as no one has proved anything else against me."

The preacher then asked him to say what he

was. The Father answered, "But, sir, I have just been telling you that very thing." The preacher said, "I did not hear, and I am here on purpose to hear and answer you when necessary." The people laughed at this, and said, "The man is deaf." The preacher, who was on horseback, at this spurred his horse against the people.

They then brought the cart, and the Father got up on it, and after him two thieves got up. After he had briefly repeated what we have said above, the preacher began to praise him and said, "Sir, you said very truly, you have behaved very well up to the present time, both in prison and on the way here, as I took notice."

The Father asked the executioner whether he could go on speaking, and where were the Sheriffs. "Sir," said the executioner, "speak freely as much as you will, and say nothing of the Sheriffs, as they are not present."

"Then," said the Father, "may God pardon the Judge, the jury, and my accusers. As for me, I pardon them heartily; but it would be better that they should make it a general rule for the future that if a man will not swear that he is not a priest, he shall be convicted of being one, even if they have only a suspicion or presumption of it. It is true that laymen can swear freely that they are not, but in my opinion they ought not to do so, but let the law take its course, so that this way of doing things should be prevented. However this may be, I acknowledge publicly before Heaven and earth, that I am, though very unworthy, a priest of the Society of Jesus, and this confession can do me no prejudice, as I have already been condemned to death without any proof, but I confess my profession openly to avoid any occasions of scandal."

The preacher here asked him several questions, viz., How he expected to be saved? Was it by the Blood of Jesus Christ, or how? The Father answered, "Sir, we are all Christians, and without doubt we all believe in Jesus Christ, that He is our Saviour, and that we cannot be saved except by His merits."

"I ask you," said the preacher, "whether you hope to be saved by the Blood of Jesus Christ alone, without the assistance of good works, and whether little children can be saved without Baptism, by means of their parents' faith alone."

The Father replied, "Sir, I am not come here to dispute; but what was it that Adam lost in Paradise? Was it this faith that you speak of? No, it was the grace of original justice. But let us talk of something more profitable to the people who are listening to us. Well, then, my friends, there is only one God in three Persons, the Father, Son, and Holy Ghost, three Persons in one God, and as there is only one God, so there is only one faith and one Church, and out of that Church there is no salvation. This is clear and evident, but the question is, Which is that Church? I answer that the true Church is that which teaches her children the end for which they were created and placed in this world, and also the means to arrive at this end, and it is only the Catholic, Apostolic, and Roman Church which teaches us these things, and to love God above all things, and our neighbour as ourselves, in order to obtain eternal life."

The preacher would not hear more, but said, "Enough, enough, sir; speak no more of that," and interrupting, caused the two thieves to speak. However, the other Father, who was by the side of the cart, said to Father Holland, in French, "Sir, the people want to know if you are a priest, and I beg of you to say so openly, as they do not understand it from what you have said."

When the thieves had spoken, Father Holland began to speak again, and published that he had been in Spain, France, the Low Countries, and Germany. "I have studied and prayed to God, I have taken all the pains I could to satisfy myself in the matter of religion for many years, and I have found by experience that there is no other way to salvation than the Catholic, Apostolic, and Roman Church. I was brought up, taught, and nourished in this faith to the present time, and now God gives me the grace to die in it, for which I thank Him from the bottom of my heart, as also for having called me to the order of priesthood, as in truth I am a priest. I am at liberty to say so now, as I am condemned to death, though without lawful proof."

The preacher now said, "Say no more about that, I beg you, sir, but pray to God quietly for yourself and think of eternity, while I dispose these other two to die well."

The preacher then made a long sermon by way of prayer, and sang the *Miserere* in English, after which the Father said, "Sir, I have not interrupted you in your prayers, and I pray you now to permit me to say mine, and to say them aloud, so that all can hear what I say." This being granted to him, he made the sign of the Cross in Latin, and knelt down and prayed in English. He made several acts of Faith, Hope, Charity, and Contrition, calling humbly on God for mercy on all the sins of his life, and asking Him also for pardon for his enemies. "I pardon," he went on to say, "Sergeant Luisant, who condemned me, the jury who found me guilty, my accusers, and all those who have had a part in my death, and also this man who has to execute the sentence. I pardon him. He is only the instrument of justice, and I give him what money remains to me, by the permission of those whom, after God, I honour the most."

In saying these words he put into his hand four pieces of silver, worth together five florins. He also prayed for his Majesty, King Charles, for our Queen, the Queen Mary, the young prince, the Duke of York, and the other children of their Majesties, praying God to bless them and draw them to His service. He also prayed for the King's Council, the Parliament, that God would reconcile them by a true and perfect union and subjection. In short, he prayed for the whole kingdom; and for the conversion and salvation of all. He offered not only his life, but said if he had as many lives as there were hairs on his head, or as there are stars in heaven on a clear night, or drops of water in the ocean, and perfections in God, he would willingly consecrate them all to this effect. Then he said, "O Father of Mercy, receive my sufferings, although most unworthy, in union with the sufferings of my Saviour; and of all those by the law of nature, the written law and the law of grace, that have been, are, or will be pleasing to Thee." This said, he shut his eyes; then opening them again a little, he turned to the Father, who gave him absolution, so that he could well hear those last words, *In nomine Patris*, &c. Immediately after, he got up, pulled down his nightcap over his eyes; they drove away the cart, and as he fell, a Catholic took the cap from him, so that we saw him, with his eyes and hands turned towards Heaven, and so he remained without moving till death. A soldier tried two or three times to close his eyes, but in vain. His face, in dying, became very red and then pale, and when the rope was cut, his usual colour returned. His quarters were carried back to the prison, to be fixed up at the gates of the city, and his head on the great bridge, according to the custom.

APPENDIX.

DECREE
OF THE CONGREGATION OF SACRED RITES
FOR THE DIOCESE OF WESTMINSTER,
CONFIRMING THE HONOUR GIVEN TO THE
BLESSED MARTYRS

JOHN CARDINAL FISHER, THOMAS MORE,
AND OTHERS,
PUT TO DEATH IN ENGLAND FOR THE FAITH
FROM THE YEAR 1535 TO 1583.

ENGLAND, once called the Island of Saints and Dowry of the Virgin Mother of God, was renowned, even from the first ages of the Church, for the sufferings of its many Martyrs. So too in the sixteenth century, when torn by dire schism from the obedience and communion of the Roman See, those were found who "did not hesitate to yield their lives and shed their blood for the dignity of this See and the truth of the orthodox faith."[1]

This noble band lacks neither fulness of numbers nor grade of honour. It is adorned with the grandeur of the Roman Cardinalate, it is dignified by vener-

[1] Gregory XIII., Constitution *Quoniam divinæ bonitati*, May 1, 1579.

able Bishops, it comprises magnanimous priests, both secular and regular; the invincible firmness of the weaker sex is also there. Eminent amongst them is JOHN FISHER, Bishop of Rochester, and Cardinal of the Holy Roman Church, of whom Paul III. speaks in his Letters as "conspicuous for sanctity, celebrated for learning, venerable by age, an honour and an ornament to the kingdom and to the clergy of the whole world." From him the layman THOMAS MORE, Chancellor of England, must not be separated; whom the same Pope deservedly praises as "excelling in sacred learning and bold in his assertion of the truth."

Accordingly, the most weighty writers on ecclesiastical history are unanimously of opinion that they all shed their blood for the defence, restoration, and preservation of the Catholic faith. Gregory XIII. even granted in their honour several ecclesiastical privileges appertaining to public and ecclesiastical worship, and chiefly that of using their relics in the consecration of altars when relics of ancient holy Martyrs could not be had. Moreover, after he had caused the sufferings of the Christian Martyrs to be painted in fresco by Nicholas Circiniani, in the Church of St. Stephen on the Coelian Hill, he permitted also the Martyrs of the Church in England, both of ancient and of more recent times, to be represented in like manner by the same artist in the English Church of the Most Holy Trinity in Rome, including those who from the year 1535 to 1583 had died under King Henry VIII. and Queen Elizabeth, for the Catholic faith, and for the primacy of the Roman Pontiff. The representations of these martyrdoms, painted in the said church, remained, with the knowledge and approbation of the Roman

Pontiffs who succeeded Gregory XIII. for two centuries, until they were destroyed by wicked men about the end of the last century.

But copies of them still remained; for in the year 1584, by privilege of the said Gregory XIII., they had been engraved at Rome on copper-plate, with the title: *Sufferings of the Holy Martyrs, who for Christ's sake and for professing the truth of the Catholic faith, have suffered death in England both in ancient and more recent times.* From this record, either by inscriptions placed beneath them or by other sure indications, many of the Martyrs are known by name, that is to say, fifty-four. They are:

Those who suffered death under King Henry VIII.:

> JOHN FISHER, Bishop of Rochester, Cardinal of the Holy Roman Church.
> THOMAS MORE, Chancellor of England.
> MARGARET POLE, Countess of Salisbury, mother of Cardinal Pole.
> RICHARD REYNOLDS, of the Order of St. Bridget.
> JOHN HAILE, priest.

Eighteen Carthusians, namely:

> JOHN HOUGHTON.
> AUGUSTINE WEBSTER.
> ROBERT LAURENCE.
> WILLIAM EXMEW.
> HUMPHREY MIDDLEMORE.
> SEBASTIAN NEWDIGATE.
> JOHN ROCHESTER.
> JAMES WALWORTH.
> WILLIAM GREENWOOD.
> JOHN DAVY.

APPENDIX.

    ROBERT SALT.
    WALTER PIERSON.
    THOMAS GREEN.
    THOMAS SCRYVEN.
    THOMAS REDYNG.
    THOMAS JOHNSON.
    RICHARD BERE,
and WILLIAM HORNE.
JOHN FOREST, priest of the Order of St. Francis.
JOHN STONE, of the Order of St. Augustine.

Four secular priests:
    THOMAS ABEL.
    EDWARD POWEL.
    RICHARD FETHERSTON.
    JOHN LARKE,
and GERMAN GARDINER (a layman).

Those who suffered under Elizabeth:
  Priests:
    CUTHBERT MAYNE.
    JOHN NELSON.
    EVERARD HANSE.
    RALPH SHERWIN.
    JOHN PAYNE.
    THOMAS FORD.
    JOHN SHERT.
    ROBERT JOHNSON.
    WILLIAM FYLBY.
    LUKE KIRBY.
    LAURENCE RICHARDSON.
    WILLIAM LACY.
    RICHARD KIRKMAN.
    JAMES HUDSON, or TOMPSON.

WILLIAM HART.
RICHARD THIRKELD.
THOMAS WOODHOUSE.
[THOMAS] PLUMTREE.

Also three[2] priests of the Society of Jesus:

EDMUND CAMPION.
ALEXANDER BRIANT.
THOMAS COTTAM.

Lastly these laymen:

JOHN STOREY, Doctor of Laws.
JOHN FELTON.
THOMAS SHERWOOD.

Until lately, the Cause of these Martyrs had never been officially treated. Some time ago, in the year 1860, Cardinal Nicholas Wiseman, of illustrious memory, Archbishop of Westminster, and the other Bishops of England, petitioned the Sovereign Pontiff Pius IX., of sacred memory, to institute for the whole of England a festival in honour of all holy Martyrs, that is to say, even of those "who, though not yet declared to be such, have in later times, for their defence of the Catholic religion, and especially for asserting the authority of the Apostolic See, fallen by the hands of wicked men, and resisted unto blood." But as, according to the prevailing practice of the Congregation of Sacred Rites, a festival can be instituted in regard to those servants of God only to whom ecclesiastical honour (*cultus*) has been already given and duly sanctioned by the Apostolic

---

[2] The Holy See has permitted the Society of Jesus to keep the feast of Blessed John Nelson and Blessed Thomas Woodhouse as priests of the Society, in addition to these three.

See, the said petition was not granted. Wherefore in these last years a new petition was presented to our Holy Father Pope Leo XIII., by His Eminence Henry Edward Cardinal Manning, the present Archbishop of Westminster, and the other Bishops of England, together with the Ordinary Process which had been there compiled, and other authentic documents, in which were contained the proofs of Martyrdom as to those who suffered from the year 1535 to 1583, and also the aforesaid concessions of the Roman Pontiffs in regard to those above mentioned.

Our Holy Father was pleased to commit the examination of the whole matter to a special Congregation, consisting of several Cardinals of the Holy Roman Church, and of officials of the Congregation of Sacred Rites,—the examination to be preceded by a Disquisition, to be drawn up by the Right Reverend Augustine Caprara, Promoter of the Holy Faith. In this special Congregation, assembled at the Vatican on the 4th day of December of the present year, the undersigned Cardinal Dominic Bartolini, Prefect of the said Sacred Congregation, who had charge of the Cause, proposed the following question:

"*Whether, by reason of the special concessions of the Roman Pontiffs, in regard to the earlier Martyrs of England, who from the year 1535 to 1583 suffered death for the Catholic faith and for the Primacy of the Roman Pontiff over the Church, and whose Martyrdoms were formerly painted, by authority of the Sovereign Pontiff Gregory XIII., in the English Church of the Most Holy Trinity in Rome, and in the year 1584 were engraved at Rome on copper-plate by privilege of the same Pontiff,—there is evidence of the concession of public ecclesiastical honour, or of this being a case excepted from the decrees of Pope Urban VIII., of sacred memory, in the matter and to the effect under consideration."*

The Most Eminent and Most Reverend Fathers, and the Official Prelates, after hearing the written and oral report of the aforesaid Promoter of the Holy Faith, and after the matter in regard to the fifty-four Martyrs above named had been fully discussed, were of opinion that the answer to be given was:

"Affirmatively, or that it is proved to be a case excepted."

The undersigned Secretary having made a faithful report of all that precedes to our Holy Father Pope Leo XIII., His Holiness vouchsafed to approve the decision of the Sacred Special Congregation, on the 9th day of December, 1886.

The present decree was issued on this 29th day of December, sacred to the Martyr Thomas Archbishop of Canterbury, whose faith and constancy these blessed Martyrs so strenuously imitated.

D. CARDINAL BARTOLINI,
Prefect of the Congregation of Sacred Rites.

LAURENCE SALVATI,
Secretary.

L. ✣ S.

DECREE

OF THE SACRED CONGREGATION OF RITES

FOR THE

INTRODUCTION OF THE CAUSE OF BEATIFICATION,

OR DECLARATION OF MARTYRDOM,

OF TWO HUNDRED AND SIXTY-ONE VENERABLE SERVANTS OF GOD, WHO WERE PUT TO DEATH IN ENGLAND FOR THE FAITH.

In the persecution which raged so fiercely in England during the sixteenth century and afterwards against the Catholic Faith and the divinely instituted Primacy of the Roman Pontiff, very many of the faithful of every rank, after enduring mockery and stripes, bonds and imprisonment, and suffering many kinds of cruel torture, courageously laid down their lives for religion. By their death the enemies of Catholicity thought to tear up the Catholic Church by its roots, in the country which in past ages was deservedly called an Island of Saints. But the blood of the slain, who from the moment of their glorious deaths were everywhere held to be true Martyrs of Christ, became the seed of new offspring in the Church, which has there day by day wonderfully grown.

The times were adverse to the drawing up of the formalities required for the process of these glorious Martyrs, and to the introduction of their cause in the Sacred Congregation of Rites, though it was greatly desired, not only in England, but also by the faithful throughout the Catholic world. But now, since the restoration of the Catholic Hierarchy in England, what was so earnestly looked for has in our day been happily accomplished. The Catholic Bishops have been able to collect together the ancient records; and by authority of the Ordinary, to institute in the ecclesiastical Court of Westminster the formal Process as to the Martyrdom, the Cause of Martyrdom, and the signs or miracles of three hundred and five servants of God who were put to death for the Catholic Faith.

The acts of this Process, supported by authentic documents, were laid before the Apostolic See, and were immediately followed by a Petition of the Bishops, and of many other distinguished ecclesiastics and laymen of the whole of England.

Our Holy Father Leo XIII. was pleased to intrust the examination of this matter to a special Commission, consisting of several Cardinals of the Holy Roman Church, and officials of the Congregation of Sacred Rites, with directions that the said examination should be preceded by a disquisition, to be drawn up by the Right Reverend Promoter of the Holy Faith; and a dispensation was also granted in respect to the introduction of the Cause before the lapse of the ten years required by the decrees, from the day of presenting the Ordinary Process in the Sacred Congregation, and in respect also to its introduction before the written documents had been revised.

Afterwards, in a special Congregation, assembled in the Vatican on the day below named, the undersigned Cardinal Dominic Bartolini, Prefect of the said Sacred Congregation, who had charge of the Cause, proposed the following question:

"*Whether the Commission is to be signed for the Introduction of the Cause, in the matter and to the effect under consideration.*"

Then the Most Reverend Fathers, and the official prelates, after hearing the written and oral report of the aforesaid Promoter of the Holy Faith, and after the matter had been fully discussed, decided:

"*That the Commission is to be signed, if it shall please His Holiness, in respect of two hundred and sixty-one, namely:*

[1537] ANTHONY BROOKBY, of the Order of St. Francis.

[1538] THOMAS BELCHIAM, and THOMAS CORT, of the Order of St. Francis.

[1539] GRIFFITH CLARK, priest; N. WAIRE, of the Order of St. Francis; ADRIAN FORTESCUE and THOMAS DINGLEY, Knights of St. John of Jerusalem; JOHN TRAVERS, priest of the Order of Hermits of St. Augustine; JOHN BECHE, Abbot of Colchester; HUGH FARINGDON, Abbot of Reading; RICHARD WHITING, Abbot of Glastonbury; ROGER JAMES and JOHN THORN, monks of Glastonbury; WILLIAM ONION and JOHN RUGG, of the Order of St. Benedict.

[1540] EDMUND BRINDHOLM, priest; CLEMENT PHILPOT, layman.

[1541] DAVID GUNSTON, Knight of St. John of Jerusalem.

[1544] JOHN IRELAND, priest; THOMAS ASHBY, layman.

[1583] JOHN SLADE and JOHN BODEY, laymen.

[1584] GEORGE HAYDOCK, JAMES FENN, THOMAS HEMERFORD, JOHN NUTTER and JOHN MUNDEN, priests; WILLIAM CARTER, layman; JAMES BELL, priest; JOHN FINCH and RICHARD WHITE, laymen.

[1585] THOMAS ALFIELD, priest; THOMAS WEBLEY, layman; HUGH TAYLOR, priest; MARMADUKE BOWES, layman.

[1586] EDWARD STRANCHAM and NICHOLAS WOODFEN, priests; MARGARET CLITHEROE, gentlewoman, RICHARD SERGEANT (*alias* LEE), WILLIAM THOMSON, ROBERT ANDERTON, WILLIAM MARSDEN, FRANCIS INGOLBY, JOHN FINGLOW, JOHN SANDYS, JOHN LOWE, JOHN ADAMS, and RICHARD DIBDALE, priests; ROBERT BICKERDIKE and RICHARD LANGLEY, laymen.

[1587] THOMAS PILCHARD, EDMUND SYKES, ROBERT SUTTON, STEPHEN ROWSHAM, JOHN HAMBLEY, GEORGE DOUGLAS, ALEXANDER CROW, priests.

[1588] NICHOLAS GARLICK, ROBERT LUDLAM, RICHARD SYMPSON, WILLIAM DEAN, priests; HENRY WEBLEY, layman; WILLIAM GUNTER and ROBERT MORTON, priests; HUGH MORE, layman; THOMAS HOLFORD and JAMES CLAXTON, priests; THOMAS FELTON, of the Order of Minims: RICHARD LEIGH, priest; EDWARD SHELLEY, RICHARD MARTIN, RICHARD FLOWER, JOHN ROCHE, and MARGARET WARD, of the laity; WILLIAM WAY (*alias* WIGGES), ROBERT WILCOX, EDWARD CAMPION, and CHRISTOPHER BUXTON, priests; ROBERT WIDMERPOOL, layman; RALPH CROCKET, EDWARD JAMES, JOHN ROBINSON, and WILLIAM HARTLEY, priests; ROBERT SUTTON, layman; RICHARD WILLIAMS, JOHN HEWETT (*alias* WELDON), EDWARD BURDEN, priests; WILLIAM LAMPLEY, layman.

[1589] JOHN AMIAS, ROBERT DALBY, GEORGE NICHOLS, and RICHARD YAXLEY, priests; THOMAS

Belson and Humphrey Prichard, laymen; William Spenser, priest; Robert Hardesty, layman.

[1590] Christopher Bales, priest; Nicholas Horner and Alexander Blake, laymen; Miles Gerard, Francis Dickenson, Edward Jones, Anthony Middleton, Edmund Duke, Richard Hill, John Hogg, Richard Holiday, priests.

[1591] Robert Thorpe, priest; Thomas Watkinson, layman; Momford Scott, George Beesley, and Roger Dickenson, priests; Ralph Milner, William Pike, Laurence Humphrey, laymen; Edmund Genings, priest; Swithin Wells, layman; Eustace White and Polydore Plasden, priests; Brian Lacy, John Mason, and Sydney Hodgson, laymen.

[1592] William Patenson and Thomas Pormort, priests; Robert Ashton, layman; Edmund Waterson, priest; James Bird, layman; Anthony Page, Joseph Lampton and William Davies, priests.

[1593] John Speed, layman; William Harrington, priest; John Cornelius, of the Society of Jesus; Thomas Bosgrave, John Carey and Patrick Salmon, laymen; John Boste and John Ingram, priests; George Swallowell, layman; Edward Osbaldeston, priest.

[1595] Robert Southwell, of the Society of Jesus; Alexander Rawlins, priest; Henry Walpole, of the Society of Jesus; William Freeman, priest; Philip Howard, Earl of Arundel.

[1596] George Errington, William Knight, William Gibson, and Henry Abbot, laymen.

[1597] William Andleby, priest; Thomas Warcop and Edward Fulthorp, laymen.

[1598] John Britton, layman; Peter Snow, priest; Ralph Grimston, layman; John Buckley (or JONES), of the Order of St. Francis, CHRISTOPHER ROBINSON and RICHARD HORNER, priests.

[1599] JOHN LION and JAMES DOWDALL, laymen.

[1600] CHRISTOPHER WHARTON, priest; JOHN RIGBY, layman; THOMAS SPROTT, THOMAS HUNT, ROBERT NUTTER, EDWARD THWING, THOMAS PALASOR, priests; JOHN NORTON and JOHN TALBOT, laymen.

[1601] JOHN PIBUSH, priest; MARK BARKWORTH, of the Order of St. Benedict; ROGER FILCOCK, of the Society of Jesus; ANNE LINE, gentlewoman; THURSTAN HUNT and ROBERT MIDDLETON, priests; NICHOLAS TICHBORNE and THOMAS HACKSHOT, laymen.

[1602] JAMES HARRISON, priest; ANTHONY BATES and JAMES DUCKET, laymen; THOMAS TICHBORNE and ROBERT WATKINSON, priests; FRANCIS PAGE, of the Society of Jesus.

[1603] WILLIAM RICHARDSON, priest.

[1604] JOHN SUGAR, priest; ROBERT GRISSOLD and LAWRENCE BAILY, laymen.

[1605] THOMAS WELBOURNE, JOHN FULTHERING, and WILLIAM BROWN, laymen.

[1606] NICHOLAS OWEN, EDWARD OLDCORNE, and RALPH ASHLEY, of the Society of Jesus.

[1607] ROBERT DRURY, priest.

[1608] MATHEW FLATHERS, priest; GEORGE GERVASE, of the Order of St. Benedict; THOMAS GARNET, of the Society of Jesus.

[1610] ROGER CADWALLADOR, GEORGE NAPIER, and THOMAS SOMERS, priests; JOHN ROBERTS, of the Order of St. Benedict.

[1612] WILLIAM SCOT, of the Order of St. Benedict; RICHARD NEWPORT and JOHN ALMOND, priests.

[1616] THOMAS ATKINSON and JOHN THULIS,

priests; ROGER WRENNO, layman; THOMAS MAX-
FIELD and THOMAS TUNSTAL, priests.

[1618] WILLIAM SOUTHERNE, priest.

[1628] EDMUND ARROWSMITH, of the Society of
Jesus; RICHARD HERST, layman.

[1641] WILLIAM WARD, priest; EDWARD BARLOW,
of the Order of St. Benedict.

[1642] THOMAS REYNOLDS, priest; BARTHOLOMEW
ROE, of the Order of St. Benedict; JOHN LOCKWOOD,
EDMUND CATHERICK, EDWARD MORGAN, and HUGH
GREEN, priests; THOMAS BULLAKER, of the Order of
St. Francis; THOMAS HOLLAND, of the Society of
Jesus.

[1643] HENRY HEATH and ARTHUR BELL, of the
Order of St. Francis.

[1644] PRICE, a layman; JOHN DUCKETT, priest;
RALPH CORBY, of the Society of Jesus.

[1645] HENRY MORSE and BRIAN CANSFIELD, of
the Society of Jesus; JOHN GOODMAN, priest.

[1646] PHILIP POWEL, of the Order of St. Benedict;
EDWARD BAMBER, priest; JOHN WOODCOCK, of the
Order of St. Francis; THOMAS WHITAKER, priest.

[1651] PETER WRIGHT, of the Society of Jesus.

[1654] JOHN SOUTHWORTH, priest.

[1678] EDWARD COLEMAN, layman; EDWARD MICO,
and THOMAS BEDINGFIELD, of the Society of Jesus.

[1679] WILLIAM IRELAND, of the Society of Jesus;
JOHN GROVE, layman; THOMAS PICKERING, of the
Order of St. Benedict; THOMAS WHITBREAD, WILLIAM
HARCOURT, JOHN FENWICK, JOHN GREEN (or GAVAN),
ANTHONY TURNER and FRANCIS NEVILE, of the Society
of Jesus; RICHARD LANGHORNE, layman; WILLIAM
PLESSINGTON, priest; PHILIP EVANS, of the Society
of Jesus; JOHN LLOYD and WILLIAM POSTGATE,
priests; CHARLES MAHONY, JOHN WALL, and FRANCIS

Levison, of the Order of St. Francis; John Kemble, priest; David Lewis (*alias* Charles Baker), of the Society of Jesus.

[1680] Thomas Thwing, priest; William Howard, Viscount Stafford.

[1681] Oliver Plunket, Archbishop of Armagh."

As to the other forty-four the decision was: "*Delayed, and further proofs must be given.*"

The fourth day of December, 1886.

The undersigned Secretary having then made a faithful and accurate report of all that precedes to our Holy Father Pope Leo XIII., His Holiness, ratifying the decision of the Sacred Congregation, vouchsafed to sign the Commission for the Introduction of the Cause with his own hand, on the ninth day of the same month and year.

D. Cardinal Bartolini,
Prefect of the Congregation of Sacred Rites.

Laurence Salvati,
Secretary.

L. ✠ S.

TABLE OF THE BLESSED AND VENERABLE ENGLISH MARTYRS.

The following tabulated results of the above decrees may be of interest:

Blessed . 54 Venerable 261 Total . 315	Under Henry VIII.		In subsequent reigns.		Totals
	Blessed.	*Venerable.*	*Blessed.*	*Venerable.*	
Cardinal	1	..	..	..	1
Archbishop	..	..	..	1	1
Secular Priests . . .	5	6	18	126	155
Carthusians	18	..	..	..	18
Bridgettine	1	..	..	..	1
Benedictines	..	5	..	8	13
Augustinian	1	..	..	..	1
Franciscans	1	4	..	9	14
Jesuits	..	..	3	27	30
Knights of St. John . .	..	3	..	..	3
Laymen and women .	3	2	3	70	78
Totals	30	20	24	241	315

The 44 *dilati*, whose fate is still in suspense, consist of 18 secular priests, 9 Jesuits, 6 Benedictines, and 11 lay persons.

Among the 54 Martyrs proclaimed Blessed by the first decree,[1] there are six whose names were not included in the Ordinary Process of 1874. These were united with the others because they are found in the English College pictures, authorized by Gregory XIII. They are the Blessed Margaret Pole, John Hailes, Thomas Woodhouse, Thomas Plumtree, John Storey, and John Felton.

The number 305, named in the second decree,[2] is made up of the 261 declared Venerable, and the 44 whose case is postponed.

The Process of 1874 contained 353 names, to which 6 were added in Rome. This corresponds with the total number of 315 Martyrs Blessed and Venerable, and 44 postponed.

[1] P. 371, seq. [2] P. 377.

INDEX.

ABBOT, GEORGE, Archbishop of Canterbury 150, 169, 193.
ADAMS, VEN. JOHN, priest 259, 285.
ADIS, HENRY 125.
AGAZZARI, ALPHONSO, FR. S.J. 250, 280.
ALLEN, WILLIAM, Card. 51, 68, 102, 104, 175, 212, 213, 218, 221, 222, 255, 280.
ALMOND, VEN. JOHN, priest (*alias* Molineux, *alias* Lathom) 170—194;
  Birth, education 170; grand act in theology, returns to England, in Newgate 171; letter of 172; his brother Oliver 173, 174; two arrests 175.
  Examined and disputes on the oath 176—179; on deposing power 178; treatment in Newgate 172, 180, 181; record of trial lost 182; other accounts of 183;
  His speech at Tyburn 184—191; king-killing 189; his courage 189, 191, 192; prays for King, &c. 190; wears Mr. Muskett's ring 191; his chastity and cheerfulness 191, 192; dies 192; consequent conversions 192.
ALMOND, OLIVER 175.
AMBASSADOR of Portugal 354, 359.

AMBASSADOR of Spain 3, 360.
AMIAS, VEN. JOHN, priest 330, 331.
ANDERSON, L.C.J., of Common Pleas 70, 71, 101, 106, 116, 119, 121, 234, 290, 301.
ANDERTON, VEN. ROBERT, priest;
  Fr. Warford's reminiscences of him and Marsden 66 seq., 257;
  At Oxford and Rheims 67; his sermon 68; prefect over younger boys, *ibid.;* nearly lost at sea 69; arrested and tried 70, 71; sent to London 72;
  Privy Council warrant for their further examination 73; ditto for the execution 74; proclamation read at the execution 75—80; its deceitfulness 81;
  Naturally timid, but brave at death 304.
ANDOVER 51, 57, 62.
ANGLESEA 118, 131.
ANTWERP 116.
APPLETREE, JOHN, priest 275.
ARMADA, year of the 286.
ARUNDEL, ANNE, Countess of 212.
ARUNDEL, VEN. PHILIP HOWARD, Earl of 212.
ARUNDELL, SIR JOHN 118.
  Brian Lacey servant to 123.
  Glynn, servant to 285.

z

INDEX.

AYLMER, JOHN, Bishop of London 101—104, 307.

B. G. (? Blackwell, George) 222, 223.
BABINGTON, Mr. 285.
BAKER 291, 304.
BAKER, ALEXANDER, FR. S.J. 352.
BALES, see Bayles.
BALLARD, a priest 285.
BANGOR, HUGH BALLOT, Bishop of 127, 130;
  Chancellor of 131, 133;
  Register of 131;
  Sheriff of 132, 133, 135, 139.
BARDICK, see Winchester.
BARKWORTH, VEN. MARK, O.S.B. 144.
BARNES, ROBERT 57, 58.
BARONIUS, CARD. 172.
BARRET, DR. RICHARD 250.
BARROWS (Barwys), haberdasher 120.
BARTLET, WILLIAM 183.
BARTOLI, DANIEL, FR. S.J. 41.
BASING 125.
BASSELIER, IGNATIUS, FR. S.J. 40.
BAYLES, VEN. CHRISTOPHER, priest (alias Rivers) 289, 291, 307, 308, 322.
BEAUMARIS 127, 128, 137—139.
BEDDAM, THOMAS 89.
BEESLEY, VEN. GEORGE, priest 103, 291, 292—294, 299, 300—303.
BELL, VEN. JAMES, priest, 218.
BELLAMY, MR. ROBERT 283.
BELLICE, CAPTAIN 242.
BELSON, VEN. THOMAS 289.
BENEDICTINES, see St. Benedict, and Convents.
BENNET, DR. 60—63.
BERNARD, GILES 252.
BETHEL, JUSTICE 225.
BIRD, VEN. JAMES, a convert 231, 232, 234.

BIRKETT, GEORGE, archpriest 51, 212, 213, 218.
BLACKFAN, JOHN, FR. S.J. 193.
BLACKWELL, DR. GEORGE, archpriest 251.
BLAKE, VEN. ALEXANDER 291.
BLANDFORD 126.
BLENERHAISET, WILLIAM, ESQ. 123.
BLOUNT, RICHARD, FR. S.J. 174, 176, 322.
BLUNTSTONE, MR. 292.
BODEY (BODY) VEN. JOHN, M.A. of New College, Oxon 49;
  imprisoned with Slade (q. v.) 50, 55;
  two trials and disputation with Dr. Humphrey 51—53;
  letter to Dr. Ely 54, 55;
  execution 62—65.
BODEY, GILBERT 54.
BOMBINO, FR. S.J. 35.
BOOKS mentioned in the text:
  Allen on Purgatory 50;
  Bible 178;
  Bristowe's Motives 247;
  Christian Exercise 50;
  De Persecutione Anglicana 8;
  Foundation of Catholic Religion 239;
  Jesus Psalter 223, 243, 274;
  Leicester's Commonwealth 307;
  Life of Genings (1st Edit.) 216;
  Life of Earl of Arundel 217;
  Manual 244;
  Mount of Calvary 246;
  Our Lady's Psalter 242;
  Reynolds against Whittaker 67;
  Second Birth of St. John 244;
  Smyth on the Mass 50;
  Supplication to the Queen 245;
  Ten Reasons 37;
  Treatise of the Church 50;
  Verepæum 274.
  see also Bridgewater, Challoner, Douay Diaries, Jessopp, Yepez.
BOSGRAVE, VEN. THOMAS, ESQ. 118.

BOULTON, *vere* YATES, priest 182.
BRAINTHWAYTE, RICHARD, ESQ. 122;
BRAMLEY, a thief 331.
BRIANT, B. ALEXANDER 54.
BRIDEWELL, *see* London.
BRIDGEWATER, DR. JOHN 213, 217, 252, 280.
BRISTOL 253.
BRUGES 321.
BRUSSELS, Bibliothèque de Bourgogne 40, 216, *see* Manuscripts.
BUCKLEY, DOM SIGEBERT, O.S.B. 144.
BULKLEY, SIR RICHARD 131.
BULL, the hangman 56, 211.
BULLAKER, VEN. THOMAS (Father John Baptist, O.S.F., *alias* Taylor), martyrdom of 353—357.
BULLOCK, PETER, bookbinder 245, 246, 248.
BULMER, SIR RALPH 212.
BURDEN, VEN. EDWARD, priest 313, 328—331.
BURGESS, a minister 130, 131, 140.
BURLEIGH, LORD 22, 90, 95, 119, 335.
BUTLER, ALBAN, D.D. 87.
BUXTON, VEN. CHRISTOPHER, priest 287.

CAERS (? Caerwys) 141.
CALAIS 209.
CAMBRIDGE 98, 143, 254.
CAMPION, B. EDMUND, S.J. his popularity 21, 33, 34, 35, 36, 39;
Brief of his life 23—34; date of 22;
Birth and education 24; at Oxford 25, 35; travels 28, 35; arrest 29, 37, 251; tortured 31; disputation and temptation 30; reports against him 22—24; trial 31, 38, 41—48; his execution 32, 48, 310; causes Walpole's conversion 40;
books by—
 Challenge 36;
 Decem Rationes 37;
eloquence 27, 30, 31, 35, 36, 42, 43, 46;
courage, &c. 29, 48;
patience 30, 31, 311;
mentioned 278, 284, 327.
CAMPION, VEN. EDWARD, priest 327.
CANTERBURY 327;
Archbishop of, *see* Abbot, Laud, Whitgift.
St. Thomas of 174.
CAPUCHIN Fathers 360.
CAREY, SIR GEORGE 74.
CARLISLE 217, 219, 220.
CARLISLE CASTLE 219.
CARVAJAL, DONNA LUISA DE 169, 170.
CARY, MR. RICHARD 295.
CAUMONT, JOHN 239.
CECIL, JOHN 97.
CHALLONER'S Memoirs 1, 2, 56, 83, 84, 87, 89, 140—145, 175, 212, 215, 231, 235, 245, 280, 285, 288, 295, 296, 318—349, 353.
CHARLES I. 190, 357.
CHEEK, MR. 312.
CHICHESTER 353.
CHILLINGWORTH, WILLIAM, apostate 358.
CHRYSOSTOM, ST. JOHN 104.
CLAXTON, VEN. JAMES, priest (*or* Clarkson, *alias* James) 287.
CLENCH, MR. JUSTICE 335.
CLITHERO, VEN. MARGARET 259.
COKE, MR. FRANCIS, J.P. 58.
COLUMBINE, FR. S.J. 76.
COMMISSIONERS, High 7, 11.
COMPOSTELLA St. James (? St. Martin) of 144, 150, 174.
CONVENTS, Monasteries, and Religious Houses—
 Benedictine, Compostella 144, 169, Douay 169;

Bridgettine, Mechlin 3;
Carthusian, Nieuport 238;
Franciscan, Abrojo 352, Taunton 169;
Institute of Mary, Munich 338, Nymphenburg 338;
Jesuit, Ghent 358, Liege 358, St. Andrea 250, 281, Watten 358, *see* Seminaries.
CONSTANTINE THE GREAT 52, 53, 63.
CONWAY 141.
COOK, MR., of Holborn 176.
COOK, JOHN 361.
COOPER 241.
COOPER, HENRY, priest 180, 182.
COPE, *see* Sugar.
CORNEFORD, FATHER 182.
CORNELIUS, VEN. JOHN, S.J. 100, 118, 266.
CORNWELL, in Oxfordshire 273.
COTTAM, B. THOMAS, S.J. 41, 280—282.
COWPER, THOMAS, Bishop of Winchester 70, 71, 74, 88, 95.
COX, DR. Bishop of Ely 7.
CRIPPS, CAPTAIN 272.
CROCKETT, VEN. RALPH, priest 287.
CROOK, JUSTICE 151.
CROW, VEN. ALEXANDER, priest 270.
CURRY, JOHN, FR. S.J. 313.
DALBY, VEN. ROBERT, priest 329—331.
DANSTIN, MR. 233.
DAVIES, VEN. WILLIAM, priest, arrest 127;
letter of 128—136;
life in Beaumaris Castle 137;
martyrdom of 137—141;
his "children" 142;
relics *ibid.*
DEANE, VEN. WILLIAM, priest 286.
DELAWARE, LORD 58.
DEVEREUX, House of 120.
DIBDALE, VEN. ROBERT, priest 285, 323.

DICCONSON, VEN. ROGER (Dickenson, Dikinson), priest, *alias* Richard Johnson 88; *alias* Welby 318;
examination 84; imprisonment, exile, and return 85;
his escapes 87; arrested 88, 318; Council warrant for his examination 89;
tortured and arraigned 90;
trial 90, 91, 319;
execution 91—97, 319.
DICKINSON, VEN. FRANCIS, priest 314, 322;
DORSETSHIRE 3, 5, 50, 125, 126.
DORCHESTER 261, 262, Judges of Assize at 7.
DOUAY, *see* Seminaries.
Benedictine Convent 169;
Catalogue of MM. 322;
Diaries 1, 175, 215, 222, 255, 257, 259.
DOUGLAS, VEN. GEORGE, priest 327.
DRIELAND 314, 315.
DUCKETT, ANTHONY 238.
DUCKETT, CATHERINE 238.
DUCKETT, ELIZABETH 238.
DUCKETT, VEN. JAMES, printer, persecution and martyrdom of 238—248.
DUCKETT, DOM JOHN, 238.
DUCKETT, MRS. (Anne Hart) 241, 243, 244, 245, 247.
DUCKETT, NICOLAS 238.
DUCKETT, RICHARD of Grayrigg 238.
DURHAM College 98;
St. Oswald's 318.
DUKE, VEN. EDMUND, priest 318.

EARTH, *see* Leigh 287.
ELEUTHERIUS, POPE 290.
ELIZABETH, QUEEN 15, 16, 17, 21, 36—70, (and Topcliffe) 119, 211, 212, 213, 217, 226, 288, 302, 307;
letters patent to keep a priest 212.

INDEX.

ELLIOT, GEORGE, a traitor 45, 46.
ELY, DR. COX, Bishop of 7.
ELY, HUMPHREY, DR. 54, 282.
EMERSON, BR. RALPH, S.J. 284.
EMPEROR OF GERMANY 36.
ENGLISCHE Fraülein, or English Ladies 338.
ENGLISH Chapter, The 280.
ESSEX, EARL OF 119, 120, 243.
EUSEBIUS 52, 53.
EVERINGHAM 176.
EXETER Gaol 352.
EXORCISMS, see Martyrs D.

FALKLAND, Lady, daughters of 358.
FARRAR, G., Notary-Apostolic 209.
FELTON, B. JOHN, martyrdom of 209—212, 213, 286.
FELTON, VEN. THOMAS, O.S.F. 286, 287.
FELTON, MRS. 210, 211.
FENN, JOHN, priest 242.
FENN, VEN. JAMES, priest, 252.
FIESOLE 41.
FINCH, VEN. JOHN 218.
FISHER, THOMAS, J.P. 58.
FITZHERBERT, THOMAS, FR. S.J. 34;
his apology 47.
FITZHERBERT, SIR THOMAS 124.
FIXER, JOHN, priest 274.
FLEETWOOD, Recorder of London 5, 6, 11, 12, 13, 102.
FLEMING, THOMAS, ESQ. 50.
FLETCHER, DR. 122.
FLOOD, a spy 242.
FLOWER, VEN. RICHARD 287.
FORBES-LEITH, W., FR. S.J. 100.
FORD, B. THOMAS, 251, 334.
FOSTER, DR. 182.
FOWLER, SIR RICHARD 130.
FOXWELL, HENRY, priest 286.
FRANCISCANS 359, see CONVENTS;
Capuchins 360;
Minims 286;
Recollects 352.
FULK, THOMAS 127.

G., Mr. H. G. 57.
GAGE, GEORGE, priest, 359;
GAGE, SIR HENRY 359;
GAGE, THOMAS, apostate 359, 361;
GAGE, WILLIAM, FR. S.J. 359.
GAOL TREATMENT, see Martyrs A.
GARNET, HENRY, S.J. 87, 120, 121, 123, 124, 128, 234, 242.
GARNET, VEN. THOMAS, S.J. 176, 180, 234.
GARROWAY, MR. 359.
GASKIN 310, see London D, Tower.
GAYES, MR. JUSTICE 225.
GENINGS, VEN. EDMUND, priest. Early life 214; missions to Mr. Layburne 214, 215; arrested 100; tried 101, 104; stripped 106, 107; executed 109; his quarters ibid.; Relation of his Life, 216.
GENINGS, FR. JOHN, O.S.F. 100, 215, 216.
GENOA 175.
GENT, JUDGE 268.
GERARD, JOHN, S.J. (alias Tomson).
life of 313, 326;
note-books of 323—326.
GERARD, VEN. MILES 314.
GERARD, GILBERT 13, 18, 19, 101.
GERVASE, VEN. GEORGE, O.S.B. 292—296.
GILFORTRIGG, Westmoreland 238.
GILLOW, JOSEPH, ESQ. 239.
GLISSON, ISAAC, of Bristol 253.
GLOUCESTER 332—336.
High Sheriff, see Tracy Paul.
GLYNN 285.
GOOD, WILLIAM, S.J. 252.
GOODACRE, THOMAS, minister 240.
GREGORY XIII., POPE 16.
GREGORY, a hangman 351.
GREEN (alias Gray), priest 311.
GREEN, VEN. THOMAS, priest (alias Reynolds).
his martyrdom 339—343.

INDEX

GREENE, priest 182.
GRENE, FR. CHRISTOPHER 34, 68, 90, 137, 175, 176, 216—219, 222, 225, 235, 253, 258, 298, 313, 322, 331.
GRISSOLD, VEN. ROBERT 321.
GROVES, *see* Thomson.
GRUFF, MR. of Carnarvon 132.
GUISE, CARDINAL OF 76.
GUNPOWDER TREASON 149, 159, 361.
GUNTER, VEN. WILLIAM, priest 289.
GUSMAN, Spanish Ambassador 3.

HALL, THOMAS 84.
HAMOND, DR. 73.
HAMBLEY, VEN. JOHN, priest 268, 269.
HAMPSHIRE 84—88.
HARDY, JOHN 53.
HART ANNE, *see* Duckett, Mrs.
HART, B. WILLIAM, priest 218, 252.
HARTLEY, ROBERT 123.
HARTLEY, VEN. WILLIAM, priest 271, 287, 288, 310.
HEATH, MR. 310.
HEMERFORD, VEN. THOS. priest 253.
HERRIES, the Lord 176.
HEWES, MR. 43.
HEWETT, *see* Weldon.
HEYDON, Sir WILLIAM 123.
HEYWOOD, GASPAR, FR. S.J. 254.
HIGGINS, ISAAC, priest 283.
HIGGINS, Scrivener 222.
HILL, VEN. RICHARD, priest 318.
HODGSON, VEN. SYDNEY, a servant 106; is believed to yield, but afterwards condemned 107, 109; executed 111; buried 115.
HOGGE, VEN. JOHN, priest, 318.
HOLFORD, VEN. THOMAS, priest (*alias* Acton, *alias* Bude) 287.
HOLIDAY, VEN. RICHARD, priest 318.
HOLLAND, VEN. THOMAS, S.J. (*alias* Saunderson, *alias* Hamond). Account of 357; trial 358, 359; martyrdom 360—367.
HOLT, MR. 2.
HOLTBY, RICHARD, FR. S.J. 313.
HOLYHEAD 127.
HORN, Queen Mary priest 273.
HORNE, Bishop of Oxford 56.
HORNER, VEN. NICOLAS, tailor. Account of 227—231; 290, 291, 308, 311, 315.
HORSEY, SIR JOHN, Knight 50.
HOUNSLOW 286.
HOWARD, VEN. PHILIP, Earl of Arundel 212.
HUGH, ROBERT AP 127, 128.
HUMPHREY, DR. 51, 52, 63.
HUMPHREY, VEN. LAURENCE 233—238.
HURLSTON, MR. 322.
HYDE, LEONARD, priest 283.

INGLEBY (INGOLBY), VEN. FRANCIS, priest 258, 304, 322.
INGLEBY, SIR WILLIAM 304.
INSTITUTE OF MARY 338.
IRELAND 44, 171, 184, 224.
ISLE OF WIGHT 67, 69, 72, 74, 76, 275;
the Needles 275.
ITALY 174, 256.

JAMES I., King 322, *see* Martyrs C.
JARDINE, DAVID, on torture 13, 122.
JENNINGS, *see* Genings.
JENNISON, MR. WILLIAM 151, 154.
JESSOP, JOHN 259, 264, 265.
JESSOPP, DR. AUGUSTUS 122, 123.
JETTER (of Layscoffe, Suffolk) GEORGE, priest 222, 224.

INDEX. 391

JETTER, JOHN, tortured in the Tower 222, 223; again in Newgate 224; and there dies *ibid.*; his claim to martyrdom not yet decided 225.
JOHN, a student 135.
JOHNSON, MR. a priest 306.
JOHNSON, RICHARD, *see* Dicconson.
JOHNSON, B. ROBERT 334.
JONES, RICHARD, printer 56.
JONES, VEN. JOHN, O.S.F., *alias* Buckley 57.
JONES, VEN. EDWARD, priest, *alias* Parker 290, 308, 315, 316.
JONES, MR. THOMAS 253.

KENDAL 213, 214, 221.
Book of Record of 214.
KING, DR. JOHN, Bishop of London 176—185.
KINGSMELL, SIR W., knight 58, 59, 63.
KIRKMAN, B. WILLIAM 218.
KNARESBOROUGH 176, *see* Manuscripts.
KNOX, DR. FRANCIS 1, 222.

LACEY, VEN. BRIAN.
tried 109, 110;
last words, death *ibid.*;
and burial, 115;
a distributer of letters 122;
warrant for his torture *ibid.*;
once betrayed by his brother 122.
LACEY, RICHARD, of Brockdish 122, 123.
LACEY, B. WILLIAM 218, 304.
LANCASTER 194, 217--219.
LANGLEY, VEN. RICHARD, account of 225—227, 305, 306.
LASSIE, MR. 304.
LAUD, WILLIAM, Archbishop of Canterbury 358.
LAYBURNE, ELIZABETH 213.
her will 214.
LAYBURNE, DR. GEORGE 218.

LAYBURNE, JAMES, ESQ. of Skelsmore, denies Elizabeth's right to the throne 212;
his martyrdom disputed 213;
his wardship 213;
generosity 214;
visited by Ven. E. Genings 214, 217;
where imprisoned 217;
described 220, 221;
date of death 218;
godfather of Ven. James Duckett 238.
LEE, a parson 195, 202.
LEICESTER, Earl of 287, 288, 311, 314.
LEIGH, VEN. RICHARD, priest (Lea, Lee, Ley, *alias* Earth) 287, 306.
LEIGHTON, JUSTICE 130, 133, 134, 137.
LEITH, W. FORBES, FR. S.J. 100.
LEWKNER MR. EDMUND 261.
LEWIS, an apostate 334, 337.
LIEUTENANT of the Tower, *see* London D.
LINCOLN 84.
LIVERDUN, DEAN OF 280.
LOMAX, JAMES 254.
LONDON. *A. Places, &c., in* 24, 72, 88, 118, 238, 255, 289, 292, 303, 353.
Bishop of, *see* Aylmer, King, Ravis;
Palace of 293;
Bermondsey [Barmesey] Abbey 209;
Chancery Lane 5;
Clerkenwell 115;
Fleet Bridge 111;
Gray's Inn Lane 291;
Guildhall 183;
Holborn 176, 295;
Lambeth Marsh 312;
Lambeth Palace 209;
Lincoln's Inn 210;
London Bridge 109;
Lord Mayor 109, 125, 359;
Paternoster Row 310;
Plague of 144;

LONDON (continued).
  River Thames 39;
  St. Catherine's 73;
  Smithfield 229, 292;
  Southwark 125, 209;
  Tower Hill 19;
  Watling Street 2.
B. *Churches.*
  St. Andrew's, Holborn 108;
  St. Edmund's, Lombard Street 240;
  St. Paul's 211, 222;
  St. Saviour's 169;
C. *Places of execution.*
  Curtain 288;
  Finsbury Fields 309;
  Fleet Street 290, 291, 302, 307, 308, 316.
  Grays Inn Fields 107;
  Hounslow 286;
  Kingston 307;
  Lincoln's Inn Fields 272;
  Mile End Green, 229, 288, 309;
  Smithfield 227, 231, 290, 308;
  St. Thomas Watering 336;
  Theatre 271;
  Tyburn 1, 19, 109, 117, 118, 121, 126, 143, 184, 194, 250, 251, 253, 254, 256, 259, 272, 280, 284, 285, 289, 306, 313, 339, 347.
D. *Prisons in.*
  Bridewell 54, 84, 89, 118, 122, 229, 240, 286, 289, 307, 312;
  Clerkenwell 289, 291, 309, 310, 317;
  Clink 222, 242, 243, 284, 287, 318;
  Counter in the Poultry 99, 245, 284, 286;
  Gatehouse at Westminster 84, 150, 175, 193, 240, 293, 335, 337;
  Marshalsea 73, 89, 271, 283, 287.
  Newgate 145, 157, 160, 172, 176, 180—183, 188, 192, 194, 224, 225, 228, 230, 242, 244, 246, 283, 285, 286, 290, 301, 306, 307, 308, 310, 339;

Newgate, escape from 182;
  hangman of 56, 211;
  Justice Hall in 81, 311;
Poultry, *see* Counter;
Sessions House (Old Bailey) 230, 322, 344;
Tower of London 6, 8, 9, 10, 13, 14, 19, 29, 37, 118, 124, 210, 222, 223, 260, 280, 291, 310; Gaskin, a keeper in 310; Lieutenant of 10—13, 17, 223, 280, 349;
Westminster (Court of Queen's Bench) 13, 15, 16, 17, 284, 336.
LOW COUNTRIES 288, 349.
LOWE, VEN. JOHN, priest 285.
LOWE, MISTRESS 287.
LUISANT, *see* Phesant.
LUKE, a pursuivant 338.
LUTTERWORTH, Leicestershire 323.

MADRID 343, 357.
MAINE, B. CUTHBERT 250.
MANCHESTER 217, 220.
MANUSCRIPT collections quoted.
  British Museum 50, 75—80, 193—207;
  Bodleian Library 22—34;
  Bourgogne, Bib. de, Brussels 40, 87;
  Fiesole, Archives S.J. 41—48;
  Guildhall 182;
  Knaresborough 176;
  Nymphenburg 338—367;
  Oscott 87, 225, 235—238;
  Privy Council Registers (Council Books) 11—14, 50, 89, 122;
  Public Record Office. *Coram Rege Rolls* 15—19, 336; *Controlment Rolls* 19; *Tower Bills* 224, 280; *State Papers* 53, 84; *Accounts of Treasurer of Chamber* 90;
  Stonyhurst. *Anglia* 51, 54, 55, 95, 100—121, 123—126, 128—137, 145—169, 172—175, 181—192, 231—235;

MANUSCRIPTS (continued).
  Collectanea A. 299—323;
  Collectanea M. 2—8, 56, 66—72, 81, 88, 90—95, 137—141, 219, 222—227, 250—278, 298—337;
  Collectanea N. 176;
  Westminster 8—11, 34—40, 51, 56—65, 68, 97, 209—212, 218, 219, 227—231, 238—248, 252, 279—297.
MARTEN, GEORGE 5.
MARTIN, GREGORY 67.
MARTIN, VEN. RICHARD, priest 287.
MARSDEN, VEN. WILLIAM, priest 66—81, 257.
MARIAN PRIESTS 121, 273.
MARTYRS. Decrees of Beatification, &c. Appendix, p. 369.
 A. *Imprisonment:*
  Prison treatment 84, 85, 180, parole 182, 219, 220, 276, 282, 345, means of communication 6, 10, 54, 85, 86, 124, 126, 140, 181, (their grate) *ibid.* 215—218, 245, 252, 262, 265, 268, 269, 276, 280, 281, free custody 327, escapes 56, 87, 129, 182, 226, 255, 286, 306, 313, 314;
  Sufferings of, chains, shackles, bonds, fetters, gyves, &c. 11, 55, 72, 106, 124, 140, 166, 172, 183, 224, 228, 236, carried on a list 245, 262, 265, 285, 303, 304, 305, common gaol 54, 84, 88, 122, 228, 230, 236, 286, 311, darkness (*see* also dungeon) 9, 173, 244, 327, food and hunger 10, 124, 173, 189, 195, 224, 345, 349 drink 163, 173, 247 *bis*, 346, stench and filth 10, 11, 244, 245, 265, pelting 332, money 10, 125, 135, 181, 345, 355, 366, dress and stripping 10, 105, 125, beds 11, 181, 220, 311, 328;

MARTYRS (continued).
  Tortures of 90, 122, 289, (with outrage) 290, 303, 314, 316, 322, rack 6, 10, 14, 31, 123, 210, 222, 223, 291, 310, 315, whip, scourge 54, 133, 142, pillory 133, manacles and gauntlets 122, described 124, 125, 229, 314, scavenger's daughter 222, dungeon (Limbo) amongst the rats 12, described 13, 136, 173, 183, 188, 195, 219, 225, 244, 285, 286, 308, 310, 311, 328, death in prison 224, 254, 265, 284 *bis*, 285.
 B. *Cause of death:*
  Examination 11—14, 69, 73, 76, 78—80, 84, 90, 122, 176, 335;
  Disputations 29, 30, 52, 53, 63, 70, 104, 126, 130, 185, 193, 237, 288, 294, 295, 305, 315, 317 &c. 344;
  Deposing power 5, 14, 15, 17, 61, 177, 213, 293, 296, the bloody question 5, 78—81, 113, 267, 297, 301, supremacy 59, 60, 64, 71, 130, 139, 216, 267, 305, 307 *bis*, 308, 315, 328, 335, oath of allegiance 145, 146, 166, 177 seq. 186 seq. 244, 295;
  Trials 15—19, 31, 38—48, 51—54, 90—92, 96, 101—107, 110, 111, 121, 133, 135, 137, 145—160, 183, 195, 226, 246, 269, 270, 290, 295, 299, 303, 320, 321, 329 *bis*, 335, 355, 359, refusing to plead 156, 183, 288;
  Offers of life 31, 93, 96, 119, 197, 200, 201, 267—270, 281, 286, 295, 300, 302, 341;
  Sentence 19, 71, 234.
 C. *Execution:*
  Via Dolorosa 58, 62, 92, 107, 109, 160, 184, 237, 281, 295, 306, 317, 332, 346, 355, 360;

MARTYRS (continued).
 Hurdle 59, 62, 92, 107, 109, 160, 199, 211, 237, 295, 317, 332, 342, ladder 59, 65, 95 bis, 97, 107, 109, 120, 141, 200, 232, 238, 307, 309, 317, cart 48, 111, 114, 140, 161—167, 185, 248, 296, 340; title on the scaffold 291, 292, 316;
 Protestant minister at 60, 107, 140, 162—164, 187—192, 195, 202, 237, 288, 295, 316, 350, 362—366;
 Executioner hard to find 139, 336, withdraws 202, 263, Bull 56, 211, Gregory 351;
 Speech at scaffold 59, 63, 93, 107, 108, 110, 114, 141, 164 —167, 185 seq. 308—310, 316, 340, 341, 347—351, 361;
 Praying for Queen and King 32, 65, 94, 112, 140, 165, 191, 232, 302, 366;
 Praying with Catholics not Protestants 48, 62, 64, 108, 167, 192, 233, 300, 302, 303, 325, 327, 331;
 Stripping 93, 109, 120, 163, 166, 185, 192, 201, 302;
 Distributing money, clothes, &c. 140, 166, 191, 192, 200, 202, 211, 313, 347;
 Blessing the hurdle, scaffold, kissing the rope, &c. 59, 63, 109, 114, 163, 237, 289, 340, 351;
 Night-cap or handkerchief 95, 166, 192, 202, 351, 367;
 Last words 48, 64, 95, 114 bis, 141, 167, 192, 300, 302, 303, 318, 337;
 Execution 6, 74, proclamation at 75—80, 109, 114, 116, 139—141, 160—168, 185— 193, 253, 295, 308, 318;
 Disembowelling alive 109, 114, 211, 253, 263, 296, 297, 302, 307, 317, 320, 337;
 Hanging till dead 114, 141, 288, 303, 309, 351, 356, unusual 167, 168, 356, till half-dead 192, of striking the breast 202, 233, 309, of pulling the legs 141, 309;
 Burial 108, 115, 168, 169, 226, 265, winding sheet 226, 235.
D. *Some consequences:*
 Relics 96, 168, 169, 203, 305, 323—326, 343, 346, 352, pictures 344, 359;
 Conversions 41, 81, 116, 162, 193, 267, 272, 303, 330, 331, 342, 343;
 Wonders: lights 203, 230, 325, 331, 333, exorcisms 256, 285, 311, 323, various 39, 56, 203, 211, 260, 306, 311, 321, 325, 334.
E. *Some characteristics:*
 Mass and sacraments 3, 7, 11, 37, 55, 63, 85, 86, 89, 91, 93, 97, 102, 105, 108, 115, 137, 142, 144, 153, 253, 261, 278, 280, 296, 316, 325, 326, 332, 356, 360, confession 167, 343, 357, 360, 367, Divine Office 257, 326, 332;
 Cheerfulness 6, 82, 96, 109, 110, 166, 190 seq. 195— 197, 220, 221, 227, 252, 281, 305, 342, 345—347, 355;
 Desire of martyrdom 55, 97 bis, 129, 138, 151, 190, 192, 254, 281, 327, 329, 341, 342, 353; cowardice 119;
 Natural timidity 260, 304, 341;
 The Holy Name 20, 65, 95, 115, 193, 211, 222, 223, 229, 233, 345;
 Jesus Psalter 223, 243, 274.
MARY, QUEEN 211.
MARY (? Fidd) exorcised 323.
MASON, VEN. JOHN 109; servant to Mr. Owen 110; tried *ibid.*; executed 111; buried 115.

MATTHEW, TOBY 271.
MAUSON, PETER 238.
MAYO (?), FR. S.J. 259.
MAYO, a pursuivant 339.
MAYLER, a priest 182.
MAYOR, THE LORD, *see* London.
MAXFIELD, WILLIAM, ESQ. 323.
MECHLIN, Bridgettine Convent 3.
MERCHANT Tailors, Company 2.
MERIONETHSHIRE 143.
MEVERELL, MR. 305.
MIDDLETON, VEN. ANTHONY, priest 291, 308, 309, 315, 317.
MILAN Cathedral 257.
MILNER, VEN. RALPH, a Hampshire yeoman, converted 85, 95; imprisonment 85; arranges for Ven. R. Dicconson (q.v.) 87; execution 95—97, 319.
MOMPESSON, MR. LAURENCE 115, 116.
MOMPESSON, MRS. 116.
MONICA'S, ST., Convent 212.
MONTAGUE Family 354.
MONTAGUE, SIR EDWARD (Recorder 1608) 294.
MOOR, VEN. HUGH 287; persecuted by his own father 323.
MORE, B. THOMAS 10.
MORGAN, VEN. EDWARD, *alias* Singleton, priest, martyrdom of 343—352.
MORGAN, WILLIAM 349.
MORTON, DR. minister 293.
MORTON HENMARSHE, Gloucestershire 336.
MORTON, DR. NICHOLAS 272.
MORTON, VEN. ROBERT, priest (Mourton) 271, 287.
MOSLY, SHERIFF (of London) 303.
MOSTON, THOMAS, Chancellor of Bangor 131, 133.
MOUNTAIN, HUMPHREY 305.
MUCH WOOLTON, Liverpool 171.

MUSH, a priest 306.
MUSKETT, MR. 192.

N., MR. 124 note.
NEELE, *see* Roche.
NELSON, B. JOHN, priest 250.
NEWTON, a pursuivant 338, 361.
NICE, Council of 52.
NIEUPORT, Convent at 238.
NORTHERN, Earls, the 213.
NORTHERN Rising, the 44, 76.
NORTHUMBERLAND 293.
NORTHUMBERLAND, EARL OF 2.
NORTON, SIR RICHARD, kt. 50.
NOTTINGHAM 2, 3.
NUTTER, VEN. JOHN, priest 304.
NYMPHENBURG, in Bavaria 338.

OATH of Allegiance, *see* Martyrdom, cause of.
ORATORY, the London 279.
OSCOTT, Seminary at 87, 225, 235.
OWEN, MR. 110.
OXFORD 2, 25, 35, 249, 251, 261, 264, 277, 278, 289.
Bishop of 56.
Bocardo 254.
Colleges, Balliol 261.
Brasenose 67.
Hart Hall 253.
Magdalen 25, 254.
New 50, 56.
Oriel 260, 333.
St. John's 254, 271.
St. Mary's Hall 67.
Trinity 249, 251, 255, 273.
Degrees 35.
Proctor 27, 35.
St. Catherine's Wheel Inn 289.
St. Mary's Church 26, 260.
Students at 254.
OXFORDSHIRE 251, 273.

PAINE, B. JOHN, priest 56.
PAINE, MR. 45.
PAGE, VEN. FRANCIS, S.J. 247.
PARIS 219, 257.

396   INDEX.

PARLIAMENT 339, 354, 360, 366.
  Committee of 355.
  Statute of 1 Eliz. 135.
  Statute of 23 Eliz. 137.
  Statute of 27 Eliz. 76, 90, 102,
    104, 119, 164, 183, 307,
    324, 340, 341.
  Statute of Persuasion 96.
PARR, a priest 182.
PATENT, Letters, to keep a priest
    212.
PATINSON, BERNARD, priest 306.
PATINSON, VEN. WILLIAM,
  priest, scrupulous 115;
  trial 116;
  converts felons and executed
    117, 306.
PAUNCEFORT, JOHN, ESQ. 239.
PENKENNEL, see Penkevel.
PENKEVEL, JOHN 283.
PENKEVEL, MARK, S.J. 283,
  284.
PENKEVEL, THOMAS 283.
PENKEVEL, PETER, O.S.F. 224,
  282—292.
  his mother 283.
PENNINGTON, SIR ISAAC, Lord
  Mayor 359.
PERSONS, FR. ROBERT, S.J. 8,
  10, 36, 50, 68, 97, 100,
  104, 121, 141, 173, 176,
  183, 218, 221, 292, 313,
  321.
PHESANT, PETER, Sergeant 359,
  362, 366.
PHILLIPS, JUSTICE 130, 131.
PHILIP II. see Spain.
PIKES, VEN. WILLIAM,
  joiner 2, 67.
PILCHARD, VEN. THOMAS,
  priest 261, 263, 269, 320,
  321.
PITTS, ARTHUR, priest 280.
PITTS, JOHN, priest 280.
PIUS V. ST. (his Bull) 5, 209, 213.
PLASDEN, VEN. POLYDORE
  (Oliver), priest 101—114;
  prays for Elizabeth 112;
  conversation with Raleigh *ibid.*
PLUMTREE, B. THOMAS
  213.

POPE JOAN 70.
PLAGUE, *see* London.
PLYMOUTH 352.
POPHAM, LORD CHIEF JUSTICE
    102, 111, 217, 245, 246.
PORMORT, VEN. THOMAS
    (Portmore) priest 118—120;
    would admit conference 119;
    Topcliffe's boasts about Elizabeth 119.
POWELL, LADY 354.
POWLETT, GEORGE, J.P. 93.
PRAGUE 28, 36.
PRICE, a student 118.
PRICE, keeper of Newgate 180,
    181, 183, 188.
PRIMERS, *see* Books.
PRIVY COUNCIL 6, 11, 13, 14,
    84, 89, 124, 125, 127, 130,
    149, 165, 282, 284, 291, 335.
    Registers of 72, 88 (*see* MS.
    collections).
PSALTER, JESUS 223, 247.
PSALTER, Our Lady's 242.
PUCKERING, Lord Keeper 99,
    116.
PYBUSH, VEN. JOHN, priest
    335, 336.

QUEEN ELIZABETH, *see* Elizabeth.
QUEEN MARY, *see* Mary.
QUEEN'S Bench, Court of 15, 101
    (*see* London, Westminster).

R.B. 57.
RALEIGH, SIR WALTER 112,
    114.
RAMESDELL, Archdeacon of
    York 225.
RAVAILLAC 183.
RAVIS, THOMAS, Bishop of
    London 295.
RAWLIN, *see* Raleigh.
REYNOLDS, MR. 285.
REYNOLDS, VEN. THOMAS,
    vere Green 339.
REYNOLDS, WILLIAM 54, 67.
RHEIMS, *see* Seminaries.
RHEIMS, St. Stephen's Church
    at 261.
RICHARD, HUMPHREY, AP 289.

INDEX.

RICHMOND 89.
RIPON 327.
RIVERS, *see* Bales.
ROCHESTER 315.
ROBERT, a student 134.
ROBERT, HUGH AP, High Constable of Llynon 127, 128.
ROBERTS, VEN. JOHN, O.S.B. at Valladolid 143;
becomes a Benedictine and labours in England 144, 149, 150;
arraignment 145—157;
condemnation 157—160;
the feast in prison 170;
execution 160—169;
relics 169.
ROBINSON, VEN. JOHN, priest 287.
ROCHE, VEN. JOHN, *alias* Neele 100, 118, 287, 312.
ROE, VEN. BARTHOLOMEW (Dom. Alban, O.S.B.) martyrdom 339—343.
ROGER, a boy student 133, 135, 136.
ROME 38, 99, 292.
English clergy at 34, 248, 250.
English College at, *see* Seminaries.
English Hospice of 292.
Roman College 172.
St. Andrea 250, 281.
St. Peter's 256.
English Penitentiary at 250.
ROPER, MR. 10.
ROWSAM, VEN. STEPHEN, priest (Rowsham) 260, 332—334.

ST. AMBROSE 257.
ST. AUGUSTINE 134, 152, 155, 158, 164, 290.
ST. BENEDICT, Ven. Order of 144, 148, 151, 154, 158, 164, 293, 297.
ST. BENEDICT, Confraternity of 154.
ST. GERMAIN in Normandy 275.
ST. GREGORY THE GREAT 152.

ST. JOHN, WILLIAM, a Justice 58.
ST. JUSTUS 158.
ST. LAURENCE 158, 189.
ST. MABYN in Cornwall 269.
ST. MELLITUS 158.
ST. OMERS, *see* Seminaries.
ST. PAULINUS 158.
SS. PETER AND PAUL 60, 66.
ST. PETER'S Cross 189.
ST. PIUS V. his Bull 5, 209, 213.
ST. STEPHEN 189.
ST. THOMAS OF CANTERBURY 24, 175.
SALAMANCA 343.
SALISBURY 268.
SALMON, VEN. PATRICK 118.
SANDER, DR. NICHOLAS 44, 102, 213.
SANDYS, VEN. JOHN, priest 333, 336, 337.
SCARBOROUGH 329.
SCOTT, VEN. MOMFORD 109, 123, 291, 299—304;
his praying with Protestants 300;
to what extent 303.
SEMINARIES AND COLLEGES:
Douay (at Rheims from 1578 to 1593) 1, 2, 8, 20, 38, 67, 68, 76, 84, 99, 100, 115, 118, 127, 143, 215, 221, 222, 249, 251, 254 seq. 270—277, 281, 324, 343.
English College, Rome 143, 172, 173, 175, 216, 252, 253, 272, 281, 343.
Rheims, *see* Douay.
Roman College 172.
St. Omers 100, 214, 216, 352, 357, 358.
Valladolid (St. Alban's) 99, 143, 144, 249, 343, 325, 357.
SEVERN River, bore on 224.
SHANDIS, LORD GILES 335.
SHAW, a relapsed priest 121.
SHELLEY, VEN. EDWARD, 287, 307.
SHELLEY, MR. RICHARD 283.

INDEX.

SHERRICK, SIR WILLIAM 242.
SHERSON, MARTIN, priest 271.
SHERWIN, B. RALPH 310.
SHERWOOD, HENRY 2, 3, 4.
SHERWOOD, ELIZABETH, his wife, 2, 7.
SHERWOOD, JOHN, DR. 3, 4.
SHERWOOD, JOHN, S.J. 8.
SHERWOOD, RICHARD, MR. 213, 216.
SHERWOOD, B. THOMAS. Not a Douay student 1; nor a mere boy 2;
birth, education, apprenticed as a draper, visits Douay 4;
arrest and examination 5;
his money stolen 9;
nakedness, hunger, &c., relieved by Mr. Roper 10;
warrant for further examination and trial 11;
ditto for his confinement "in the dungeon amongst the rats" 12;
ditto for racking 14;
tortured 6, 10; his verbal treason 13; wishes to retract it 14; his trial 6, 15—19; execution 6; writs for 19, 20;
his character and cheerfulness 6, 7; his patience 20; mentioned 215.
SHIRT, ANTHONY, priest 274.
SHIRT, B. JOHN 334.
SHREWSBURY CASTLE 337.
SIKES, VEN. EDMUND, priest 328, 329.
SIMPSON, MR. RICHARD 35, 47.
SINGLETON, see Morgan.
SIXTUS V., POPE 272.
SLACKSTEAD, Hampshire 89.
SLADE, VEN. JOHN, of New College, Oxon 49;
becomes a tutor 50;
Council warrant for his arrest 50;
books found in his cell *ibid.*;
first trial 51;
second trial and disputation 52;

solitary and in irons 55;
incident at his execution 56;
execution 57—62.
SMALLMAN, NICHOLAS, and family 337.
SMITH, VEN. RICHARD, *alias* Newport, priest 292.
SMYTH, *see* Floyd.
SOCIETY OF JESUS 8, 34, 35, 171, 172, 250, 283, 343;
Archives of 41, *see* Manuscript Collections;
General of 234.
SOISSONS 282.
SOMERS, VEN. THOMAS, priest 144—169.
SOMERSETSHIRE 252, 268.
SOUCHE, DR. 126.
SOUTHALLERTON, Liverpool 171, 185.
SOUTHAMPTON, Sheriff of 73, 90, 92.
SOUTHWELL, VEN. ROBT., S.J. 246;
his supplication to the Queen 246.
SPAIN 2, 142, 174;
Ambassador of, *see* Gusman;
Court of 34;
King of, Philip II. 44, 271, 315;
Seminaries of 127.
SPENSER, VEN. WILLIAM, priest 273—277.
SPRAT, MR. EDWARD 323.
STAFFERTON, DR. 334.
STAFFORD 323.
STAFFORDSHIRE 271.
STAMPE, MR., a priest 5.
STANFORD, MR. EDWARD 274.
STANHOPE, DR. EDWARD 244, 245.
STANLEY, house of 119.
STANWAYE 337.
STATUTES, *see* Parliament.
STOKES, MR. GEORGE 310.
STONYHURST College 173, 231, 280, 299, 323, *see* MS. Collections.
STOREY, B. JOHN 213.
STRANGE, Earl of Derby 120.

INDEX.

STANNEY, FR. THOMAS, S.J. 85, 86, 90.
STRANSAM, VEN. EDWARD (Stransham, Transom) 254—257.
STRANSAM, GEORGE 257.
STRANSAM, THOMAS 257.
STRICKLAND, a lawyer 43.
STUBBES, MR. JOHN 123.
SUCQUET, ANTHONY, FR.S.J.41.
SUGAR, VEN. JOHN (*alias* Sweet, *alias* Cope) priest 321.
SUPREMACY, *see* Martyrdom, cause of.
SUSSEX 283.
SUSSEX, EARL OF 211.
SUTTON, VEN. ROBERT, priest, once Protestant rector of Lutterworth 323 ; converted by his brother 324 ; arrested 323, 324 ; his relics at Stonyhurst 323—326.
SUTTON, WILLIAM 323.
SUTTON, ABRAHAM 324, 326.
SUTTON, VEN. ROBERT, schoolmaster 287, 289, 309, 310.
SWEET, *see* Sugar.
SWYNNERTON 34.
SYDNEY, R., *see* Hodgson.
SYDNEY, SIR PHILIP 36.
SYMONDS, *alias* John Harrison, Martyr 289.
SYMONS, *see* SYMONDS.

TARUGI, CARDINAL 172.
TAUNTON Convent 169.
TAYLOR, THOMAS, pursuivant 73.
TAYLOR, *see* Bullaker.
TERTULLIAN 104.
THIRKELL, VEN. RICHARD, priest 218.
THOMAS, JOHN, martyr 232.
THOMSON, *alias* Groves, prisoner 332, 333.
THOMSON, *see* Gerard, John.
THOMPSON, martyr 218.
THORNBERY, MR. FRANCIS and his brother 323.

THULIS, VEN. JOHN, priest 194—207 ;
in the dungeon with thieves 195 ;
disputes 195, 200 ;
offered his life 197, 200, 201 ;
offered the oath 197, 201 ;
forced to church 198 ;
farewells 198 ;
execution 200—202.
TICHBORNE, HENRY, S.J. 259.
TICHBORNE, VEN. THOS., priest 247.
TICHBURNE, MR. BENJAMIN, J.P. 58.
TOPCLIFFE, RICHARD 90, 101, 102, 103, 107, 108, 109, 110, 112, 113, 114, 119, 120, 122, 223, 229, 230, 285, 289, 290, 301, 303, 306, 308, 309, 315, 317, 322, 335.
TOWER, the, *see* London D.
TRACY, PAUL, ESQ. of Stanwaye 337.
TRANSOM, *see* Stransam.
TREASURER of the Chamber 90.
TREASURER, Lord, *see* Burleigh.
TREGONNELL, LADY 6.
TRENCHARD, GEORGE, ESQ. 50.

UPHOLLAND 357.
USSHER 193.
VALLADOLID, *see* Seminaries.
VAUGHAN, JUSTICE 225.
VENDÔME, DUC DE 360.

WADE, WILLIAM, Clerk of the Council 101.
WADSWORTH, pursuivant 339, 352, 361.
WAFERER, MR., Q.C. 8.
WALES 121.
WALES, North 127.
WALKER, MR. 121.
WALPOLE, CHRISTOPHER, FR. S.J. 321.
WALPOLE, VEN. HENRY, S.J. 40, 306, 310.
WALPOLE, MICHAEL, S.J. 176, 321.
WARCOPPE, THOMAS 213.

INDEX.

WARD, VEN. MARGARET 100, 118, 286.
WARD, MARY 338;
WARD, VEN. WILLIAM, priest 354.
WARFORD, WILLIAM, S.J. 55, 66, 72, 74, 81, 223, 224, 249 —278.
WARWICK 321, 322.
WARWICK, EARL OF 43.
WATKINSON, VEN. ROBT. priest, 246, 247.
WATSON, WILLIAM, priest 312.
WEBB, Lord Mayor of London 109.
WEBBE, LAURENCE, LL.D. 209.
WEBLEY, VEN. HENRY 287.
WEEKES, a priest 240.
WELBY, *see* Dicconson.
WELDON, VEN. JOHN, *alias* Savell, *alias* Hewett, priest 228, 229, 287, 288, 309.
WELLS in Somerset 252.
WELLS, MRS. 100, 101.
WELLS, VEN. SWITHIN, ESQ. 100, 101, 107, 108.
WELSH 347.
WEST, THOMAS 58.
WESTCHESTER 139, 268.
WESTMINSTER, CARD. ARCHBISHOP OF 279.
WESTMINSTER Archives, *see* MS. Collections.
WHITE, VEN. EUSTACE, priest, 101, 109, 114, 115.
warrant for his torture 122; his letter describing his sufferings 123, 126.
WHITE, MRS. 289, 311.
WHITE, MR. THOMAS, High Sheriff of Hampshire 60, 63;
WHITE, THOMAS, Kt. 25.
WHITE, widow 91.
WHITE, MR. ROBERT 58.
WHITGIFT, JOHN, Archbishop of Canterbury 119, 150.
WHITTLE, MRS. 307.
WIDMERPOOL, VEN. ROBERT, priest 287.
WIGGS, WILLIAM, priest 283.
WILCOX, VEN. ROBERT, priest 287.

WILLIAMS, VEN. RICHARD, Queen Mary priest, martyred 120, but *see* Preface, pp. xvi —xix.
WILSON, JOHN, priest 216.
WINCHESTER 57, 58, 62, 83, 85, 87, 236, 259.
Dean of 53.
Bishop of, *see* Cowper, Thomas.
Bardick of 95, 231, 232, 233.
Winchester Martyrs 231, 235.
Warden of the College of 53.
WINDSOR 11.
WIPER, MR. 212, 213.
WISBECH 289.
WOLSEY, JOHN, ESQ. 323.
WOODFEN, VEN. NICHOLAS, priest 284.
WOODHOUSE, B. THOMAS 213.
WORCESTERSHIRE 85.
WRAY, LORD CHIEF JUSTICE 12, 39, 42, 101, 105, 106, 107.
WRENNO, VEN. ROGER (Wrennol) 194, 199.
WRIGHT, WILLIAM, ESQ., J.P. 50, 58.
WYCKLIFF 323.

XAVIER, ST. FRANCIS 345.

YATES, *alias* BOULTON, priest 182.
YAXLEY, VEN. RICHARD, priest, *alias* Yeats 289, 314.
YEPEZ, BISHOP 140, 142, 213, 217.
YORK 225, 227, 252, 273, 304, 313.
Bishop of 322.
Bishop's Palace at 258.
Bishop's fields 304.
Castle 276, 304, 305, 328.
Council at 322.
YORKSHIRE 115, 258.
YOUNG, JAMES, priest (Younge or Younger, *alias* Dingley, *alias* Christopher) 98—121, 190.
YOUNG, JUSTICE 116, 122, 125, 284.
YOUNG, a priest 182.

Works on the English Martyrs
BY THE
REV. JOHN MORRIS, S.J.

The Life of Father John Gerard, S.J. Third Edition, re-written and enlarged. 14s.

Father Morris is one of the few living writers who have succeeded in greatly modifying certain views of English history, which had long been accepted as the only tenable ones. . . . To have wrung an admission of this kind from a reluctant public, never too much inclined to surrender its traditional assumptions, was an achievement not to be underrated in importance. And yet it may be doubted whether Mr. Morris would ever have obtained a hearing at all, or got people to read many pages of the later volumes, if it had not been for the happy chance, or the foreseeing sagacity which induced him to print, as an introduction to the series which was to follow, the remarkable biography which is now re-published as a separate work.—Rev. Dr. Augustus Jessopp, in the *Academy*.

Father Gerard's narrative not only carries on its face all the appearance of artlessness, but its details are so minutely confirmed from contemporary documents, now in the Public Record Office, that a defence of his veracity is wholly unnecessary. . . . The Life is full of interesting particulars, both as regards the writer and many other Jesuits who were employed on the English Mission during the reign of Elizabeth.—*Saturday Review*.

This volume is certainly a literary curiosity. The life of Father Gerard is in the main an autobiography, as full of exciting details as the most sensational of novels. . . . The narrative of the Plot is thoroughly well worth reading, as throwing light on a portion of English history which most students feel has not as yet been thoroughly explored.—*Guardian*.

The autobiography, extending from about 1580 to 1606, should rather be called, "Condition of the Catholics during the latter part of the reign of Queen Elizabeth," of which it presents a very curious and interesting picture. . . . Extreme pains have evidently been taken to render this book as complete as possible. —*Pall Mall Gazette*.

The life is full of the most interesting details of personal adventure and suffering, recounted in the simplest, and therefore in the most telling manner. If any one wants to know what was the life of a Seminary priest in England in the days of Elizabeth, or to visit in imagination the torture-chamber of the Tower or the secret labyrinth of Henlip, he cannot find a better guide than in Mr. Morris's volume.—*Athenæum*.

We have been able to give within our necessary limits but a very imperfect and faint idea of the interest and value of the volume before us, though we have, perhaps, said enough to send our readers to the work itself for a more particular knowledge of its contents; but we cannot conclude without thanking Mr. Morris for his intelligent and unobtrusive editorship, or without speaking highly of the moderate and candid tone of his remarks.—*Spectator*.

Life and Martyrdom of St. Thomas Becket.
Second and enlarged Edition. In one vol., cloth, large post. 8vo, pp. xxxvi., 632 - - - - 12s. 6d.
Or bound in two parts. Cloth - - 13s. od.

Father Morris has succeeded in producing a biography worthy of his great and sainted subject. It is full without being voluminous, and possesses all the attractions of an agreeable style. No one can read over its six hundred pages without appreciating the more the saintly grandeur of that character that is there so faithfully described, and at the same time feeling how unjust is the estimate which those have formed of St. Thomas who, as Mr. Froude, have been accustomed to view him as the "proud and ambitious priest." . . . In the Appendix is added a series of historical notes, in which many incidents but briefly referred to in the previous portion of the book are discussed at greater length; as, for instance, the legend of his Saracen parentage, the fate of his murderers, and other subjects of a not less attractive character.—*Irish Ecclesiastical Record.*

The author is especially at home on the congenial subjects of the monasteries and churches which the Saint is said to have visited, of the traces of his presence on the Continent, and of his relics, some of which are extant, though many more have disappeared in "the various storms which have assailed religion." On these topics he brings together information which the ordinary English reader would probably have difficulty in finding elsewhere. . . . Its fulness and precision of details make it a valuable work.—*Saturday Review.*

The services rendered by Father Morris to the Church in connection with the Beatification of the English Martyrs are so remarkable that they are well known not only to Catholics, but to every student of history, as it is now being re-written in the light of the fuller information which was denied to Englishmen of the last generation. . . . For twenty years this admirable book has been out of print, and therefore known only by name to most men of the present generation; and the second and enlarged edition, which is before us, has all the charm of a new work. Father Morris has not written a panegyric, but a faithful biography; he has no theory to support, and his manifest aim has been to tell the plain truth. Hence, as portrayed by him, the career of St. Thomas does not present any of those perplexing problems which beset those who approach the subject under the influence of foregone conclusions. . . . Father Morris has done much more than any previous writer to help to the gradual formation of a correct public opinion on an important period in English Church history. For his co-religionists he has done a service of inestimable value, by giving them a sketch of the life of one of England's greatest Catholic sons that is no less attractive in style than it is accurate in detail. . . . It need only be added that the Notes which compose the Appendix will repay careful study, and that the addition of an excellent Index renders the book most useful for purposes of reference.—*Tablet.*

The Troubles of our Catholic Forefathers, related by themselves; from hitherto unpublished manuscripts. Second Series, Father Weston's narrative and the falls of Anthony Tyrrell. Demy 8vo, cloth, 14s. Third Series, Persecutions in the North of England. Demy 8vo, cloth, 14s. Each series complete in itself.

On the actual working of the penal laws much new information has been given us in the series of contemporary narratives published by Father Morris under the title of *The Troubles of our Catholic Forefathers.*—Mr. John Richard Green, in his *History of the English People,* authorities for Book VI.

Volume after volume of that painful series of *Troubles of our Catholic Forefathers,* which contains some of the most pathetic and some of the most shameful chapters to be found in our country's annals.—Rev. Dr. Augustus Jessopp, in the *Academy.*

The mass of documents which Mr. Morris has printed constitutes a body of evidence which no historian of the sixteenth century can hereafter ignore. If they do not prove that the Catholics were right, they, at any rate, go far to prove that the treatment they endured at the hands of the stronger party was immensely more cruel than was heretofore believed. They reveal a system of the most elaborate espionage that could well be conceived—a truculent barbarity which had hardly been suspected, and an organized persecution, which, as it lasted much longer, so during its course was more crushing and inquisitorial than the previous persecution of Protestants in Queen Mary's days —*Athenæum.*

Father Morris's second series of *The Troubles of our Catholic Forefathers, related by themselves,* contains two very interesting biographies. The first is the Life of Father William Weston, *alias* Edmunds, taken chiefly from a later autobiography, and carefully completed from two other MS. sources, namely, Grene's collections of Father Parsons's unpublished works at Stonyhurst, and a Spanish Life of Weston by Father de Peralta, a MS. from the Gesù at Rome. Wherever they serve the purpose, the State Papers in the Public Record Office have also been quoted. . . . The second part of Father Morris's book is an autobiographical narrative of the fall of Tyrrell, a Catholic priest who became a hired spy of Elizabeth's Government, and who several times repented and relapsed. . . . What Father Morris—and I must add Brother Foley—have already given us from the treasures of Stonyhurst makes us all the more desirous of further instalments.—Mr. Richard Simpson, in the *Academy.*

The Letter-Books of Sir Amias Poulet, Keeper of Mary Queen of Scots. 1874. Demy 8vo, cloth, 10s. 6d.

We close reluctantly the pages of an interesting and instructive book, of which we can only say that were there more such upon this and kindred historical topics, our history would not labour, as it too frequently does now, under the disadvantage of incomplete or incorrect materials.—*Athenæum.*

In the volume before us are published for the first time a number of letters of Sir Amias which were preserved by his descendants, and are now deposited in the Bodleian Library. Many of these are highly interesting, and Mr. Morris has done good service to the cause of historical truth in placing them before the public. . . . Mr. Morris has both ably and honestly performed his duty as editor of these interesting letters. He is thoroughly acquainted with the history of the period; and in addition to the correspondence of Poulet, he has printed a number of original papers from the Record Office.—Mr. Hosack, in the *Academy.*

These interesting letters, many of which have been hitherto unknown, throw much light on that part of the captivity of Mary Stuart which was passed under the rigorous keeping of Sir Amias Poulet. . . . Mr. Morris deserves the thanks of those students of history who prefer plain facts to picturesque fiction for publishing these very important letters. In editing them he has done his work with great exactness and impartiality.—*Saturday Review.*

In this most interesting volume there is more to be learned of the house life of Mary, during her last years in England, than in any detailed history of her career.—*Notes and Queries.*

The valuable volume of Father Morris on the Letter-Book of Sir Amias Poulet, keeper of Mary Queen of Scots, for extent and originality of research, acuteness of criticism, and breadth and comprehensiveness of view, may claim the very highest rank in the long array of literature, Latin, French, Italian, and English, devoted to the vindication of this ill-fated lady.—The Very Rev. Dr. Russell, President of Maynooth, in the *Dublin Review.*

The Devotions of Lady Lucy Herbert of Powis,

formerly Prioress of the Augustinian Nuns at Bruges. Cloth, gilt, 3s. 6d.

The volume before us contains a great variety of prayers, all of them breathing a spirit of intense piety; and the reflections and meditations with which the book abounds, will render it a favourite in every religious house.—*Weekly Register.*

A very full manual of forms of prayer and meditations, and gives admirable instructions on the latter Divine art. For a long time we have seen nothing which has given us so much pleasure and is calculated to be of greater spiritual profit. Prefixed is a most interesting account of Lady Lucy's Life.—*Church Review.*

London: BURNS AND OATES, Limited.
Roehampton: JAMES STANLEY, Manresa Press.

www.ingramcontent.com/pod-product-compliance
Lightning Source LLC
Chambersburg PA
CBHW051741300426
44115CB00007B/647